Campus Computing Strategies

Campus Computing Strategies

John W. McCredie, *Editor*
President, EDUCOM

DIGITAL PRESS

Printed in the U.S.A.
10 9 8 7 6 5 4 3 2

Documentation Number: EY-00009-DP
ISBN: 0-932376-20-7

Production Notes
EDUCOM delivered this electronically-prepared manuscript to Digital Press on magnetic tape. Copyediting and generic coding were added to the manuscript tape, which was then automatically typeset via a translation program on Digital's DECset Integrated Publishing System. Production time from receipt of the magnetic tape to delivery of bound books was eight weeks. The book production was done by Digital's Educational Services Development and Publishing group in Bedford, Mass.

Library of Congress Cataloging in Publication Data

Campus computing strategies.

    Includes index.
    Contents: Introduction / John W. McCredie --
Hamilton College / David Smallen -- Dartmouth
College / William Y. Arms -- [etc.]
    1. Education, Higher--United States--Data
processing--Case studies--Addresses, essays, lectures.
I. McCredie, John W.
LB2324.C35   1983   378'.0028'5   82-19888
ISBN 0-932376-20-7

Trademarks appear on page 311.

Credits

Figure 2, Page 288
Reprinted by permission. From Frank Greenwood, *Information Resources in the Office of Tommorrow*, Association for Systems Management.

Preface and Acknowledgments

Campus Computing Strategies is intended for everyone interested in the impacts of converging information and communications technologies in higher education. This book answers one of the first questions asked by individuals interested in learning more about this subject: "What are people doing, or planning to do, about these technologies at other campuses?" Faculty, students, planners, administrators, board members, computing center staff, and computer scientists from all types of institutions will find the information contained in the ten case studies a valuable resource for their campuses. Individuals from corporations that are designing future information-technology products should learn what several leading colleges and universities are planning. Corporate, foundation, and government managers as well as potential college students and secondary-level educators should know what steps are being taken in higher education to prepare students for an information-based society.

The book evolved from a study conducted during the 1981-82 academic year in which EDUCOM's staff examined how ten colleges and universities are creating strategic plans in the information-processing area. Instead of examining hardware, software, or budgets, the participants concentrated on ideas, goals, objectives, and plans—the underlying strategies shaping the various implementation decisions. The conclusions of this effort are presented here as a coordinated set of case studies that describe both the planning processes and the strategies used by these institutions for computing and communications systems. These results are important to all of higher education, because most colleges and universities are not organizing to take advantage of converging information technologies.

In the ten chapters, individuals directly involved in strategic planning describe the information-processing planning activities taking place in diverse organizations. The authors are not unbiased scholars; they are computing professionals. Clearly they see the world in general, and higher education in particular, from a different vantage point than the typical student, faculty member, or administrator. An interesting image emerges from their different approaches. It is a mosaic of traditional academic institutions struggling with technologies that many people believe will cause waves of change comparable to the development of movable type.

The study was not designed to be statistically significant. The ten participating colleges and universities do not represent typical institutions. They are a non-random selection of innovative schools actively planning to confront the information revolution. Although the participants included a wide range of institutions (small liberal arts colleges, large state universities, independent doctorate granting, church-affiliated, and technological) there was no attempt in the selection process to be comprehensive in scope. The prerequisites for inclusion were (a) an innovative campus approach to information processing, and (b) a willingness to describe the internal strategic planning processes used by the organization.

After an introduction, the chapters appear in the order of increasing size of the college or university. Although this presentation is somewhat arbitrary, it does create an interesting view of the information. Certain management problems increase exponentially with size and complexity, and planning for information technology appears to be in this class.

Many individuals and organizations contributed a great deal of time, energy, and intellectual effort to the creation of this book. Certainly the authors deserve the appreciation of all readers for finding time in their very busy schedules to create coherent descriptions of what seem to be hectic processes in most institutions. The participating colleges and universities were most generous in making information about their internal operations and management style available to other organizations. As always, the authors' assistants, on campus and at home, deserve even more appreciation for keeping on-going activities from flying apart, while the authors worked on such an interesting special project.

American Telephone and Telegraph, Control Data, Digital Equipment, International Business Machines, and XEROX corporations supported the development of the book and other dissemination activities related to the project through generous grants to EDUCOM. Such cooperation is important, since rapidly changing technology causes new interdependencies between industry and education. EDUCOM is most appreciative of the corporate support.

The opinions expressed in the book belong to each author and are not intended to represent policy statements of Digital Press, EDUCOM, the participating colleges and universities, or the supporting corporations.

The individual chapters were created on 11 different local text processing systems, and then transferred (mostly by electronic means) to the EDUCOM computer system. After several editing passes, the manuscript was delivered to the Digital Press on magnetic tape. Several EDUCOM staff members worked long and hard to coordinate these efforts. Diane Coleman, Carolyn Landis, Sheldon Smith, and Phoebe Wechsler deserve special mention and thanks. The surprising result that this complex process worked reasonably well among so many independent organizations located from coast to coast is at least partial testimony that academic institutions are moving toward the information age mentioned so frequently in the book. However, the fact that it worked at all is even greater testimony about the power of human ingenuity in the face of barely cooperating electronic "assistants." We still have a long way to go!

John W. McCredie
President, EDUCOM
November 1982

Contents

1

educom

Introduction

JOHN W. McCREDIE
President, EDUCOM

Higher education in this decade will be rocked by waves of change caused by the converging technologies of computing, high-speed local and satellite digital communication, video disc and other large-capacity information-storage devices, graphics, two-way cable systems, and artificial intelligence applications. The information-processing challenges and opportunities presented by these changes are profound, particularly for higher education where most institutions are unprepared to deal with them effectively.

While some universities and colleges are organizing to take advantage of these opportunities, most seem oblivious to the challenge. Nevertheless, future technological trends are just as predictable as the widely recognized demographic changes altering the pool of potential post-secondary students. Most institutions have made plans to react to the demographic forces of the 1980s, but only a few have strategies to face the inevitable technological changes on the horizon. If these changes are not planned for, the opportunity cost to all of higher education will be very large.

1

This book describes the information-processing planning activities taking place on ten campuses from the perspectives of individuals directly involved in the planning process. Although the case studies cover a wide range of different types of institutions (small liberal arts colleges, large state universities and systems, independent doctorate granting, and engineering) there was no attempt in the selection process to be comprehensive in scope. The prerequisites for participation were an innovative campus approach to information processing activities, and the willingness to describe the internal planning processes used by the organization.

This chapter summarizes several current and future effects of the rapid spread and integration of computing and communication technologies and discusses their implications for academic administrators. It represents a description of the environment in which the ten institutions have done their planning.

The Power of Computing Technology

Information-processing technology, particularly in the academic environment, is fundamentally different, in both character and range of impact, from other technologies, past and present. Certainly inventions like the steam engine, the automobile, antibiotics, and television transformed society, but they did not radically change higher education. Why is the computer so different?

Computing capabilities have made important and complex tasks much more economical to perform, but so have other technologies. Every successful new idea must sustain itself in the marketplace. Therefore uniqueness cannot be claimed simply on the basis of cost effectiveness. The truly unique capabilities of the digital computer come from the tremendous generality and power of its underlying basic process—the manipulation and transformation of abstract symbols with extraordinary rapidity. Early applications of computers to tedious and repetitive arithmetic tasks failed to suggest this potential power. This is why many people still view computers as nothing more than incredibly fast mechanical calculators. But computers are much more than that; they are in fact information-processing systems that rival existing educational delivery systems for many applications.

The ability to recognize a particular state or arrangement of symbols, and to take actions based on that state (including modifying the state and/or the instructions governing the system) enables computers to exhibit characteristics defined as intelligence when present in humans. For example, cognitive scientists routinely use the symbolic manipulation capabilities of computers to simulate human thought processes. Computer scientists working in the area of artificial intelligence have implemented systems that understand limited vocabularies of human speech, play chess at the master level, prove theorems, and compute structural descriptions of complex organic compounds from data such as mass spectrograms.

The capability to execute complex, and adaptive, sets of instructions places computers at the center of many converging technologies. Intelligence is easily added to common household systems by combining them with powerful and inexpensive microcomputers. For example, the integration of telephones, television, and computers creates powerful new teletex and videotex systems capable of delivering individualized interactive education into almost every home in America. The synergy of these technologies is beginning to be explored in dozens of new ways, and computers are the key to making new applications adaptable to the needs of individuals.

Programmers, after only a year or two of experience, can write applications that simplify tasks in every domain of modern life. It is this incredible generality that is pushing information-processing systems into every corner of society—from wristwatches to energy monitoring systems to robots exploring uncharted planets. In addition to this general growth, the special features of the academic world dovetail more closely with the capabilities of computers than with many of the traditional manual ways of processing information. This close match between computer capabilities and academic functions guarantees even larger impacts in the educational domain.

Creation, storage, retrieval, processing, use, and dissemination of information are at the core of academic effort. For this community, the convergence of computing and communication represents perhaps the most profound technical development since the invention of movable type and the modern printing press. Because information processing is so central to academics, systems that amplify human cognitive capabilities will have tremendous consequences, some of which are already visible in a few organizations.

Taking Advantage of the New Wave

About 30 years ago, computers began to make an impact at large universities as expensive batch-processing systems were introduced for advanced research, and later, administrative applications. Approximately 15 years ago, conversational timesharing systems placed person and machine into a new interactive, and expensive, problem solving environment. During the last 10 years rapid decreases in hardware costs have caused mini- and microcomputers to spread into every area of higher education. The new, and potentially largest wave will result from the integration of low-cost computing and communication technologies.

Although information-processing technologies have an entertainment dimension—witness the great popularity of computer games—in the academic community their primary focus is on the intellectual processes central to scholarly disciplines. Computing systems are partners in the teaching and research process. Their wide applicability ensures that computing systems may be used in the research process of every discipline—from collecting, analyzing, and storing data to simulating complex systems to proving theorems.

Modern computer-aided instructional systems have courseware available in hundreds of different topics that allow students to take individualized paths through different learning environments and assessment programs. The literature about innovative applications ·of computing to almost every subject imaginable is growing rapidly. Students may now receive customized career counseling though systems that help them make explicit value judgments and select appropriate courses to meet their long-term educational goals.[1] They may learn about computers in programming and other computer science courses, or they may use them as a tool to learn other disciplines. A modern graphics terminal connected to an inexpensive computer can provide a flexible laboratory in which a student may experiment with simulations of physical and social systems of all types. Students may even change the basic laws of physics in such labs to observe what might happen in hard-to-imagine universes.

As external agencies impose costly administrative requirements on colleges and universities, administrative applications will continue to grow. Newer support areas such as text processing, financial modeling, and electronic mail and teleconferencing applications will aid central administrations, departments, and individual scholars. For example, independent word processing systems have demonstrated an ability to reduce the costs of writing individualized letters to thousands of alumni and potential applicants, and of revising scholarly papers and internal memoranda. Adding communications, larger storage capacities, and more logic to such units turns them into advanced messaging systems that can change the way organizations function.

The unique features of information-processing technologies explain why they are becoming ubiquitous in higher education. Their generality and power come from the capability to process abstract symbols in ways that make them active *participants* in teaching and research activities. Many technologies help to store, retrieve, and communicate information; information-processing systems are unique in that they enable people to discover new knowledge in addition to communicating information. An unusual example is the computer system DENDRAL at Stanford, which is the first nonhuman co-author of a paper in a refereed scientific journal.[2] While it may be argued that similar discoveries could have been made by hundreds of people working with pencil and paper for years, the point is that society could not afford such a process. Creative people working closely with modern information-processing systems guarantee discoveries that otherwise would be unimaginable.

The Campus Computing
Environment of the 1980s

Examples of current innovative efforts to integrate new information-processing technologies with traditional academic objectives merely suggest the potential impact of this technological revolution on teaching, research, and administration. Such examples are rarer today than they should be. Evidence of this as yet untapped potential surfaces continually at meetings of academic computer professionals, such as the annual conferences of the Association for Computing Machinery Special Interest Group on University and College Computing Services, EDUCOM, CAUSE, the Snowmass Academic Computer Center directors meeting, and others. Many of the same points have been raised during campus consulting assignments and meetings of visiting committees. The summary of these themes presented in the following paragraphs is taken from many such sources and does not represent a formal consensus of any one group.

1. The United States is fast becoming an information-based economy, and computer technology is central to this movement. Studies such as Marc Porat's 1977 effort, show that in the U.S., information-based activities now account for almost half of the gross national product.[3] In this work, Porat describes the shift of the predominant work in the U.S. from agriculture to industry to information processing. Many sectors of the economy (e.g., banking, airlines, communications, hotels, etc.) have moved faster than education to integrate computers into the basic fabric of the organization.

2. More students each year are demanding courses in information-processing fields. The number of undergraduate majors in computer science doubled between 1975 and 1981. By the end of the decade almost every student, not just those in computer fields, will expect the full range of computer-related services to be available at colleges and universities. However, there is no well-defined notion of what constitutes a reasonable level of information-processing literacy for individuals majoring in other subjects, preparing for other professions, or just learning to function well in an information based society. The University of Iowa reports that instructional computing grew by about 40 percent last year and that the university is not yet close to meeting the demand for services.

3. Computer applications will grow rapidly in new areas as the relative costs of automated and human information processing continue to shift dramatically. The prices of computer hardware capable of performing at a specified level will continue to decline during the next 10 years, as they have for the last 30, at a compound yearly rate of approximately 25 percent. This trend means that a 1982 medium-scale computer costing $100,000 will be available in 1987 for $15,000 to $30,000. However, the cost of a technical person or faculty member will increase by 75 percent assuming 10 percent yearly inflation. In 5 years, the relative cost of a skilled person will go from one-fifth the cost of a powerful minicomputer to twice its cost.

4. Trained information-processing professionals (faculty, analysts, programmers, technicians, etc.) will be more expensive, harder to recruit, and more difficult to retain than they are now, or were in the past. Salary policies will make these problems more severe in the education and non-profit sectors of the economy than in the business sector.

Recent studies show that the number of graduates with degrees in computer-related fields lags behind the number of available openings at the following rates [4]:

a. a BA/BS by a factor of four (13,000 vs. 54,000)
b. an MS by a factor of ten (3,400 vs. 34,000)
c. a PhD by a factor of four (330 vs. 1,300)

The shortage of computer professionals is part of a much larger gap in trained scientific and engineering professionals described in a *New York Times Magazine* article by William Stockton. He reports that the number of doctorates awarded in engineering in this country declined by one-third during the last decade. In 1980, an estimated 10 to 15 percent of the nation's faculty positions in engineering were vacant. Stockton also reported that Japan, with half the population of the United States, graduated 19,257 electrical engineers with bachelor's and master's degrees or doctorates in 1977, while the United States turned out 14,290. He adds that the gap is believed to have been widening.[5]

5. There is a current personnel and facilities crisis in academic computer science departments throughout the country.[6] Insufficient experimental facilities on campus and significantly higher salaries in the private sector make it almost impossible to hire and retain enough faculty to teach the courses demanded by students or to perform needed research. The same high salaries lure students into the work force before they have completed enough graduate training to help with departmental teaching and research. However, they often do not have enough training to fill many of the vacant higher-level industrial and academic positions. Peter Denning, president of the Association for Computing Machinery, summarizes the problem: "We are eating our seed corn."[7]

6. The rapid development and spread of microcomputers is accelerating the decentralization of computing resources on campuses. Many students now have their own microcomputers and there are several predictions that during this decade, 30 to 50 percent of students and faculty will have personal systems. Such estimates may be conservative. These owners will require ways to link their systems to other microcomputers and to large local and remote campus or non-campus facilities for access to data, large storage capacity, and high-quality printing capabilities, and for communication with other scholars. Current telephone systems cannot handle this growth in digital communication requirements, but it is the linkage, or networking, of many distributed systems that is needed to utilize fully the growing capabilities of personal computers.

7. Libraries and computer centers will draw closer together. Similarities in information-processing functions and needs are emerging and will become more important than historical differences in organization. As library materials increase in cost by yearly rates of about 20 percent and computing hardware costs decline by about 25 percent per year, information systems will be used in more

innovative ways. This trend will accelerate as more commercial organizations publish and distribute materials in electronic ways. Access to bibliographic data and archival information through common terminal networks will allow faculty and students to search on-line catalogues or use several computers, both local and remote, for such standard current applications as statistical analyses and simulations.

8. Nationwide discipline-based computer networks will draw geographically dispersed academic communities together in new ways. Computing and communications opportunities strengthen scholars' ties with their disciplines and weaken their ties to departments, colleges and universities. Experiences in the computer science community with computer networks and in many innovative applications of EDUNET (EDUCOM's cooperative computer network linking 17 campus facilities to more than 170 institutions) indicate that the community of scholars will extend far beyond an individual college or university.

9. Administrative computing in general is much more difficult and costly than most university administrators believe. Recent studies show that budgets for all types of computing services are now more than one billion dollars per year, which is slightly more than 2 percent of total higher education budgets; that approximately 90 percent of colleges and universities have access to some form of computing capability; and that about half of total academic computing expenditures is for administrative data-processing applications.[8] Ten years ago administrative computing accounted for only about 34 percent of the total. Standardized software for many important academic applications, when it exists, remains expensive and difficult to install.

10. Instructional computing is funded at an inadequate level. In 1967, the President's Science Advisory Committee submitted *Computers in Higher Education* (the Pierce Report), which estimated that about 30 hours per year of instructional computing, averaged over all students, would be required for undergraduate use.[9] Recent studies indicate that only a very few schools are now achieving this level of support, and they spend $100 to $200 per student per year for instructional computing. Most provide less than one third of this amount. During the last 10 years, instructional computing dropped from 30 percent of computing budgets to 25 percent. To improve this situation, large capital investments are required from an educational system that has been traditionally people, rather than capital, intensive.

11. New economic partnerships are needed to capitalize on the technological opportunities available now and in the near future. Federal support for campus computing is less than it was 10 years ago. New relationships among institutions of higher learning, government, foundations, and industry must be developed to generate the human, technological, and financial resources needed to move forward. Countries such as Japan and France are implementing nationally coordinated information-system plans. At the very least, we in the U.S. must forge new and innovative partnerships to support academic computing or face the probability that several other countries will pass us in technological leadership.

Organizational Implications for Colleges and Universities

Whether or not information technologies are unique, the demands they place on academic institutions are clearly proliferating at a quickening pace. Therefore, the argument as to why higher education must create new strategies for information-processing activities in the next decade is in part a very practical one. Such strategies are central to the convergence of several related campus activities that use new technologies (e.g., video discs, graphics, broad-band cables, etc.) in instruction, research, administration, telecommunications, mail, printing, institutional planning, and library services. The integration of parts of these activities for capital planning purposes and priority setting will be sound business policy because of the great potential for waste if they are handled separately. For example, the implementation of a new telephone system or broad-band TV cable network is likely to be an economic mistake without a thorough investigation of the implications of rapidly increasing digital needs from terminals and distributed mini- and microcomputer systems.

Effective models of integrated planning and priority setting do exist. Several universities have created positions with titles like vice provost for information services (e.g., Carnegie-Mellon and the University of Washington) or organizations with broad technology responsibilities such as Stanford's Center for Information Technology or Harvard's Office of Information Technology. With this approach, responsibilities for planning and managing campus information technology are identified with one group or one position.

Another solution is the creation of a high-level task force charged with planning responsibility in these areas. An example of the type of problem that can be attacked by such planning groups is that in many institutions, different individuals are responsible for campus voice, data, and video networks. In most cases, they communicate with each other infrequently. Often directors of these functions report to different vice presidents, and the first opportunity for coordinated planning sometimes occurs at the presidential level when competing requests for capital improvements are discussed.

Planning Issues

Perhaps the most fundamental area that requires campus-wide discussion and planning is computer, or information-technology, literacy. An important policy question is how to prepare students for a world in which computing will have an ever increasing impact. Dr. Richard Van Horn, Provost and Senior Vice President of Carnegie-Mellon University, has defined four approaches, or viewpoints, for students and schools trying to determine the appropriate levels of computing for different scholarly communities[10]:

- *Elective.* Computing is viewed as an interesting subject which students may elect to study if they so wish.
- *Literacy.* Computing is a basic area of knowledge and every student should understand its essential features.

- *Skill.* Computing is viewed as an intellectual skill similar to natural languages or mathematics.
- *Foundation.* Computing is viewed as the key technology for information processing, and information processing is viewed as the fundamental process in learning.

Determining which level is appropriate for an entire institution, a department, or a program is a key policy question that many institutions have not faced. Potential students are beginning to ask about the existence and the content of such policy statements while they are selecting the school they wish to attend. The appropriate policy for an institution should not be determined by the director of the computer center, but by careful deliberation of academic and administrative long-range planning committees representing the entire academic community.

Many policy issues center on money. A key policy question is salary administration for computer-related support staff and for computer science faculty and research staff. There is a serious drain of individuals trained in these areas to the industrial sector. Market factors are not likely to correct the situation, and, in fact, may make it worse.

Salary administration in higher education is not governed by the general free market because there are constraints imposed by governmental agencies for public institutions and internal equity problems with faculty and staff from other disciplines. As the external market for skilled computing professionals pushes salaries up faster than the general inflation rate, institutional constraints will not allow an equity in many higher education organizations. Several universities have innovative plans to solve similar problems in the medical and legal professions, and they must start to deal with information-processing professionals in similarly creative ways.

Perhaps the most difficult problems in this area are the financial issues concerned with generating the investment capital required to move forward. Even though the underlying economic trends are reducing hardware costs by yearly amounts of 25 percent, the investment required to deliver a modest amount of interactive computing to every student is still very large. Hardware will cost less in a few years, but building innovative programs and recruiting staff take time and hardware and software investments are required to accomplish either goal.

In the 1960s the National Science Foundation took a leadership role in investing in computing in higher education. There is no such leadership today. Robert Gillespie and Deborah Dicaro, from the University of Washington, recently completed the final report of a study sponsored by the National Science Foundation titled *Computing and Higher Education: An Accidental Revolution*.[11] As part of this study a panel on computing and higher education created a consensus statement to recommend programs and policies addressing the major national issues affecting computing in higher education. These issues need to be discussed at many levels, and they need to be on the agendas of university planning committees.

What is needed for tomorrow is a set of new partnerships among higher education, foundations, industry, and government to meet these challenges. New interdependencies among these groups are emerging. Resource sharing of people, ideas, software, and hardware is one dimension where a great deal more can be done. Information-technology challenges are national priorities in a few countries. However, much can be done by individual institutions, and consortia where they are appropriate, to create innovative strategies that are both workable and fundable.

Common Strategies

The extent and type of planning in a college or university are reflections of both its academic character and management style. Planning procedures, to work effectively, should be consistent with the general management structure. Therefore, it is not surprising that several different strategies and planning styles are evident in the ten chapters that follow.

Given the diversity of institutions and styles, it may be surprising that there are important common denominators to their information-processing strategies for the 1980s.

- *Organizational Structure.* Eight of the institutions have a single administrative office or individual to coordinate information-processing related issues. Of the remaining two, one is actively considering the creation of such a position.
- *Decentralization.* All of the organizations are moving to a more decentralized information-processing environment. This trend does not necessarily imply that centralized facilities will cease to exist, or even get smaller. It does mean that an increasing amount of information-processing activity will occur outside of a centralized facility.
- *Personal Computers.* All of the organizations have, or are formulating, plans related to the growing potential of personal workstations for students, scholars, and administrators. Rather than resisting the avalanche of these systems (the way many organizations resisted minicomputers in the early 1970s) the ten campuses are actively encouraging innovative uses of personal computing systems.
- *Networking.* All ten campuses are involved with both local and national networking activities. They are investigating, and a few have installed, experimental, high-capacity, digital, local-area networks. Some are even designing their own networks. Five of the universities have facilities connected to national packet switched networks, and all use such networks to share remote hardware and/or software resources. Several of the larger organizations are studying combined voice, digital, and video networks. Many face major investments in telephone systems and are seeking to make sure such investments serve more than one purpose.
- *Library Automation.* Once again, all of the schools have plans to deal with the convergence of computing and communications to help provide access to library resources. Many project participants are using local computer systems for circulation and serials control. Several are using national networks and resource-sharing organizations for cataloging, bibliographic, and interlibrary loan services.
- *Information Processing Literacy.* Groups or task forces in each of the colleges and universities are studying what level of literacy for computing and communications activities is required of a well-educated graduate in the 1980s. This definition will vary for each institution, but all are working on the problem.

- *Text Processing.* In all ten institutions, text processing services are seen as important to academic computer literacy and to administrative support. In fact, text processing is the most important service that can be provided to many humanities faculty and students whose work deals with words, not numbers.
- *Electronic Mail.* Several of the campuses have extensive electronic mail systems in operation, and most are actively considering how to provide this service in the future. Today these systems are used locally to allow convenient communications among faculty, students, and administrators. Many individuals are also using national computer-based mail systems for task forces to reduce travel costs and increase the effectiveness of communications.

Conclusions

Each of the ten colleges and universities is in the midst of a major evaluation of how it should participate in the information-processing revolution taking place throughout modern society. Some of the strategies propose a position of leadership, while others suggest that a competitive stance with respect to peer institutions is reasonable. About half of the institutions have decided which strategy will be followed and have determined the broad outline of how it will be implemented. The remaining organizations are still developing strategies. In all of the chapters, the word "plan" is not really appropriate. A better term is "planning process" because of the dynamic nature of the activities and the topic. Given the present financial environment in higher education and the conservative nature of most colleges and universities, the process is much more complicated than seeking a consensus and implementing a simple plan. A fundamental property of the exciting concepts proposed in these case studies is that large financial and human resources are required to make the ideas come alive. A combination of new resources and a reallocation of existing resources is implied by these strategies.

There have been some negative, as well as positive, reactions to the planning activities on the campuses. An inherent danger to long range planning, in general, is that some expectations may be raised to unattainable levels. In addition, there is often a backlash effect when major new ideas are proposed in an organization because existing subgroups try to protect their positions. Finally, some fear that a plan will stifle opportunities to move in new directions or take advantage of developments that could not be foreseen, rather than providing a framework within which to exploit such opportunities. The fact that such reactions are taking place on some of the participating campuses does not mean that the strategies are poor or that they will not be adopted. It does imply that these planning activities are being taken very seriously, and it reinforces the assertion that information-processing strategies are crucial for the futures of colleges and universities.

Acknowledgements

Significant portions of this chapter were published in two articles by the author titled "Campus Information Processing: A New Wave,"*Educational Record*, Fall 1981; and "Strategies for Campus Computing," *Perspectives in Computing*, Vol. 2, No. 3, October 1982. The permission of the American Council on Education and IBM to include this material is appreciated.

References

1. "Career Guidance by Computer," *Mosaic* (the magazine of the National Science Foundation). January/February 1979, pp. 17–22.
2. Feigenbaum, E. A. "The Art of Artificial Intelligence: I. Themes and Case Studies of Knowledge Engineering," *Proceedings of the 5th International Joint Conference on Artificial Intelligence* (2 vols). Cambridge, MA: Massachusetts Institute of Technology, August 1977.
3. Porat, M. A. *The Information Economy.* U.S. Dept. of Commerce, Office of Telecommunications, Washington: GPO, 1977.
4. Hamblen, J. W. *Computer Manpower—Supply and Demand by States,* Fourth Edition. St. James, Missouri: Information Systems Consultants, 1981.

5. Stockton, W. "The Technology Race," *The New York Times Magazine.* June 28, 1981, pp. 14–18, 49–56.
6. Denning, P. J. ed. "A Discipline in Crisis," *Communications of the ACM,* Vol. 24, No. 6, June 1981.
7. Denning, P. J. "Eating our Seed Corn,"*Communications of the ACM,* Vol. 24, No. 6, June 1981.
8. Hamblen, J. and Baird, T. *Fourth Inventory: Computers in Higher Education 1976-77.* Princeton, NJ: EDUCOM, 1979
9. President's Science Advisory Committee. *Computers in Higher Education* (Pierce Report). Washington, 1967
10. Van Horn, R. L. "How Much Computing is Enough," *Proceedings of 11th Annual Seminar for Academic Computing Services.* Oregon State University: Division of Continuing Education, 1980
11. Gillespie, R. G. and Dicaro, D. A. *Computing and Higher Education: an Accidental Revolution.* NSF Grant, SED–7823790

2

Hamilton College

DAVID SMALLEN
Director of the Computer Center

With the transformation of society brought about by widespread application of computer technology, liberal arts colleges must prepare students to compute in the broadest sense of the word. This means educating students to participate actively in an information-based society by offering an appropriate computing environment in which learning can take place. In the context of the small liberal arts college, several barriers to supplying this computing environment are more severe than in larger institutions. Among these are: the inability to take advantage of economies of scale; stiff competition from universities and industry for qualified personnel; and a more constrained financial environment in which to operate. All of these factors limit the ability of the small institution to react to rapid changes in technology. Within this framework Hamilton College is taking a flexible approach that features the use of modern technology, supports several diverse forms of computing, and minimizes obstacles to its mission of properly educating students.

At Hamilton, the process of providing computing services has four major components:

1. A close association with a major research university—Cornell.

2. A microcomputer facility to provide a user-friendly environment for general computing.

3. Administrative computing on a small-business system utilizing a local terminal network.

4. A variety of communication links that integrate various resources.

The combined utility of these four components enables Hamilton to provide a flexible computing environment that supports teaching, research, and the information needs of administrative offices.

Computing in the Liberal Arts Setting

The Hamilton College catalogue states:

> The central purpose of the college is to develop in its students an understanding of the value and uses of the intellect, and by so doing, to prepare them for a life of enrichment and constructive influence free of the twin provincialisms of ignorance and arrogance.

Further, students are expected to strive to achieve seven goals, two of which are:

> ...an ability to think, write, and speak clearly, with precision and cogency...and...an informed acquaintance with, and a critical appreciation of, the ways in which knowledge of nature and man is gained through experimental or quantitative methods of analysis.[1]

In this context, what then is the role of computing? At Hamilton it is the ability to extend the intellect and open new paths of knowledge. While the second goal mentioned above speaks to the traditional view of computing as a means of assisting in the analysis of data, it is perhaps the first goal that can be most dramatically influenced by understanding the power of the computer. The widespread use of the computer holds great promise for improving the ability to think with "precision and cogency."

Hamilton College is not alone among liberal arts colleges in seeking to define a role for computing in the college curriculum. The role of technology in general and computing in particular in the liberal arts curriculum is currently a topic of considerable discussion. In his recent paper, Stephen White of the Sloan Foundation states: " . . . to believe in this era that a man possesses a liberal education who is ignorant of analytic skills and technological skills is to make a mockery of the central concept of liberal education and to ignore the nature of the world in which the graduate will live, and to which he hopes to contribute."[2] In a similar vein Nannerl Keohane, in her inaugural address as president of Wellesley College, spoke of the need to ensure that students acquire both the technological skills and methodology to be " . . . informed users of the powerful tools at their disposal, capable of appreciating and taking advantage of their powers. These persons will also be perceptive and responsible critics of such tools and techniques."[3] How information technology will be integrated in the liberal arts setting is an issue Hamilton College is addressing.

The first step in developing understanding among Hamilton College students is to encourage computer literacy among faculty members. By this we mean developing and encouraging teachers and researchers to view computing as an important tool for understanding their disciplines. Computing must not be a topic one goes to the computer center to learn about, but rather an integral part of the classroom experience. Many faculty at Hamilton view computing in this light and integrate computing into their courses, with the most notable applications made in the social science areas—political science, psychology, and sociology.

An Historical Perspective

Although Hamilton College has a long tradition of excellence in the liberal arts, its history with respect to computing services is modest, dating back only about ten years. At that time administrative data processing was accomplished by means of an IBM 407 accounting machine and associated unit record equipment, while academic facilities consisted of two small minicomputers and three Teletypes connected to the local air force base computer.

During this period, two quite different changes were taking place at the college which would have important implications for computing. First, due to upheavals in the educational job market, Hamilton was able to attract many more faculty from large graduate-level institutions. These faculty had been trained in the use of computer facilities and found that a proper level of computing support was necessary to continue their teaching and research interests. This was particularly true in the social sciences where statistical packages were viewed as essential tools. Secondly, more students were becoming interested in learning about computer science.

Also at this time, the college realized that administratively it was operating as if there were still 600 students enrolled rather than 1600. The data processing department had all it could handle with payrolls, class lists, and necessary bills. The most crucial offices with respect to the ultimate well-being of the college—admissions and development—were still operating in a predominantly manual fashion.

Thus, a committee was organized by the president to recommend a future course of action for computing at Hamilton. The committee predicted that administrative applications would be relatively homogeneous, for the most part involving data storage and retrieval, while already diverse academic needs would become even more diverse in the future. In fact, the level of teaching and research support that Hamilton College faculty needed was not qualitatively different from that found at large research universities. The committee recommended that academic and administrative computing resources be jointly managed.

To comprehend fully the manner in which decisions about computer services are being made at Hamilton, it is important to understand both the formal and informal planning processes currently in existence. Traditionally, the mechanism of achieving curricular change has been a system of standing faculty committees that recommend changes to the entire faculty and, by faculty vote, to the president. In addition, ad hoc committees are often set up by the president to advise on matters of immediate concern. As chief academic officer, the dean of the college participates, ex officio, on most committees. Academic program changes generally receive careful consideration and proceed slowly. Hamilton prides itself on the quality of its instructional program, the responsibility for which rests on the favorable faculty-student relationships of advisor-advisee, teacher-student, and researcher-research assistant. The fact that all students have the opportunity to develop such relationships is central to the ethos of the institution.

Administratively, planning is centered in the president's cabinet, which, in addition to the president, consists of the Dean of the College, Dean of Admissions, Vice President for Administration and Finance, Vice President for Communication and Development, and Dean of Students. Currently, no separate planning office exists.

The director of the computer center is responsible for overseeing both academic and administrative computing services. He formally reports to the Vice President for Administration and Finance. Informally, he advises the Dean of the College on matters relating to computing services that support the teaching and research interests of the faculty. In addition, the director serves as a resource person to both officers on matters relating to the use of computer technology in the college. No formal committees currently exist to recommend policy changes to the director, although he meets informally with academic and administrative users, both individually and in groups, to receive suggestions for improving computing services.

The location of the computer center—on the lower level of the library—has served to encourage considerable dialogue between the librarian and the director on problems relating to the application of computer technology to general information processing. One result of this communication has been a procedure for assisting faculty and students in the use of data acquired from the Inter-University Consortium for Political and Social Research (ICPSR). Here, the reference librarians serve as resource persons for the location of appropriate data, while the computer center staff provides support for accessing and working with data. It is clear that the future direction of information technology at Hamilton will result in similar, and even closer, integration of library, computing, and audio-visual resources.

Goals for Computing

As Hamilton's goals set high expectations for the accomplishments of undergraduates, so do computer center goals provide direction in planning for the provision of computing services. Three goals characterize the direction that Hamilton is taking. They are:

1. To achieve a computer-literate faculty, administration, and student body; specifically, individuals who understand from actual experience how the computer can be used to assist in the management and discovery of knowledge.

2. To develop in the academic community an appreciation of computer resources analogous to other predominant college information resources (e.g., the library), and, as a result of such appreciation, to foster applications of computer technology significant to the learning process.

3. To increase the overall efficiency of Hamilton's administrative operations by utilizing automation that cuts paperwork, enhances the ability of administrators to deal in a "personal" manner with constituents, and increases the accuracy of the information being maintained.

These goals provide both a framework for computing to enhance the overall educational goals of the college and a direction for administrative operations. Each of these goals can be transformed into short- and long-term objectives. Progress in achieving these goals is measured on a yearly basis.

Association with Cornell

Hamilton began using Cornell University's computing services in 1974. Initially, use consisted of a remote job entry (RJE) connection using a leased telephone line. During the mid 1970s, when this link provided Hamilton's major computing resource, the school averaged over 30,000 batch jobs each year. Later, services were expanded to include access via interactive terminals, with both facilities now available over 100 hours per week, and alternative dial-in facilities available 20 hours per day. Over 400 students and 20 faculty members currently use the connection with Cornell annually. However, the association provides far more than equipment use. The long-term approach for providing computer services at Hamilton is interwoven with this association.

Cornell provides Hamilton with access to a diversity of computer resources of the type found only on large computer systems. For example, faculty and students currently use more than five different statistical packages, an equal number of programming languages, and other application software. It can be argued that one statistical package will suffice, but this is not the case. Some statistical procedures are only thoroughly accomplished by certain statistical software packages. Any one such package is, in fact, severely limited for full analysis of data and teaching of statistical concepts. This diversity has positive benefits in preparing students for similar situations in the "real" world where there is no one approach that works in all cases.

More important than access to hardware and software is access to a staff of computer professionals. Every small institution must face this problem. In computing, the shortage of qualified personnel is severe, with no significant improvement indicated in the 1980s. By many estimates, personnel costs will rise about ten percent per year[4], causing personnel sharing to have strong economic incentives. In light of recent economic conditions, a higher than average annual salary percentage increase is likely. There is no substitute for being able to talk to a knowledgeable consultant when first using computer software. As computer technology advances, those who have access to personnel who understand that technology will have the best chance of successfully applying it. It is not possible for the small liberal arts institution to acquire enough in-house expertise to keep up with the rapidly changing information-processing field. Only by association with larger institutions committed to a high level of computing can the small liberal arts college hope to stay abreast of the latest technological changes.

In addition to understanding technological change, one must also be able to provide written documentation for a variety of uses, a skill that is rarely a part of computing resources at a small institution. Interestingly, during the 1960s the model of the small college utilizing remote computing resources was feasible due to the high cost of hardware. In the 1980s a similar model may be feasible because of the high cost of technical personnel and the range of computing needs that must be supported.

Generally, if a small institution like Hamilton makes a capital expenditure for equipment, it is committed to that equipment for an extended period of time. Unable to achieve economies of scale, it is quite common for the small institution to acquire computer hardware to accomplish all of its computing and to have the equipment overloaded in a relatively short period of time. This is followed by a period of dissatisfaction with the system until the next capital expenditure can be made. The original system, which perhaps reflected the latest in computer technology at the time of purchase, is soon not as cost-effective as more modern equipment. By maintaining a close relationship with Cornell, Hamilton can benefit from frequent capital investments of the larger university and avoid the purchase cycle described above.

Ideas as well as data are shared through the Cornell-Hamilton association. Hamilton faculty have developed computer-based materials which have proved to be of interest to the Cornell community, and such exchanges encourage scholarship among both faculties. Currently, the two institutions have formed a federation arrangement in the ICPSR (mentioned earlier) which results in economies of time and resources for both institutions. Data are maintained in one location, ordering is centralized, institutional charges are reduced, and potential interdepartmental associations are enhanced.

Clearly, it would be impossible for Hamilton to be at the forefront of the field in information technology. Nevertheless, association with Cornell has enabled the college to apply some of the most recent advances in the field to a liberal arts setting. By focusing efforts on those areas most heavily impacting the college curriculum—namely, assisting faculty with their teaching and research—we are able to maintain a position of excellence among comparable educational institutions. One prominent example of Hamilton's uniqueness among small colleges is the use of special software for teaching computer science courses, described later in this chapter.

In addition to association with Cornell there are a number of other affiliations that Hamilton must consider if it is to address computing needs. Among these are interuniversity arrangements through special activities like the EDUNET computing network and cooperation with local companies. Each has a potential for ameliorating some of the problems Hamilton will encounter in the near future.

Currently, via EDUNET, Hamilton utilizes the EFPM modeling system, a computer-based software system that assists the college decision makers during the annual budgeting process. Access to specialized resources via organizational arrangements such as those provided by EDUNET enable Hamilton to provide a wider range of services without having to wait until enough users exist to cost-justify acquisition of the resource locally. Additionally, such services as MAILNET (an electronic mail system) and teleconferencing, will enable faculty and administration to maintain closer contact with current developments in their fields of interest.[5] These computer-based communication services are attractive alternatives, especially for the small college, when considered in light of the high cost of transportation for meetings and the inefficiencies of traditional methods of correspondence.

Although the shortage of faculty to teach computer science courses at small colleges is acute, an intimate educational environment and Hamilton's progressive approach to hardware and software services have enabled the college to attract a trained computer scientist for its faculty. Nevertheless, the existing shortage of computer science instructors has provided an opportunity for Hamilton to rethink its approach to the traditional faculty appointment. Within twenty miles of the Hamilton campus are several internationally known computer research firms. Many of the employees of these companies are interested in college teaching, but remain in industry due to the great disparity in salaries. One feasible alternative to full-time employment, however, is a cooperative arrangement which enables computer specialists to take on part-time teaching assignments at the college. This could have great benefit for both the companies and the college; it would provide the college access to knowledgeable computer professionals, and an interactive environment for the qualified computer experts who want to teach. Of course, this arrangement must preserve Hamilton's high standards that emphasize personal contact between students and faculty.

Microcomputers

Microcomputer technology offers both a promising and problematical situation for the small institution. On one hand, the initial technology costs are now affordable, while on the other hand, the types of applications feasible on such systems are limited. The costs associated with widespread use of microcomputers can be substantial.

At Hamilton, a microcomputer facility provides a major portion of current computing needs. Over 250 students used the facility this year in connection with offerings in computer science, and an additional 150 students used the microcomputers for instruction in biology, psychology, and chemistry. In the process, Hamilton has learned that the microcomputer can be an ideal environment in which students and faculty are first introduced to computing technology. In Hamilton's case, the facility, consisting of twelve Teraks, one Radio Shack TRS-80, and four printers, has been the major resource for teaching introductory computer science courses. In addition, the versatile, medium-resolution graphics packages on these systems have proved to be cost-effective for teaching more advanced computer science courses as well as providing support for computer simulations in biology, real-time experimental learning in psychology, and word processing for faculty and students. There are many things that the microcomputer can do well. However, it is important that it be used to expand the level of computing resources rather than being a limiting factor, which would be the case if it were the only available computing resource on campus.

Developing a computer-literate faculty and student body has been the focus of recent discussions at many institutions. At Hamilton, faculty have chosen to teach about computing by having students actually use a computer in a variety of settings. The microcomputer provides a user-friendly environment in which initial learning can take place, and we currently use a software system called the PLC synthesizer for teaching introductory computer science courses. The synthesizer, developed at Cornell by Professor R. Tietelbaum and initially tested at Hamilton by Professor R. Ellison, provides students with an easy-to-use system with powerful debugging tools set in a structured programming environment. The synthesizer has been acknowledged by many faculty as one of the most important advances in the teaching of introductory computer science in the last decade. Additionally, the use of the Teraks is cost-effective when compared to the alternative of interactive programming costs on a large system. With interactive computer costs averaging from five to ten dollars per hour on many large systems, well equipped microcomputers can pay for themselves in less than two years. Moreover, they provide a substantially better learning environment for the student than many large timesharing facilities.

Another important consideration in managing microcomputer growth on a small campus is compatibility. While several microcomputers exist for dedicated applications such as laboratory control, Hamilton's emphasis has been on maintaining as much compatibility among systems as possible. In particular Hamilton has encouraged the acquisition of systems that are supported by Cornell's Decentralized Computer Services and are capable of communicating with larger facilities. In this manner we have been able to utilize newly developed software and to develop on-campus expertise for simple hardware maintenance.

Microcomputers also provide a means for the small institution to add computing resources incrementally. In this way, the institution can take advantage of hardware and software advances and budget for microcomputer purchases much the same as it would for equipment replacement or the purchase of books and periodicals in the library. Failure to provide sufficient resources for microcomputer purchases will destroy the continuity of the approach and lead to frequent user overloading.

In addition to the centrally provided microcomputer facility several departments have acquired their own microcomputers for several purposes. For example, the psychology and chemistry departments use Apple II microcomputers for laboratory control of experiments and analysis of experimental data, and the physics department uses Commodore Pet microcomputers for similar purposes. The biology and mathematics departments use the Terak microcomputer for instructional computing. Each of these systems was acquired through the standard budgeting method used at Hamilton for other instructional equipment. Advice was often sought from the computer center on what equipment to buy, but the decision on approval or disapproval was made by the appropriate budgetary officer of the college. Thus requests for microcomputer equipment compete with requests for other educational equipment. Not surprisingly, in the last two years requests for microcomputers have begun to come from the humanities faculty members as they learned to use word processing software.

The growth of microcomputer use around campus is a natural outgrowth of the increased understanding of the capabilities of the equipment. Given that the systems require no special conditions for operation, it is a simple matter to provide microcomputer systems in many small areas around campus. The major problem of such growth is the need for hardware and software support for the great (and growing) variety of potential users. Users themselves must also be willing to take greater responsibility for hardware problem recognition if equipment is to remain functional. Additionally, the college must budget for both maintenance and servicing. As hardware is dispersed, demand will rise more quickly than supply. The college must try to provide timely access to equipment for the greatest number of users. One short-term solution to this problem is a concentration of several units in areas where use can be supervised, and expensive peripherals such as printers and disk devices can be shared. Space for such clusters of machines is often difficult to obtain. The costs of space, maintenance, security, and software must be considered when evaluating microcomputers.

For the near future, microcomputers are expected to provide a major component of instructional computing at Hamilton. With an ever-growing need for instruction in computer science, greatly increased use of computer-based instructional materials, and the expanded use of word processing, the microcomputer will become not only the most friendly piece of equipment on which to learn, but the most cost-effective. The graphics capabilities of Hamilton's microcomputers have already resulted in large-scale conversion of instructional materials previously only implemented on large systems. Hamilton currently purchases these materials from organizations like CONDUIT, the software transfer center at the University of Iowa. The growth of similar organizations will likely result in many new materials being used in support of Hamilton's academic and administrative computing needs. Because of the high ratio of development time to actual instructional time, it is reasonable to expect that Hamilton will be a user rather than a developer of such materials.

Library Automation

For several years the Hamilton College library has been involved in computerization of traditional library functions. Five distinct but interrelated areas of library operations have been identified by the college as amenable to computerization in cost-effective ways. These are: original cataloging, maintenance of the catalog, inter-library lending, on-line data base searching for reference services, and circulation.

Since 1974, through a contractual arrangement with OCLC, a national computer-based bibliographic network, the library has been able to obtain, quickly and inexpensively, cataloging data for

new materials or materials reclassified from present library holdings. With more than 8 million bibliographic records, the OCLC data
base satisfies more than 90 percent of the library's needs for cataloging information. Catalog cards are supplied to the library directly
from OCLC and are manually added to the library's card holdings.
By 1985, all of Hamilton's 350,000 holdings are expected to have
been entered into the on-line data base system maintained on the
OCLC central facility.

Consisting entirely of members' bibliographic records, the OCLC
data base is used very efficiently for determining the location of
materials and electronically transmitting interlibrary loan requests
to holding libraries, a process that circumvents delays inherent in
traditional mail requests. A greatly increased volume of requests,
both incoming and outgoing, can be handled through this system
with improved speed and efficienty. To assist faculty and students,
an OCLC terminal is available in the campus library for public use
approximately 80 hours per week.

In addition to OCLC, other computerized data bases containing
both bibliographic and nonbibliographic information relating to a
broad range of subject areas have been used by staff in the library's
reference department for several years. More than 200 data bases are
now available for bibliographic search with more being added each
month. Reference librarians specially trained in on-line searching
techniques perform searches on a library terminal linked to computers about the country by the Telenet telecommunications network.
The OCLC bibliographic data base is also used heavily for reference
purposes to determine bibliographic and location information on
books and other library materials.

The computerization of circulation and reserve reading functions
of the library is highly desirable as it will result in a vastly improved
record-keeping ability and easy charging and discharging of library
materials. Such a system, currently being considered for Hamilton
in the near future, will most likely run not on the college's main
administrative computer system, but rather on a stand-alone minicomputer linked to a large external data base.

Improvements and enhancements to the computerization of
library functions will inevitably occur at Hamilton in the future. In

the meantime, cataloging data will continue to be obtained from a computer data base, and the expectation is that the library will completely replace its manually updated card catalog with a fully computerized on-line catalog. Access to catalog records will continue to include author/main entry, title, editor, etc., but subject access will be greatly improved with the possible application of Boolean, keyword, and multiple-entry searching. Hamilton plans to make library catalog terminals accessible in various campus offices and other locations as well as in the library itself.

Hamilton's interlibrary lending services will continue to have improved access to non-owned materials as the OCLC data base grows. Reference data base searching will become much more common as more data bases become available, and much heavier use will be made of nonbibliographic data bases for fast, factual reference information.

A computerized circulation control system will also improve access to library materials at Hamilton and may be linked with neighboring college libraries so that the location and disposition of library materials will become readily ascertainable.

The library's present computer-based systems require relatively inexpensive computer terminals linked to remote computer data bases via telephone lines. Costs involved include the purchase of terminals and printers, network and OCLC services, and data base searching time.

Hamilton's future development of an on-line catalog and circulation system will require considerable investment. The total amount of these expenditures will depend not only on the type of hardware/ software combinations used, but the extent to which other colleges will share in the development effort. Here again, associations with other institutions may play an important part in making it possible for Hamilton to automate information services.

Administrative Computing

Administrative information systems present additional challenges to the small college. While the volume of transactions does not compare with that of larger institutions, reporting needs are often as complex. Fund accounting systems are basically the same throughout higher education, and the success of the fund-raising and admissions offices in the small college is critical to the success of the institution. Additionally, maintaining a personal approach in dealing with its constituency is often expected and traditional. In this context, the keys to providing computer services at Hamilton are fourfold. These include:

- Acquiring powerful programming software tools.
- Providing management with a flexible inquiry language and reporting scheme.
- Providing on-line access to user files for timely information.
- Integration of word and data processing functions via local communication.

As in the academic computing arena, the shortage of qualified personnel greatly affects administrative computing support. Again, shortages make it difficult for the small institution to maintain continuous staffing. As a result, it is common to hire only inexperienced personnel when positions are vacant. It is therefore mandatory that the software tools be facile enough for effective utilization by such personnel. By trading sophistication of software for experience of personnel, the small institution thus provides continuously effective administrative computing services.

In the programming realm, productivity is a critical necessity at Hamilton, given the fact that the programming staff consists of two people. In order to improve productivity—as measured by the time necessary for our staff to address requests for administrative services —Hamilton must provide powerful software tools including on-line program development, data base management software, and easy-to-use teleprocessing interfaces. While packaged software meets some needs, it is illusionary to think that needs do not change.

To understand fully current administrative software choices, it is important to understand the manner in which administrative applications at Hamilton have developed. When Hamilton established its computer center in 1974 the emphasis was on setting up effective automated accounting systems including consolidation and automation of the existing payroll system. A package was acquired from a hardware vendor and modified to handle various payroll functions. This package is still being used. In other administrative areas with needs not so pressing, customized software was developed as each office's needs were identified. This customized software operated in a batch environment with all offices being served by 1980. Had the same offices been able to clarify their needs in 1974, and had the college decided to meet those needs immediately, it would have been necessary to acquire packaged software in almost all areas. But regardless of the manner in which the original software was acquired, we now know that change is the rule rather than the exception. The question now for Hamilton is, "How can this change best be managed?" Even with a small staff it must be possible to react to modifications in a timely manner and ultimately to allow the user the flexibility to implement desired reporting changes without having a major impact on other users' service. More than other factors, changing needs have motivated the acquisition of the above-mentioned software tools.

Allowing administrative computing to cope with change, flexible software packages will enable administrators at Hamilton to utilize the college information data base in order to assist in the decision-making process. Hamilton's management will need access to a powerful inquiry language to interrogate the data base and a flexible report writer for producing ad hoc printed reports that involve full file searching. These software tools will allow us to provide a 24- to 48-hour turnaround capability while avoiding extensive program writing. Additional help in analyzing administrative data can be provided by extracting data from administrative files and transmitting that data to Cornell for analysis by large statistical packages. By utilizing remote facilities in this manner, Hamilton avoids maintenance of extensive local resources, or worse, the creation of such resources.

Related to this need to provide administrators with useful and timely information from the institutional data base, is the need to provide administrators with the tools to ask questions about future planning. As Hamilton's administrators are asked to plan for the future, they must learn to use tools that help in the planning process. Computer-based modeling is one such tool. As was mentioned above, EFPM (a computer-based modeling system) is currently used for forecasting and budget planning. Additional applications to financial aid, admissions, and personnnel areas are also important.

The offices of the college that need immediate access to timely data will acquire it through our local terminal network. High-speed, short-haul modems are being used for office-to-computer center connections. Higher speed cable communications may be feasible once this rapidly changing field has matured. In Hamilton's case, the lack of available conduit space coupled with the inherent vulnerability of such conduits to failure on an old campus make the use of this technology for the future somewhat problematical except for intrabuilding functions.

While several offices have used magnetic card typewriters, office automation is in its infancy at Hamilton. Most offices use the traditional electric typewriter as the means of producing written material. Word processing software has been used on the Terak microcomputer for the last two years by students and faculty, but this software is not sufficiently user-friendly for general office use. Given the variety of word processing equipment currently available and the advances that are being announced almost daily, Hamilton's approach to automating the text processing functions of its offices may be considered conservative. Only two offices utilize word processing systems on a rental basis, and these systems operate in a basically stand-alone fashion. At the same time the computer center is examining methods of communication between word processing systems and the main administrative computing system.

This integration of word and data processing functions will be important to the administrative offices because it will enable administrators to utilize directly files of data. Targeted mailings as well as fast response to prospective college applicants require this integration of resources to avoid duplication of effort. In general, such integration of the various administrative functions at the small college provides not only cost reductions but higher levels of service.

Managing Computer Services

Joint management of academic and administrative computer services results in significant benefits for the small institution. It appears that most smaller four-year institutions have chosen this method of providing computer services[6], although they probably have done so by utilizing one machine for both academic and administrative purposes rather than using remote resources. In Hamilton's case this choice results in a considerable sharing of equipment and personnel. Not only does such sharing create cost savings for the institution, it also enables Hamilton to provide a more challenging environment for computer center personnel. The total computer center budget has amounted to slightly over 1 percent of the institutional budget over the last several years (e.g., in 1980-81 it was 1.08 percent of the budget) with administrative computing being only 0.7 percent of the total institutional budget. According to the recent CAUSE survey, Hamilton's expenditures for administrative computing are among the lowest of comparable institutions. However, almost all equipment at Hamilton was chosen because of its ability to provide service to both academic and administrative users. Administrative data can be transmitted to Cornell for statisical analysis, while academic users have benefited from the multiprogramming nature of Hamilton's NCR system by being able to send and receive batch jobs throughout the day.

While computing services at Hamilton have been treated in much the same way as library services (the services exist for the benefit of the academic community with no charge-back system to distribute usage costs), budgeting processes have followed several different approaches. At Hamilton there is a need to reconsider these processes to provide for greater continuity of services.

The rationale behind a charge-back system should be to encourage proper behavior on the part of the user community rather than to create an artificial currency system.[7] At a small institution this can often be more effectively accomplished by informal procedures rather than by internal accounting. Whether the expenditures show up in the computer center line or in individual departments is not particularly relevant.

More important is the means of allocating funds to ensure the continuity of services that the computing organization provides to the college. In a library, in order to ensure continuity of service, regular expenditures are budgeted for books and periodicals (adjusted for price increases). This is done without specifying exactly what items are to be purchased; rather, the administration understands that knowledge in written form is ever-expanding and, in order for the library to continue to reflect this, it must acquire a portion of new materials. This is well understood and traditional. Unfortunately, computing services are not traditional. In order to ensure a similar continuity, the acquisition of hardware and software must be annually budgeted to encourage the application of current technological advances to information services. More importantly, this strategy encourages long-term rather than short-term planning.

Communication

One component of Hamilton's success in providing computing services is communication between the various computing resources. With communicating computing systems, information can be processed using the most cost-effective approach. Figure 1 shows a schematic drawing of the resources available at Hamilton, with communication linkages indicated. In this environment considerable sharing of computing devices and peripheral equipment is possible. As computing facilities pervade the campus, interaction of local systems will continue to provide a timesharing environment, including access to personal data bases and microcomputer technology. This will enable users to satisfy many individual computing needs close to offices or classroom environments.

At Hamilton, the hookup among microcomputers and between microcomputers and larger systems is heavily emphasized in the effort to provide a total computing resource. While stand-alone applications such as laboratory control of experiments are impor-

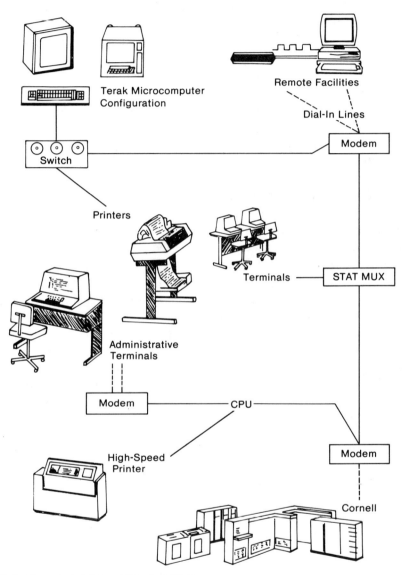

Terak Microcomputer
Configuration

Remote Facilities

Dial-In Lines

Switch

Modem

Printers

Terminals — STAT MUX

Administrative
Terminals

Modem ——————CPU——————

High-Speed
Printer

Modem

Cornell

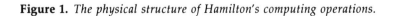

Dotted lines represent phone line connections;
solid lines represent local wire connections.

Figure 1. *The physical structure of Hamilton's computing operations.*

tant, the ability to transmit data to a larger system for analysis completes the system. For example, a Terak microcomputer programmed in Pascal by a student was used in a psychology course to collect data from a real-time experiment. The data were transmitted to a larger system at Cornell for data analysis by a statistical package, and then the final results were documented using a microcomputer-based word processing system.

Summary

The decade of the 1980s will present many challenges for small liberal arts colleges. In times that are sure to test the financial well-being of such institutions, small colleges must face the need to prepare graduates for a society heavily based on computer-processed knowledge. It will be a time in which small colleges find the formation and strengthening of associations with other institutions a tremendous help in providing the additional resources that are too expensive to maintain on their own campuses. And such associations will be made even more feasible with future advances in communications technology. Communication will be the link that makes possible distributed approaches to computing without sacrificing availability and accuracy of information. For Hamilton, such associations and communications have already provided a direction for the 1980s.

References

1. *Hamilton College Catalogue 1981-82*, p. 10.
2. White, Stephen. "The New Liberal Arts," An Occasional Paper, A. P. Sloan Foundation, 1981.
3. Keohane, Nannerl O. "Inaugural Address." Wellesley, MA, September 18, 1981.
4. Van Houweling, Douglas. "Meeting the Challenge of Diversity and Change: Cornell Computer Services." *EDUCOM Bulletin*, Fall 1979.
5. Heller, Paul S. "MAILNET: A Strategy for Inter-Campus Exchange of Electronic Mail." *Proceedings of 1981 CAUSE conference.*

6. Thomas, Charles. "Administrative Information Systems: The 1980 Profile," *CAUSE*, 1981.
7. Bernard, Dan, Emery, James C., Nolan, Richard L., Scott, Robert H. "Charging for Computer Services, Principles and Guidelines." *PBI*, 1977.

3

Dartmouth College

WILLIAM Y. ARMS
Director, Computing Services

Introduction: A Time of Change

For almost twenty years computing at Dartmouth College has been synonymous with timesharing and the DTSS operating system. This is changing. Timesharing has not been abandoned, but its central role is disappearing steadily. The future centers around the Kiewit Network, a high-speed local network connecting all terminals and computers, small or large, to each other.

None of this was foreseen in 1976 when the Kiewit Computation Center at Dartmouth was ten years old. In fact, a report which was written to mark this event announced " . . . the end of an era of spectacular growth and . . . the beginning of a period of growing maturity and stability." Few prophecies have proved more false.

One by one, the assumptions used during the 1970s have had to be dismantled or revised for two major reasons.

1. The first comes from success. Computing has penetrated into every corner of the campus, and its applications are spreading everywhere. When computing expertise was in short supply on cam-

43

pus, it made sense to have it centralized in a single computer center. Now that expertise is widely spread, no single center can have a complete overview of all the opportunities. This implies that the management of computing should be partially decentralized, but it is far from clear how responsibility should be divided. Some departments are highly capable of managing their own affairs, others have a little knowledge, some are still beginners.

2. The second reason for change is technical. In 1970, the cost of computing was dominated by the cost of mainframe computers. Moreover, mainframe computers had large economies of scale. Today these economies of scale have disappeared in some areas but remain in others. For example, microprocessors are very cheap, but large economies of scale remain for on-line file stores. Since medium-size, or small computers can be cost-effective, it often makes sense to buy a machine to run a specific software package or to serve a single department.

These two factors lead to the conclusion that, although computing is becoming increasingly decentralized, for the foreseeable future there will be major central activity. The problem is how to combine centralization with decentralization at a time of rapid change. This would be difficult even starting with a clean slate. In practice however, Dartmouth has to move steadily, without interruption of service, from the present highly centralized structure to an unknown destination.

The movement from complete dependence on a single timesharing system has been guided by a few people, without any overall planning by the college as a whole. Perhaps this is the best way to manage a short period of rapid change. It is certainly not the way to handle the long term. As a result, a major review is now taking place of the technical, managerial, and financial methods needed for a future of decentralized computing.

Standardization is a good example of the problems. There are strong reasons why a university should standardize on a small number of operating systems, computer manufacturers, applications packages, etc. Each new type of computer or operating system is a major expense, and a thankless learning process for users who use more than one machine. On the other hand, there are many software packages which run on one operating system only, many machines that are good for one type of work but not for another, and a hundred and one reasons for buying special-purpose computers. What decision making process will best weigh the advantages and disadvantages of standardization?

Finally, computing causes problems because its special needs require a style of management which is foreign to most universities. Higher education is a static or declining industry. Computing, as a rapidly growing field, is continually forcing awkward decisions to be made. Effective management of computing requires rapid decision making, flexible budgeting and active personnel policies, combined with strict reporting and accountability. Private universities are in a better position than state schools to respond to the opportunities and challenges of computing, yet even the best managed are hard pressed.

Background

Academic Computing

To understand computing at Dartmouth a certain amount of history is needed. When interactive computing came to universities in the early 1960s, there were no commercial timesharing systems on the market, and so several universities developed their own. These universities included MIT, Michigan, Edinburgh, and Dartmouth. Of these, Dartmouth is unique in not being a major research university, and as a result, the design and application of timesharing at Dartmouth has followed a route which is markedly different from the work done at the other schools.

Since the principal users of computing at Dartmouth were students, and not funded researchers, the organizational structure which developed has always emphasized computing as a service to all. It is provided freely, rather than on a cost-recovery basis as in most large universities.

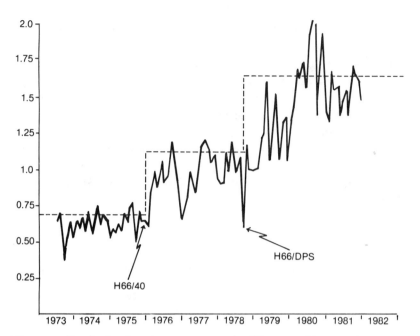

Figure 1. *Graph showing the use per month of Dartmouth's central processor (in millions). The dotted line shows estimated capacity.*

The Dominance of DTSS

The Dartmouth Time Sharing System, universally known as "DTSS," was developed to serve students. It concentrated on fast, flexible, user-friendly software. The BASIC programming language was developed by mathematics professors John Kemeny and Tom Kurtz, whose primary interests lay outside computing.

The DTSS operating system has been developed continuously since 1963, and is one of the most cost-effective timesharing systems for general academic work. The present service runs on a Honeywell 66/DPS-3 computer. A second computer, a Honeywell DPS 8/44 system, is on order. Together these computers will eventually be able to handle about 500 simultaneous users. The early days of DTSS emphasized ease of programming and this remains its par-

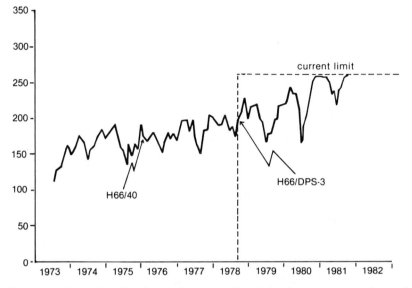

Figure 2. *Graph showing the maximum number of simultaneous users observed by month. Dotted line shows the current limit, or maximum number of users.*

ticular strength. The compilers and other system programs are particularly friendly to users, with excellent error messages, and the amount of on-line information available to help the casual user is impressive. Recent efforts have been aimed at making the system as convenient for word processing and text handling as it is for programming.

Using these facilities, Dartmouth has generated a particularly computer-literate body of students, faculty, and administration. A survey in 1981 showed that about 95 percent of students use computing while at Dartmouth. Perhaps more impressive is the fact that 24 percent of students claim to have written programs for personal use, rather than for course work. The majority are comparatively inexpert, doing a small amount of computing every year without developing any deep expertise, but the general level of awareness of the capabilities of computing is impressive. Figures 1, 2, and 3 show the growth in total demand for timesharing over ten years. The number

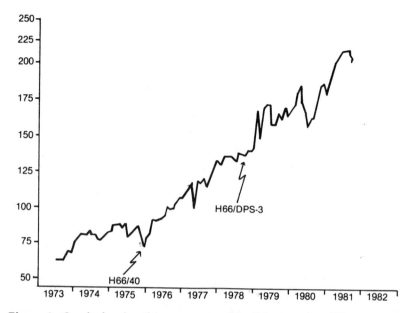

Figure 3. *Graph showing the average monthly disk usage in millions.*

of terminal hours has grown at a compound rate of about 10 percent, but the demand for central processing, and above all for on-line storage, has increased much faster. This reflects the increasing complexity of the work being done—longer programs, in larger programming languages, doing more complex manipulation of ever more data. Table 1 shows the main categories of users and the resources that they use.

From 1962 to 1978 academic computing had one theme—DTSS. Since DTSS runs on a big computer, the college built the Kiewit Computation Center. Since timesharing uses terminals, 800 are presently scattered around the campus including about 150 in public clusters.

During this period the management of computing developed into a routine covered by the college's standard policies. Decision making became institutionalized, revolving around the preparation of the annual budget. Things became so routine that for a period Computing Services reported to an associate dean. The senior officers knew little of what was going on except when major equipment purchases were needed.

Table 1. *Use of Dartmouth College computing 1980–1981*

		Total Dollars Used	Percent
Academic			
Student personal		204,508	8.04
Graduate personal		140,000	2.93
Faculty personal		104,793	4.12
Courses		303,464	11.93
Departmental		298,365	11.73
Sponsored research		91,274	3.59
	Sub-Total	1,076,929	42.33
Administration			
Administrative personal		26,142	1.03
Administrative departments		705,985	27.75
Academic departments		6,121	.24
Computing Services		372,101	14.63
	Sub-Total	1,110,349	43.65
Off-Campus		356,646	14.02
	Total	2,543,924	100.00

First Steps Toward Decentralization

In the late 1970s a single home-grown operating system was recognized as no longer adequate for all academic needs. Groups of users realized that their needs could be best met in other ways and non-DTSS equipment and packages crept onto the campus. Since the movement began as a reaction to gaps in the DTSS services it naturally caused some friction, but fortunately this did not get out of hand. There were four primary areas in which computing facilties grew within departments.

1. Real-time computing. Timeshared computers cannot be used for real-time computing. Rather than go their independent ways, four science departments and the Thayer School of Engineering pooled their efforts and won a CAUSE grant from the NSF to develop real-time minicomputers for science laboratories. This project was coordinated by physicist Arthur Luehrmann. It proved a great success. Working together using New England Digital mini-

computers, the various departments produced user-friendly software and hardware which has been widely used throughout the
college. Currently about 30 New England Digital minicomputers are
in use for real-time laboratory work.

Computing Services joined this project only near the end of its
life span, but has been able to share in the spirit of cooperation
which it generated.

2. Number crunching. The DTSS system cannot handle large
number crunching jobs. In 1979 the chemistry department (with
funds from the NSF), and the Amos Tuck School of Business pooled
resources with Computing Services to buy a PRIME 750. This sits in
the Kiewit building and is operated by the Computation Center for
number crunching and selected academic packages.

3. Statistical and other applications packages. This area remains
a problem. Although several major academic packages have been
imported to run either on DTSS or the PRIME 750, the service given
in this area is still weak. It is the penalty that the college pays for not
supporting any major academic operating system. The declining
price of hardware and the widespread acceptance of SAS as the
standard statistical package have led the college to wonder whether
it has the resources to support a small IBM system specifically to run
academic packages.

4. Computer science. The first significant departmental minicomputer was a Digital Equipment Corporation (DEC) PDP-11/60
in the Thayer School of Engineering. Although acquired for real-
time image processing it rapidly acquired importance as a small
UNIX system. The college is currently evaluating a major commitment to UNIX which would be used to support computer science
teaching and research.

These moves towards decentralized computing have shown the
strengths and weaknesses of centralized management. Computing
Services has a reasonably good overview of the whole of Dartmouth, and some budget flexibility, which can be used to stimulate
and coordinate work in other areas. As a result, on several occasions
Computing Services has been able to seed new developments. On
the other hand, there is a large gap between purely local needs

Table 2. *Computers at Dartmouth*

Date	Computer	Operating System	Use
1978	Honeywell DPS-3	DTSS	General timesharing
1979	DEC PDP-11/60	UNIX	Engineering research
1979	PRIME 550	Primos	Alumni records
1980	PRIME 750	Primos	Academic research
1980	DECSYSTEM 2020	TOPS-20	Medical research
1980	PRIME 550	Primos	Financial records
1981	DEC PDP-11/70	UNIX	Library catalog
1982	DEC VAX-11/750	VMS	Gift recording
1982	Honeywell DPS 8/44	DTSS	General timesharing

which an individual department can address, and global needs which are clearly the task of Computing Services. One reason for the slow progress in bringing statistics packages onto campus is that the demand is spread over many departments. No individual department has the drive or resources to coordinate the needs of the whole college. Table 2 lists the principal computers owned by the college.

Administrative Data Processing

Administrative data processing has always had lower priority than instructional computing. Its recent history began in 1978, when a complete overhaul of all administrative data processing was begun. It was characteristic of the style of computing management at that time that this plan was developed by Computing Services and the middle-level administrators who actually use computing. No senior officer of the college was involved. After evaluating a very wide set of alternatives, it was decided to base future development around five groups of data which are central to the administration of the college. These five groups are:

- Financial
- Student
- Personnel
- Alumni
- Library

The plan is that each group of data will have its own minicomputer. These will be on the Kiewit Network with connections to each other and to the central computers. The DTSS system remains available for other administrative applications and word processing. The aim was, and still is, to install these five minicomputers and overhaul all administrative systems within seven years, that is, by the end of 1985. After three years, one of these five systems is completely operational, two are well developed, and two are in the early planning phase:

1. The financial systems were mainly batch systems. They ran on an ancient Honeywell H200 computer and a vintage collection of punched card equipment. These systems have been converted to on-line input, with batch updating on a PRIME 550 computer. As a second phase, the general ledger system has been replaced by the FAS package from Westinghouse DataScore Systems.

2. At present, most student records are maintained on DTSS. The on-line registration system is excellent, but some other systems are a mess. Work has begun on overhauling the entire area, but it is a long task.

3. Personnel records pose an interesting dilemma. At present, personnel and payroll are handled by separate offices with different computer systems. A new payroll system is badly needed, but most commercial packages combine personnel and payroll. Should the college reorganize its operations to fit a new package?

4. Alumni records are now maintained on a second PRIME 550, with the master data base on DTSS. A new gift recording system has been authorized which will run on a DEC VAX-11/750 computer.

5. The library has its own DEC PDP-11/70 running UNIX. This area is so important that it has its own section later in this chapter.

The most interesting development over the past few years has been the rapid acceptance of packaged software for administrative data processing. Until 1980 all systems were locally developed. In 1980 two small packages were acquired, telephone billing, and menu planning for the dining hall. In 1981 the president personally authorized the use of a package for the general ledger; the new payroll system will almost certainly be a package; gift recording will follow the same route. The biggest package of all is the on-line library catalog. This rapid acceptance of packages is a major change which comes from several things coming together:

1. The packages on the market have improved steadily over the past few years.
2. Minicomputers have reached a price where it is reasonable to buy a computer to run a specific package.
3. The college administration is more knowledgeable and better prepared to adapt procedures to fit packages.
4. The computer center personnel are more flexible.

Computer Science

Despite its early and continuing involvement with instructional computing, Dartmouth was very late in recognizing computer science as an academic discipline. In part this came from a belief in the sanctity of a liberal arts education, with a corresponding dislike of anything vocational. Even now the college does not have a computer science department. Teaching and research in computer science are carried out in four areas:

1. The mathematics department runs a high-quality undergraduate major in computer science. Although begun only in 1978, this major has rapidly established itself as one of the most demanding, yet popular in the college. About 35 students per year major in computer science, but perhaps more important is the fact that nearly half the undergraduates take at least one of the introductory courses.

2. Computer engineering, at both undergraduate and graduate level, is taught at the Thayer School of Engineering. As already mentioned, Thayer School made an important contribution to com-

puting at Dartmouth when in 1979 it introduced the first UNIX system on campus running on a Digital Equipment Corporation PDP-11/60.

3. Since professional graduate schools are a particular strength of the college, when the decision was made to introduce a first graduate program in computing it was decided to emphasize professional training. This led to the imaginative introduction of a masters program in computing and information science, which is intended for those who will be the leaders of data processing, rather than pure computer science. It has proved popular with students and industry. IBM gave a major gift to cover the start-up costs. This course had its first students graduate in 1982.

4. The Kiewit Computation Center teaches non-credit courses and has the most active research and development program on campus. This began in the early 1960s with the development of DTSS, and the BASIC programming language. Currently the group is particularly strong in programming languages, telecommunications, and distributed editing.

The rapid growth in computer science has put considerable strain on the faculty, despite successful recruiting efforts over the last few years. As an example, the average number of students taking each undergraduate course is approximately double what was expected when the major was approved in 1978. One consequence of this growth is that academic research in computer science has not had the emphasis that it deserves. This is a major worry.

Despite the lack of a computer science department, there is good community spirit among the four groups. Computing at Dartmouth was founded by members of the mathematics department and cooperation between the computer center and the faculty has always been strong. Faculty members have regularly worked on computation center projects, and recently members of the center have taught advanced courses in the mathematics department. Many of the faculty in mathematics and engineering have struck up good working relationships.

Recently there has been a growing feeling that computer science is too important at Dartmouth to rely on ad hoc working relationships. The Task Force on Computing has recommended that these fragmented activities should be brought together into a single department, but the area is still uncertain.

The Management of Computing

Long Term Planning

During the late 1970s computing ran itself. Timesharing was king, and business as usual, the order of the day. Planning was informal and everything worked well.

Decentralized computing caught the college by surprise and the initial reactions were private initiatives by key individuals, rather than any coordinated policy. This could not last, and organizational changes began in 1980, when the director of Computing Services was moved to report directly to the provost, a position that he shares with the librarian among others. Since then a series of important steps has been taken which is transforming the way that Dartmouth looks at computing.

In the past the college had no formal mechanism for the long-term planning of computing. In practice the director of Computing Services has always had very great power to select areas of priority and to choose the technical means used to address them. From time to time, working groups have been established to study specific areas, report and disband. Administrative data processing priorities went to the departments which were most energetic in making their needs known. In fact this procedure worked quite well. A single individual with access to a wide range of information has several advantages which are lost in a more formal structure. The most important of these is flexibility.

For this approach to be successful, there must be good communication between the users of computing and the computation center. This is both formal and informal. The formal channel is the Computing Council, but the informal channels are probably more important: Several members of the computer center have adjunct academic appointments. Every director of Computing Services has been an active member of the faculty, teaching courses which use computing. Members of the faculty have held part-time appointments in the computer center. President Kemeny, who was one of the founders of computing at Dartmouth, taught courses throughout his time as president.

With this good communication, planning by informal consensus has proved generally effective for instructional computing. Very little has been formally placed on paper, but the service has been quite responsive to the changing needs of users. However, there are a few important areas which this process has neglected. The most notable of these is support for statistical computing. Current opinion favors the establishment of a user-group of academic users to guide the selection of priorities.

Consensus planning works less well for administrative data processing. Only too often it resulted in no planning, and major decisions being made by junior people. Over the past few years several changes have been made which lead in the right direction. The first was to improve feedback between the administrative data processing department, and the major administrative users. This is done through a Data Processing Steering Group which meets once or twice per term. When set up in 1978, one of the first acts of the group was to develop the plan to overhaul all the major systems over seven years as described above. At the same time, Computing Services began to collect consistent data of the cost and time used to develop new administrative data processing systems. Without this data, planning was inevitably mainly guesswork.

In 1981 the provost set up a procedure for selecting administrative projects. He brought together a group of vice presidents to survey the proposed projects with estimates of cost, benefit, and time-scale. At about the same time, he established a word processing steering group. This group has succeeded in coordinating a previously fragmented area. Its work is described below.

In June 1981, David McLaughlin became president of Dartmouth. He immediately took personal control of the selection of administrative data processing projects, using the information which was being provided to the provost. A few months later he and the provost set up a Task Force on Computing to advise on the long-term directions which the college should take. The brief of the task force was to look at seven areas.

1. Academic computing—services and opportunities in instruction and research.
2. Administrative data processing—priorities and procedures.
3. Library computing.
4. Word processing.
5. Financial control.
6. Organization and management structure.
7. Interactions between different areas of computing.

The last of these items is seen as crucial. Action in any area of computing tends to interact with every other area. The plan is that by looking at all areas together, the college will handle these interactions successfully.

Management of Central Computing

Big computer systems inevitably lead to centralized management. So long as core memories ruled the world of computing, the economies of scale forced Dartmouth and other universities to buy very large computers, and centralize the management of them. The Kiewit Computation Center represents a major concentration of computing expertise and experience in providing service. It also represents a vested interest, which could easily become a barrier to change.

In 1976, the DTSS operation and the administration data processing group were brought together, and since then have had a single reporting structure. The director of Computing Services reports directly to the provost.

The Computing Council, which also has a parallel in the Council on Libraries, is a council of the general faculty. It is a group of approximately twelve academics, administrators, and students who meet four or five times a term. The chairman, who is a faculty member, is appointed by the president and reports to him. Although most of the time the council acts as a discussion forum, it has proved that when the members disagree with the direction taken by Computing Services, they have the power to change the course of events.

As shown in Figure 4, Computing Services is organized into four divisions, and a research and development group:

1. *Technical Service.* This group is responsible for all computers, system programming, quality control, and trouble shooting.
2. *Academic Computing.* This group provides all academic services except computer time. It covers user services, applications programs, documentation, and word processing.
3. *Administrative Data Processing.* This group develops and maintains administrative systems.
4. *Network Support and Administration.* This group looks after off-campus users, telecommunications, budgets, purchasing, and bookkeeping.
5. *Research and Development.* This group comprises three senior technical people who have no management responsibility, and four managers with technical expertise.

Management of Decentralilzed Computing

Although the timesharing system is by far the principal source of computing power at Dartmouth, every year it is supplemented by more mini- and microcomputers. On the academic side the PRIME

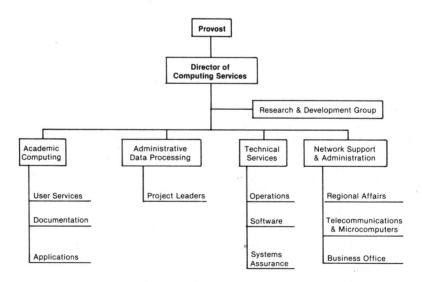

Figure 4. *The organizational structure of Dartmouth's computing services administration.*

750 has already been mentioned. This machine is run by Computing Services on behalf of all academic users, but particularly for researchers with large problems. Several departments have smaller minicomputers which they operate themselves. Typically these have been bought with grant money, and the selection has been based on the availability of suitable software.

To ensure that purchasing decisions are made on a sensible basis, the provost and treasurer have a formal policy that any computer purchase which is likely to cost more than $5000 has to be discussed with the director of Computing Services. In practice Computing Services provides support to people buying their own systems. This expertise is available to help draw up requests for proposals, evaluate needs and responses, negotiate financial or legal questions, site preparation, training, and so on.

Several of the large departments now have considerable expertise in computing. The Task Force on Computing has been asked to recommend whether the departments should take full responsibility for their computing. One possible route would be for these departments with their own computers to take financial responsibility for their computing. For the next few years the most likely outcome is to see a wide range of arrangements. Several departments, notably the library and the medical school, have excellent computing staffs, but rely on Computing Services to operate computers for them. Others, such as the Thayer School of Engineering and the alumni office run their own machines.

Technical Factors

Innovation

Dartmouth's intention to lead in student and instructional computing cannot be achieved by sitting back and waiting for other people to develop products. Such products are likely to be too expensive and too complex for widespread use on campus. Innovation is therefore prized in its own right. Trends in computing are not necessarily followed because other universities are going in that direction. New areas are entered before they are generally accepted. Software is built in anticipation of hardware coming on the market.

Being a user of an operating system which is not widely used has some interesting features, both good and bad. Because Dartmouth has written its own software, the college must have strong system programming and telecommunications divisions. These divisions have enabled new developments to be added and experiments made that have improved the quality of service and kept down its cost over the years. On the other hand, any applications package has to be imported before it will run on the system, and despite efforts to standardize programming languages this often involves a substantial amount of work.

Timesharing and Personal Computers

Today is a time of change. As demand increases year after year, computing is a growth area in the declining field of higher education. This creates stress, but fortunately, technological advances provide a partial solution. Most of the services provided for the academic community require processing power or file storage. The costs of these resources are coming down rapidly. Unfortunately, processing power is likely to be cheapest when provided in the form of a large number of personal computers, while the big economies in file storage look like they will remain in large, centralized file stores. The problem is how to take advantage of these technological improvements when they push in directions contrary to current practice.

Between the time engineers develop a new product in laboratories and the necessary support in software is available to use a system for general academic services, there are delays of many years. Moreover, few universities are able to use a single vendor to supply all their needs, and interconnections between software and hardware of different vendors is a major problem.

In 1985 the college will need to make a major decision on hardware purchases. At present it is not clear whether this acquisition will be further extensions to the current timesharing operations, separate minicomputers, or large numbers of personal computers. If personal computers are chosen, there are some very big design decisions to be made. It is also not clear what criteria or planning mechanism should be used to make the right decisions.

Calculations in 1979 showed that for general student use a typical personal computer (the Apple II Plus was used for comparison) costs about the same per student hour as timesharing service. This total cost estimate, including purchase, and all supporting facilities, is based on simple assumptions about the utilization of various types of equipment. Today's 8-bit microcomputers do not provide the high quality of service for general purpose uses of a good timesharing system, but it is clear that the 16-bit machines now coming on the market are superior to timesharing.

The Kiewit Network

Telecommunications is perhaps Dartmouth's strongest area. The need to satisfy large numbers of off-campus users led to the creation of a very strong group. Telenet, both inward and outward bound, has been available for many years; remote concentrators, running a slightly modified version of the DTSS front-end software, are scattered over four states; and the college is just completing development of an ultra high-speed, on-campus network. This network of New England Digital minicomputers provides RS232 and X.25 ports linking any terminal to any computer and any computer to any other computer. The backbone of the network will be four miles of coaxial cable operated at ten million bits per second. This high-speed, cheap, error-free transmission of data throughout the campus and over the regional network is the building block behind all computing plans for the next ten years.

The Distributed Editor

One particularly elegant use of the Kiewit Network is the development of a screen-editing, microprocessor-based workstation, which is known as the Dartmouth Avatar. This is a terminal, supported by a small microprocessor with a substantial amount of random-access memory. The total cost for the terminal and microprocessor is $1,300. It is used to edit files which can be on any computer. If the file is too big to store in the workstation, it is transmitted back and forth over the network at high speed. This workstation is just coming into production.

The microprocessors are standard Z-80 systems. Although their primary use is to support a low-cost but high-performance terminal, the plan is that 25 percent of users will add floppy disks so that they can run their workstation as a free-standing microcomputer, using the CP/M operating system. This will be the bridge into the networks of personal computers which will dominate the world of university computing in the late 1980s. The probable steps in their development are:

1. Eight-bit microprocessors editing centrally stored files with a screen editor held in read-only memory.
2. The same eight-bit microprocessor running CP/M. The editor can be used to edit centrally or locally stored files.
3. Sixteen-bit microprocessors running a more powerful operating system, probably UNIX. The same screen editor will be used.
4. The same operating system will be modified to handle a distributed file system over a synchronous link, probably X.25.

One of the major tasks of Kiewit Research and Development is steady migration through these stages while maintaining existing services.

Word Processing

Word processing is the most exciting area of computing growth to a liberal arts college. It has tremendous potential both for improved service and for high levels of expenditure. The recent history is a good example of how the college's centralized management structure makes decisions in complex areas.

Coordination of word processing began in the fall of 1980 when the provost and the director of Computing Services decided that the field needed overall guidance. An ad hoc steering group on word processing was set up, with two faculty members, and two administrators, and chaired by the director of Computing Services. A recent Dartmouth graduate was employed to support this group. The initial meetings of the group showed that the college did not have the information to make sensible decisions. Six months were spent gathering information. This included a study by business school students of faculty needs, surveying the literature (in particular the excellent reports from Stanford University), and local studies in several areas. The needs and technical options were summarized in a preliminary report dated March 1981. This report recommended two technical routes as the basis for word processing at Dartmouth.

1. General users, particularly students and faculty, who do not spend their entire life in writing and preparing documents, can use the screen-editing microcomputer which is described above. This is used to edit documents that are stored on the timesharing system's file store. Formatting programs will be used on the central computers. In this way, the same workstation will be used for regular computing, for word processing, and to access the library catalog. Everything depends upon the Kiewit Network.

2. In addition to this general service there are some departments that have an intensive need for dedicated word processing equipment. The report recommended that a standard word processing system be chosen and supported by Computing Services and the purchasing department for these applications. If experience with typewriters, photocopiers, and terminals is a guide, no compulsion will be needed for everybody to accept these standards recommended by this working group.

Work continued during the summer of 1981 and the group was able to disband in September with a report to the provost which addressed not only these technical recommendations, but also made some organizational proposals. As might be expected, these include recognition of the importance of coordinating word processing with related areas such as printing and library automation. In addition, the report focuses on the problems of providing good word processing equipment for individuals unable to pay for it from available funds. These include those faculty whose subject areas are low in funded research, and student users.

The key recommendation in this area is that the college should not attempt to provide public workstations for everybody, but should encourage individuals to acquire their own screen editing workstations. Computing Services has a plan for selling low-cost workstations and setting up a second-hand market in them. At the same time the possibility of wiring every office and dormitory room on campus is being actively studied.

In this way, with a minimum amount of effort, the college has developed a cogent plan for providing good quality word processing to all. Follow-up work is continuing in the mathematics area and the interface to printing. Meanwhile the IBM Displaywriter has been selected as the standard dedicated equipment, the screen-editing workstation is nearing readiness, and a UNIX system is being considered for mathematical word processing. The organizational and long-term questions are being examined actively by the relevant departments and progress on all fronts is surprisingly rapid.

The Library

An area in which cooperation between departments has been particularly fruitful is the joint work done by the library and Computing Services. The college was a very early member of OCLC, and for ten years all cataloging has been machine readable. In addition, literature searches using commercial data bases have been freely available for many years. In 1979, the college joined the Research Libraries Group and is now using the RLIN network for much of its cataloging. These activities were brought together, first in a pilot study, and in 1981 in a formal commitment to work with Bibliographic Retrieval Services of Scotia, New York in a joint project to develop an on-line library catalog available to every terminal on the Kiewit network.

This cooperation shows several characteristics which might be generalized to other areas. First of all, both parties have senior members of their staff who are experts in the other's area. Sympathetic understanding of each other's operation has been the basis for an ambitious, but realistic, program. This has led to the next reason for cooperation. By working together, the library and Computing Services have been able to approach foundations for external funding. The on-line catalog project in particular appeared too uncertain to justify purely from Dartmouth resources, but sustained and generous support from the Pew Foundation has made it possible. Finally, the organization of Dartmouth has simplified this project. Since both the library and Computing Services report to the provost, he has been personally involved in the key decision making and his office has coordinated relationships with foundations.

The Future

This chapter was written during the academic year 1981/82. The year proved to be one of change. The installation of the Kiewit Network, the distributed editor, the imminent arrival of the library online catalog, continuing spectacular growth in undergraduate computer science, a realization of the power of word processing—all these and many more have found a focus in the deliberations of the Task Force on Computing. This year Dartmouth College timesharing has been overloaded and the number of student terminals has lagged behind the demand. This problem has stimulated interest in computing. People have realized just how important good computing is to Dartmouth. Finally the imaginative planning papers coming from other universities, particularly Carnegie-Mellon and Stanford, have been read with great interest.

Many people believe that the next five years will see the most rapid growth in the history of computing at Dartmouth. While some universities are looking for a great leap forward, evolution is the route that the college has chosen, but the result will still be dramatic. As ever with evolution, natural selection will take its toll. Some projects will not survive, or stand the test of time, but the trend is clear. By the end of this decade most faculty and students will have their own personal workstations. By the end of this century, universal computing will be routine. In the interim, in an imaginative university judicious use of computers can make a great contribution to the quality of academic life.

4

Pepperdine University

JOHN McMANUS
Director of Academic Computing

JAMES PENROD
Vice President for Systems and Planning

The University Setting

In the fall of 1969 Pepperdine was located on a crowded thirty-five acre site in south central Los Angeles. The institution did not own an electronic calculator, and the only available computing access was through a dial-up Teletype terminal located in a closet in the School of Business and Management building. Today the Pepperdine campus is located on 820 acres in the Santa Monica Mountains overlooking the Pacific Ocean at Malibu. There are four schools and colleges now, and the total enrollment is about three times that of the late sixties. In addition to the central program at Malibu campus, courses are offered at four educational centers in the Los Angeles basin and through a European program in Heidelberg, West Germany. Pepperdine's progress toward modern and sophisticated computer services in a little over a decade is in complete harmony with the dramatic transformation of the university as a whole during this same brief period.

The university was established in 1937 by George Pepperdine (1886–1962), founder of Western Auto Supply Company. From its inception, Pepperdine has been affiliated with the Church of Christ. The institution's stated purpose remains the same today almost 50 years after its establishment: " ... to help young men and women prepare themselves for a life of usefulness in this competitive world and to help them build a foundation of Christian character and faith which will survive the storms of life."[1]

In 1972 Seaver College was established on the Malibu campus. This undergraduate, residential, liberal arts college, the heart of educational life at Pepperdine, was made possible by generous gifts from a dozen friends of the university, and included historic gifts from Mrs. Frank Roger Seaver. Beyond its physical expansion, the university, which has always maintained "a serious commitment to a rigorous academic program in concert with concern for spiritual matters,"[2] has set further goals for extending academic achievement during the 1980s. It intends to elevate the quality of students admitted, to attract exceptional faculty, and to place greater emphasis on research as a fundamental methodology for improving the quality of instruction at this teaching institution.

With all its recent growth, the institution still recognizes that its own heritage lies in a free-market economy. It also recognizes that the appreciation of the abundance of goods and resources produced by this economic system, and the value of sharing and providing stewardship for these goods, are fundamental values in educating its students for "a life of usefulness in this competitive world."

Background of Computing

The initial step toward modernization of computing at Pepperdine University was taken in 1970 when the School of Business and Management installed its first computer. This was an IBM 1130, which offered limited batch processing capabilities for business students. In 1972 the university joined a National Science Foundation-sponsored timesharing network, and two remote terminals were installed on the Los Angeles campus. As the Malibu campus developed, additional terminals were added to the Seaver College laboratory, and eventually, ten terminals were connected to the timesharing network. Between 1974 and 1976 University Computer Systems (UCS), an external service bureau, developed initial administrative systems. Soon, on three campuses, Four-Phase minicomputers collected data which were then transmitted for processing to an IBM 360/50 mainframe, located off campus. With the growth of the university and its increasing reliance on computers, this system became inadequate, and need for a major on-campus computing facility became evident.

The university realized this goal in 1977 with the completion on the Malibu campus of the Pendleton Computer Science Center, a specially designed 7,000-square-foot building. With the installation in this center of a UNIVAC 90/60 central processor, all university computer services were placed under the supervision of the Pepperdine University Information Services Department. From early 1977 to October 1979, Systems and Computer Technology Corporation, a facilities management firm located in Malvern, Pennsylvania, provided personnel to fill the directorship and several computer services positions. In 1979 the university terminated the facilities management contract and assumed full management of the computer services.

Since assuming operational responsibility for computing services, the university has replaced the 90/60 central processor with a UNIVAC 90/80 and has continued new systems installations (see Tables 1 and 2). The university-approved Five Year Plan for Computer Services mandates a move from batch-oriented systems to online systems designed to serve the university better. The plan calls for all major administrative divisions of the university to be able to input data and retrieve information from their files by 1984. The university will have developed a Decision Support System (DSS) to permit access by the client community to information that will assist them in decision making. The DSS, supported by the existing Management Information System, will afford access to appropriate reformatted files through a proposed broad-band, local-area network.

Table 1. *Computer Services hardware overview*

Equipment	Description
1 Mainframe processor	UNIVAC 90/80; mod-3, 3-meg, 800 kop
9 Disk drives	UNIVAC 8433; 200 megabytes per pack
6 Tape drives	Uniservo 32 tape drives; 9-track 6250/1600 bpi tape
3 Other mainframe peripherals	card reader, 1000 cpm; 2 printers, 1400 & 2000 lpm
1 Multichannel Communications Controller (MCC)	64K, handles 32 synch/asynch ports
2 Miniprocessors	1900 Cade - data entry, 128K; Prime-environmental control
27 Microprocessors	Terak (16), 56K, for education; Apple II (10), 48K, for education, office use, and administration; Cromemco Z2D, 192K micro for Physical Plant office use
61 On-line terminals	UNIVAC (6), U-200, UTS-400; Harris (33); TeleVideo (14); Hazeltine (4); Texas Inst. (4), dial-up; all used for education, office work, and development
11 On-line printers	NEC (5); DTC (2); DECwriter (2); Malibu (1); Printronix (1); use is same as for On-line Terminals

Further, the five-year plan anticipates that user-friendly modeling systems and query languages will be used by their computer clients.

In addition to the computer facilities for administrative systems, academic computing laboratories on the main campus and at four educational centers provide instructional computing to Pepperdine students. These laboratories are equipped with microcomputers

Table 2. *Computer Services software overview*

Software	Description
UNIVAC 90/80 Student Information Applications Software	From SCT: integrated student information system; development retrieval; In-house: on-line admissions and recruiting; on-line alumni records; financial aid; 4 retrieval packages (INDEX, POWERS, Development, Mark IV)
UNIVAC 90/80 Financial Applications Software	In-house: on-line accounts receivable; From ISI: payroll personnel; From IAI: accounts payable (AP); general ledger (FAS); From SCT: integrated business information system (IBIS)
Other UNIVAC 90/80 applications software	Statistical packages (SPSS, BMD, BMDP); mail system
In-house micro software	Statistics (PEPSTAT); class grades (GRADES); optical test information scoring (OTIS); plotting (PLOT10); ecology modeling (FISHER)
Purchased micro software	VISICALC (budget); VISIPLOT (graphics); VISITREND (statistics); VISIDEX, DBMASTER (both data base management), and other commercial software

(Teraks and/or Apple IIs), which are capable of stand-alone processing or of serving as intelligent terminals to the UNIVAC 90/80. The locations and capabilities of these several systems today stand in sharp contrast to the crude beginnings in the late 1960s.

Philosophical Stances

The university is unequivocally committed to information-technology literacy. This commitment is obvious in a recent statement by Pepperdine's president, Dr. Howard White:

. . . It is evident that the wave of the future demands that all students graduating from Pepperdine University become literate in the usage of information technology. Students should understand computing, word processing, communication devices and the integration of these to the extent that they can use this technology to solve problems, thus enabling them to compete in and contribute to the world in which we live.

I am therefore appointing a small Strategic Planning Task Force to provide the administration with recommendations as to how best to accomplish this institutional goal by 1984 . . . The Task Force will solicit input from faculty and students, staff, administrators and industry leaders.[3]

Furthermore, the Academic Computing Advisory Committee formally recommended to the University Academic Council "That all graduates of Pepperdine University, regardless of school, both graduate and undergraduate be required to be computer literate as a requirement for graduation." The committee defines computer literacy as having "the ability to write a simple computer program to solve a problem, to understand the basic components of a computer, and to demonstrate abilities to utilize software packages, including word processing."[4]

In the past, and currently, the institution has devoted major resources to the computing enterprise. In developing its computing facilities the university is somewhere between the competitive and intensive stages of technological development. The computing facility has been built, space for academic learning facilities has been established, and computers have been installed. The institution also plans to hold to its current policy of purchasing software where possible rather than building it internally. It plans to develop a network of microcomputers and word processors which will facilitate the administrative and educational decision-making processes of the institution. With such an extension of major decentralized services not currently available, the university intends to provide adequate tools to the client community while at the same time maintaining strict centralized controls on the university data base and on the purchase of hardware and software.

So that the university community might adequately employ and successfully develop its computer capacity, the Systems and Planning Division seeks to act as an agent of change within the university. This is partially accomplished by supporting the needs of faculty, staff, and students through helping promote continual progress toward more effective and efficient administrative systems and through envisioning the Computer Services Department as a library-type resource. Thus, any student, faculty member, or member of the staff will be granted a computer account for personal use by submitting a request form to the Academic Computing Laboratory supervisor. These accounts are for personal and/or professional development, and are not for funded research, commercial consulting, or developing material for a commercially funded book. (Accounts for funded use are available on a charge-back basis.)

As part of the commitment of the university as a whole, the Computer Services Department attempts to integrate the goals of the institution and the personal needs of individuals. The department is committed to a philosophy which recognizes and supports the professional standing of the university, yet respects the dignity of individuals, the honor and value of work, and the necessity for a high degree of accountability. To fulfill this philosophy, Computer Services, as part of the Systems and Planning Division, believes that a defined and formal structure provides effective and efficient management. The department also believes that management primarily derives its authority from knowledge, skill, and achievement and that decision making, rather than being the prerogative only of management, is most effective when it occurs among people closest to a particular activity. A project approach to problem solving is felt to be most effective. Computer Services feels that groups, constituting the basic organizational unit, should participate in setting goals and should provide controls and feedback for management. Furthermore, the department believes in and encourages free, unfiltered, vertical and horizontal communication—among group members, between groups, and between groups and management —and is wholly committed to maintaining an atmosphere receptive to internal change. An attempt is made to be personalized at every level of the organization. Because of the technical nature of many of the services rendered by Systems and Planning, the Computer Services Department is committed to the continual process of staff development, constantly encouraging personnel to update their knowledge of technological advances, to develop new and additional skills, and to pursue advanced studies. Mutually beneficial to the employee and the institution, this program of staff development guides individuals toward achieving their full potential.[5]

To maintain the best possible working relationship within the university, and to encourage effective use of computer facilities and capabilities, Computer Services underwrites all aspects of its operation with a philosophy of service and accountability. Within the organization, management by set objectives exercised through groups, and zero-based budgeting practices enable the department effectively to serve its client community and achieve a high level of accountability. Outside the department, close interaction with users effects accountability and service. Users participate in setting policy, users assist in developing systems and procedures, and users participate in a monthly evaluation process to provide feedback.

One final philosophical goal of the Computer Services Department is its policy of seeking special vendor relationships in which the university serves as a showcase account. This ties directly to the university's belief in a free-market economy and proves beneficial to the institution, its various vendors, and the public which the institution serves. This may best be illustrated by noting that approximately 15 percent of the direct costs of a national summer institute on computer literacy for college administrators, sponsored by the university in cooperation with CAUSE and EDUCOM, is underwritten by vendor sponsors. Thus the institute, which operates on a break-even cost basis, can be offered to participants for a fee substantially less than actual cost.

Organizational Structure

The President of Pepperdine University is the school's chief executive officer, while the chief operational officer is the Executive Vice President. Three operational vice presidents, including the Vice President of Systems and Planning, and four deans report to the

Executive Vice President. The Systems and Planning division consists of the departments of Computer Services, Data Administration, Strategic Planning, Institutional Research, the registrar, and an administrative staff. The director of Academic Computing and the director of Administrative Computing report to the Assistant Vice President for Systems and Planning. The directors are responsible for all daily operations in their respective areas. The academic director supervises the departments of Academic Support, Academic Programming, and Academic Centers. Departments managed by the administrative director include Systems and Programming, Technical Support, and Operations.

The university's committee structure, believed to be a major factor in the systems' success experienced at Pepperdine, is integral to the implementation, and operation of computer-related systems. This thoughtfully designed structure, using Likert Linking Pin Theory[6] (see Figure 1) and fine tuned over a period of years, includes the Systems and Planning Committee (SPC), the Data Administration Group (DAG), the Academic Computing Advisory Committee (ACAC), and the Interoffice Coordination Committee (ICC). The Systems and Planning Committee for the university is chaired by the Executive Vice President and consists of the operational vice presidents, the Executive Assistant to the President, the controller, and the Vice President of University Affairs (the chief development officer). The Vice President of Systems and Planning serves as vice-chair, records the minutes, and prepares the agendas. This group meets biweekly and is responsible for strategic planning for the university, all systems policy, and approval of all university-wide, systems-related expenditures. It also recommends to the Budget Committee the level of funding for Computer Services and prioritizes all systems-related projects. The Assistant Vice President for Systems and Planning, assisted by the directors, presents a written report which includes major accomplishments, major problems, utilization statistics, and user ratings to the SPC each month. A full discussion with questions and answers accompanies the written document.

The Data Administration Group consists of middle managers of the institution: the registrar, the director of Business Services, the director of Personnel, the Assistant Vice President for University

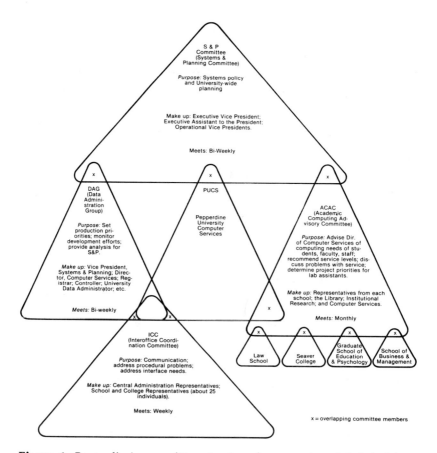

Figure 1. *Pepperdine's committee structure for computer-related decisions.*

Affairs, the Administrative Computing director, and others. The University Data Administrator (UDA) chairs this committee, and the Vice President of Systems and Planning normally attends. The DAG meets biweekly and is charged with the duties of setting priorities for systems modifications called Technical Service Requests (TSRs), providing analysis for the SPC, monitoring progress of major projects, and approving systems-related procedures.

The Academic Computing Advisory Committee meets monthly and consists of representatives from each of the schools and colleges, the library, Institutional Research, and Computer Services. The chair is a Seaver College faculty member recommended by the Executive Vice President and appointed by the Vice President of Systems and Planning. This committee provides communication and feedback links with the academic community, makes recommendations concerning items to be included in the instructional computing budget, prioritizes and monitors instructional projects, recommends policy, and oversees such computer-related training as faculty seminars.

The Interoffice Coordination Committee (ICC) is made up of supervisory level personnel from all major administrative offices, representatives from the schools and colleges, and the Decision Support Coordinators (DSCs) from Computer Services. This committee, which meets weekly, sets the computer production schedule, makes recommendations regarding procedures, addresses interface concerns, prepares the university's administrative calendar, and raises issues for discussion by the Data Administration Group and/ or the Systems and Planning Committee.

Three other university groups, although not directly related to management or policy for computing, also need to be mentioned: the Operations Committee (OC), the University Academic Council (UAC), and the Management Advisory Council (MAC). The Operations Committee is a council of senior administrators responsible for all administrative university policy that is not systems related. It is chaired by the Executive Vice President and works very closely with the SPC. The University Academic Council, made up of deans, the admissions officer, the director of libraries, the registrar, and elected faculty members, is responsible for all academic policy at the institution. The Executive Vice President also chairs this committee. Overlapping members ensure coordination among the UAC, SPC and DAG. The Management Advisory Council, which works closely with the Data Administration Group, consists of all the institution's middle managers. This council is charged with such administrative responsibilities as planning registration.

In addition to the organizational bodies discussed above, three other distinctive structures are significant in the overall design. The first is the Decision Support Coordinator position. The four DSCs serve as liaisons between user departments and Computer Services.

They have technical systems analysis backgrounds but also have worked in user departments such as the Office of the Registrar or Office of Finance. Their primary responsibility is to represent the user within Computer Services, but the DSCs are also deeply involved in systems design and implementation, user training, problem resolution, and a continual evaluation of the efficiency of computer services.[7] The office of Data Administration, the second unique organizational entity, is directed by the University Data Administrator, who reports directly to the Vice President of Systems and Planning. This office, which is independent of Computer Services, has the responsibility for assuring the integrity of the data base and implementing related policy. In many respects, the UDA serves as an internal auditor for computing. Finally, two members of the administrative staff for the Vice President of Systems and Planning serve in ombudsperson roles within the system. Any member of the division or of the university community may call upon these individuals (confidentially if desired) to seek the resolution of problems which have not been satisfactorily addressed through established channels.

The Planning Process

Successful completion of projects to fulfill immediate and long-term goals requires careful planning, and successful planning requires input from as many involved parties as possible. At the highest level, the university has a published mission statement with long-term goals and short-term objectives. Each school, college, or major administrative unit has derived statements of its goals, and objectives which fit within the overall parameters specified in the university's mission statement. The annual preparation and review of the fiscal year's budget is closely coordinated with this planning process. All university units must tie their budget requests to their goals and objectives.

Because Systems and Planning Committee members possess overall responsibility for strategic planning for the entire university, as well as full responsibility for systems policy, the committee assumes a central role in the planning process, and assures the integration of university and systems planning. Computer Services approaches the planning process from two directions:

1. Hierarchical standing committees that represent a broad spectrum of university management.
2. Ad hoc task forces consisting of representatives from multiple offices. The task of such ad hoc groups is to define needs, buy or design and code systems, and test, implement, and post-test (or "baby-sit") these systems until the clear and apparent need for the task force is no longer present.

Understanding the functional operations of the previously addressed committee structure is essential to a full appreciation of how deeply these committees participate in the planning process, particularly as they relate to Computer Services. In addition to reviewing the Computer Services monthly report and client community forms for appraisal of services, the SPC must prioritize all major system-development proposals, thus establishing long-term goals for the university. This committee also discusses budget and personnel. The directors of Computer Services frequently meet with this group in a reporting and advisory capacity. The success of the SPC lies in the representation of all sectors of the university. Within the committee these various sectors in a sense compete for increasing information needs in their departments while at the same time they support Computer Services, whose resources remain fairly constant. This process requires that they must, in fact, negotiate and compromise and ultimately agree on a plan of activity. Guiding these deliberations are the university's mission statement and a set of specific operational goals. The work of the SPC is not easy; hard decisions must be made and favorite projects often delayed to meet the goals of the university. The process is often painful, but it works.

At a middle-management level the Data Administration Group (DAG) meets every other week to discuss policy and procedures regarding all computer systems. There is usually a report on any hardware development and computer system enhancement, but major discussion centers around client needs, perceptions of service, and suggestions for improvements. The directors of all major administrative departments attend DAG.

Computer Services, like any other major administrative unit, participates in the same planning framework as other units, but in a more extensive way. The Assistant Vice President of Systems and Planning formulates a five-year plan which he updates annually. The Data Administration Group and the Management Advisory Council review this document, which is then sent to SPC to be approved and issued. It is through this process that Computer Services derives its immediate and long-term goals. Besides helping prepare and update the five-year plan, the directors of Computer Services each year present to the SPC a zero-based budget with four levels of service specified. The committee then decides through full and open discussion which levels of funding will be requested through the Budget Committee. The SPC also resolves questions of budget versus value and addresses questions of compromise, e.g., should a new library system be installed at the expense of funds for faculty development? When SPC determines which budget requests should be made, the directors of Computer Services, working with Computer Services managers, specify Management by Objectives (MBOs) for each request. The MBOs become the fiscal year objectives for the departments. Progress toward MBO completion is monitored throughout the year, and a formal mid-year adjustment or correction takes place within departments. At the end of the year the assistant vice president submits to the Vice President of Systems and Planning a written analysis of MBO accomplishments. This analysis becomes part of the formal personnel evaluation process.

Computer Services interacts with client community committees both in the long-term planning process and in ongoing system modification. By agreement with the SPC, Computer Services dedicates a certain percent of DSC and programmer/analyst time to the modification of existing systems. All requests are made in writing on a Technical Service Request, and Computer Services makes time estimates for job completion. Every six weeks, progress on TSR work is reported to DAG. Completed TSRs are removed from the task list. At this review meeting all open TSRs are prioritized by majority rule; DAG ranks all outstanding requests from first to last. Computer Services committee members do not vote, but can advise.

Here again the client community, agreeing by mutual consent, determines the priorities, in this case for systems modifications. The impact of the client community determining its own service priorities cannot be overemphasized. Taking direction from university goals, stated and adhered to, each appropriate committee member must lobby, negotiate, and plead his or her case with a peer group member, not with the administrative director, to establish long-range goals for system development. This provides Computer Services with at least 20 to 30 planners, external to the Computer Center, who establish goals and timelines. The university feels this is a credible, productive, and perhaps unique system which enables Administrative Computing effectively to meet the needs of the client community.

On the academic side, the Academic Computing Advisory Committee is becoming increasingly active in defining and implementing computer literacy. This group initiated the long-term commitment to a computer capability requirement for all university graduates. The ACAC reviews annual budget proposals, recommends the distribution of hardware and personnel to the various laboratories and centers, coordinates such events as workshops and computer fairs, and prioritizes all academic computing requests. This group, drawing membership from the faculty, the library, Institutional Research, and Computer Services, is essential to strategic planning because its members are in a position to foresee needs, potential, and opportunities for academic use of computers. They bring, in a sense, a new network to bear on the strategic planning process and act as a direct complement to the Data Administration Group.

Working to support the efforts of the standing committees are several ad hoc task forces whose responsibilities are intermediate, rather than long term. These task forces implement projects approved by the Systems and Planning Committee. Their responsibilities include definition of scope, possible alternatives, design, development, testing, implementation, and evaluation of a new system. Currently, there are four active task forces working on computer-based systems. Members include managers, DSCs, programmer/analysts, and key individuals of the client community. It should be noted that the chair of such committees is not always from Computer Services. For example, the chair of the Financial

Accounting/ Accounts Payable Task Force was the university controller; the head of the Payroll/Personnel Task Force was the Director of Administration from the office of the Vice President of Systems and Planning. Although not employed by Computer Services, these persons are able through the task forces to assure that systems have been installed on time, with minimal disruption to offices during conversion. Other active task forces include Financial Aid, Word Processing, and Library Systems.

The task force approach at times appears to be a process of endless meetings, constant education, deciding and redeciding. The work of a system task force whose members represent varied and vested interests is very draining. The approach is valuable, however, because it provides divergent views on computer services and enables conclusions, specifications, and implementations of plans with these views in mind. Moreover, when all appropriate points of view are heard and assessed and decision responsibility is broadly based, the results are usually substantial and rewarding. The task force itself becomes a system support structure during testing and implementation. This tenacious overseeing function greatly assists Computer Services and the university.

The strategic and tactical planning processes described above have resulted in major systems awareness at the university during the past years. Standing committees and task forces, combined with the capabilities of Computer Services personnel, have produced the implementation of six new major systems within the last three years. Eight more systems will be completed by 1983. Much of the success of this enormous effort must be attributed to the planning process within Computer Services through its Five Year Strategic Plan. But this plan does not belong to Computer Services alone; designed to meet university goals and supported by the more than fifty administrators, managers, and professionals who reviewed and approved it, the plan belongs to the university.

Despite the significant advancement of computing development at Pepperdine, some of the needs of the university are still unmet. Because a vice president or committee yields to a greater good and postpones one project in deference to another, the worth of the deferred project is in no way demeaned. Currently, many application system-related needs of the university are on hold because of finite Computer Services resources. Computer Services feels that the long delivery schedules resulting from these holds do not represent a desirable level of service; thus, it has recommended long-term plans to assure that every unit of the university will eventually benefit from the computer resource. These plans will be discussed after a careful assessment of the fundamental consideration for the success of Computer Services—personnel.

Computer Services Staffing

The most important component of Computer Services operations is the people who carry out those functions critical to the department's success. In planning organizational structure and in filling approved positions, management and staff realize that job functions and emphases shift and, at times, even disappear. Consequently staff roles are fluid. For some staff a new role is easily defined; for some positions a new role evolves easily; for others redefinition requires substantial analysis and planning.

Management planning assumes a twofold role in staff considerations:

1. It must foresee the job requirement change as clearly and as early as possible.
2. It must establish training programs to assure that dedicated, competent, and motivated employees can grow with the organization.

Assuming the worth of each of its employees, Computer Services is committed to a program of skills development that will make obvious to each person a career path that he or she may follow. To identify areas of educational interests and needs, a permanent Career Development Task Force has been developed within Computer Services. The task force analyzes shifting needs for personnel and develops programs for career training and job placement. Chaired by the director of Academic Computing, this group includes all managers and supervisors, as well as the University Data Administrator and the Assistant Vice President for Systems and Planning.

Because of the development of computer systems, several changes in personnel requirements can be foreseen for the immediate future. The university, remaining in a strong system development mode for the next thirty months, will require a large number of programmers for design, coding, and maintenance. The need for programmers, however, should drop significantly within three years as systems become fully operational and as Decision Support Systems are installed in the client community. Because of the competition in the computer industry for skilled programmers, Computer Services expects that the number of programmer positions can be reduced with normal attrition. Options for career advancement other than leaving the university are also available to programmer/analysts. Computer Services would readily consider raising a qualified programmer/analyst to a DSC position or shifting the person to a technical support position. Outside the department, these persons could serve as consultants in client offices helping to define Decision Support Systems.

Currently a large professional data-entry staff uses a key-to-disk system, which will be removed in 1983. Computer Services is formulating preliminary plans to find positions for these persons within the department or in the larger university community. One or two persons in data entry will be necessary for back-up data entry, but others could serve important data entry, modeling, and retrieval functions in the client community. On the other hand, as the university installs networks and implements DSS, and as microcomputers proliferate, technical support requirements will grow. Computer Services hopes to accommodate this growth from within the department.

A major growth area for the next three to five years will be academic computing. The expressed university commitment to computer literacy for all students and, necessarily, for faculty and staff will create major training and educational burdens in the academic computing division. The university-wide Task Force on Computer Literacy will prepare a detailed framework for the literacy plan. While the recommendations will most likely be broad in scope, ranging from curriculum to space considerations, a major burden of work will certainly fall on academic computing, increasing the demand for programmming and training personnel. The functions of the librarian and the software evaluator will be expanded, and student staff will increase. Fortunately, the increasing number of computer science students at the undergraduate level will provide a pool of bright, motivated personnel who understand the Pepperdine system.

One of the strengths of Computer Services' planning program is that Pepperdine cares about its personnel and will take reasonable steps to assure that education and training are made available. The concept of redefining positions and maintaining a visible career path is critical to Computer Services' success. Every loyal and competent employee must know that there is a career for him or her within Computer Services or within the university. Every member of the organization has been chosen because he or she is an outstanding professional, and everyone is welcomed for his or her talent.

Increased Service—A Planned Evolution

Some of the goals for Computer Services have already been mentioned: university-wide computer literacy, a microcomputer-based orientation, extensive usage of word processing, development of a university-wide network that will support word and/or data processing, and the eventual development of a DSS with units in all major administrative offices.[8] Other future expectations include the installation of a UNIVAC 1160 AVP to replace the 90/80 as the university's mainframe computer, the installation of a dedicated minicomputer supporting an automated library system, and the development of an electronic mail system to work in conjuction with the word-processing network. Subjects under discussion which may lead to future developments include the acquisition of a laser printer, the integration of copying services into the computer network, microcomputer/video disc applications, and an organizational restructuring that would transform the Systems and Planning Division into an Information Resources Management Division.

The UNIVAC 90/80 has served the university well, but more

than a year ago it was recognized that a new technology would be needed to support information processing past 1984. Thus, a contract was negotiated with Sperry-UNIVAC in 1981 that scheduled the installation of a UNIVAC 1160 processor in August 1984. To facilitate any desirable conversion of application systems, the 1160 will be accompanied by an Attached Virtual Processor (AVP), which is basically a 90/80. Current systems will operate on the AVP until the conversion is completed, and the hardware configuration will permit sharing of jobs and communications protocols. By selecting this option, Computer Services is overcoming a major conversion problem.

As the 1160 moves into full operation, the broad-band cable network will be in place. Several buildings on campus and all of the student dormitories are already connected by a cable that is used to transmit television and radio signals. Space remains on the cable for data transmission. In addition, plans call for the connection within the next year of all buildings to the cable. This cable provides a possible solution to the major problem of planning and installing a network. What does remain is the task of identifying communications protocols common to all devices desiring to use the cable. Once the identification is completed, the hardware connections must be installed and all communications software designed and implemented. Although initial planning has begun on the network project, details of implementation are not yet available. The established initial planning guidelines will permit:

1. All Malibu and Educational Center terminals to access the network.
2. Every terminal on the network to access every other terminal.
3. The 1160 to act as a single user of the network rather than the focal point.

Thus, the network could be categorized as a loop configuration.

As presently planned, microcomputer-based word processing equipment will serve as the basis of one of the major network projects. At Pepperdine, word processing was, for a considerable length of time, in somewhat of a state of flux. In some offices there has been significant use of the mainframe editor to generate documents, in other offices stand-alone units were employed, but until fall 1981, no university plan on word processing existed. At that juncture the SPC appointed a Word Processing Task Force to identify those vendors who could produce word processors with the following characteristics:

1. An upward compatible family of processors.
2. The ability to communicate using standard network protocols.
3. A CP/M operating system, or one similar to it.
4. An interest in developing a "relationship" with the university, possibly as a Beta site.

Vendors were identified who met the requirements, and in late spring 1982 a product was selected for the university's word processing. Broad client community representation on the task force, direction and approval from SPC, and, especially in this case, an opportunity for large numbers of university personnel to view and test equipment from various vendors all resulted in the selection of a family of products from the CPT Corporation which met the university's needs and created a relationship with a vendor who thus became involved with the university.

An early product of the word processing technology marriage with the network will be an executive electronic mail system that will link key administrative offices in the university. No specific system has yet been designed or selected, but the characteristics of Contact-EMS at Stanford and Telemail will be examined. CPT possesses its own electronic mail capacity that will also be evaluated. As the executive electronic mail system is more fully developed, Computer Services, in conjunction with the SPC, will explore expansion of the project. Top administration was selected initially for the mail system because these persons are most likely to require constant and timely communication with each other and because they will be the first offices in the institution to be tied into the Decision Support System, a technological extension of the electronic mail system.

Access to the main storage through microprocessor terminals will permit either direct file manipulation or down-loading capabilities at the client location. Subsequent use of a retrieval language and modeling systems, where appropriate, will permit client access to information when they want it and in proper format to support timely administrative and academic decisions. Full implementation of a Decision Support System should permit users to avoid many of the changes now requiring the TSR process that is monitored by the Data Administration Group. Installation and maintenance of new systems will remain the responsibility of Computer Services; however, the ability of the client to access well-designed files will dramatically reduce the need for system development and modification.

Just as client involvement in system design increases the client's positive attitude toward the system, the awareness of computer potential—especially with networks, word processing, electronic mail, and decision support systems—heightens the client's expectancy and acceptance level of a new mode of operation. The success of this transition from basically batch to client-controlled information processing is facilitated by four factors that motivate all long-term planning within Computer Services:

1. Top administrative support.
2. A client-based committee and task force system.
3. Appropriate training.
4. A participative strategic/tactical planning process.

The question of what happens when centralized processes once totally within Computer Services are distributed to the client community, and when new hardware, software, and networks make services routinely available to users that are now only dreamed about, is one of great significance. Computer Services will surely emerge in the next three to five years as a quite different organization. The change will not be sudden and dramatic, but will be more of a metamorphosis, regulated and planned. The many significant changes that will occur within Computer Services, as well as in the user community, and the burden of dealing with these changes must be addressed by the whole university. A look at the changes and the means of achieving that end are described in the final section.

Computer Services as a Utility

Plans are already in place to change the role and character of Computer Services at Pepperdine University. In addition to the idea of a Computer Center, data center, or even information-processing center, Computer Services will project the image of a utility whose function is not to provide electricity, water, or gas on demand, but to provide data and information on demand to a group of clients or customers who will come to expect constant and improving service from that utility. Such key functions for Computer Services as computer operation, application software and file maintenance, training, and consulting will remain, as well as the administrative functions of general administration, budgeting, and planning. Obviously, these key functions of operation and maintenance lie at the center of any utility's success. To ensure success, Computer Services will maintain a high-caliber professional staff in these areas. Operations and maintenance personnel will work chiefly with the mainframe processor, its peripherals, and the micros/terminals/word processors that link with the network. Management will work closely with technical support and maintenance people to review distribution patterns and consider repair versus replacement of hardware.

The network promises to become a major development project over the next several years. Most offices will have access to the network for electronic mail and decision support systems by 1984; however, other uses of the cable will be explored. For example, the mix of television transmission and data processing, or of radio and data processing, especially in the areas of instruction and public opinion assessment, is extremely intriguing. The university will also explore possible inclusion in the educational environment of graphics transmission capabilities of such emerging technologies as the Canadian Telidon[9] and the French Antiope.[10]

As the technological advances increase, so will the need for counseling and training, particularly in the client community's use of equipment in its environment. Within the next five years most current procedures will be changed, equipment replaced, and attendant skills needs updated, so that training may well become a major service provided by Computer Services. A training center containing a multimedia repository of training materials that would facilitate individual and small group instruction may be established. A successful training center of this nature would require an appropriate support staff whose development would be the result of careful planning and top administrative support. It is envisioned that the nucleus for such a service is already in place with the DSCs for administrative clients and the academic computing consultants for instructional users. These consultants aid clients, whether academic or administrative, in selecting appropriate tools available through the computer utility for use in solving the challenge before them. The tools might be modeling packages (micro, mainframe, or national network accesses through the utility), retrieval languages, preformatted or free-formatted reports of basic university data, and graphics packages.

An important capability of any utility is to provide timely repair or replacement of worn-out equipment. A parts and service capability, therefore, will need to be established to take care of client hardware needs. As the use of microcomputers increases dramatically among faculty, students, and staff, a university strategy must be established to keep these devices operable. Computer Services will have to analyze the repair needs to determine which would be more efficiently and effectively handled by professional maintenance contracts and which would be better processed in a repair shop operation.

Despite all the extended roles, Computer Services will still assume the traditional information-processing functions. Computer Services will continue to need computer operators to monitor the machines and respond to tape mount requests. Technical support will become increasingly important as most of the integrated systems become self-sustaining. The goal is that the system, i.e., network, processor, communications equipment, and client equipment, must always work. Such a goal can be attained by proactive planning, not simply reactive repair. Thus, technical support personnel must become planners and visionaries and work closely with management to ensure that the human aspect of information processing is appropriately supported by a sound technical base designed to meet human needs. Job scheduling, overflow data-entry problems, abnormal job endings, difficult restarts, and serious applications software failures are all problems that Computer Services must and will address. No intent to diminish the importance of these traditional tasks is implied here. What is implied is that such tasks will be handled in a manner perhaps quite different from today's.

The ambitious change described above will be accomplished through a significant amount of hard work and planning by a professional staff dedicated to doing their jobs more effectively and efficiently—in short, through participative strategic and tactical planning. Technical management will be responsible for recommending the major changes of the next three to five years; administration will be responsible for approving them. But the entire professional and support staff will have input. In effect, it will be their plan.

Summary

Pepperdine University is thus actively confronting the task of strategic planning in a computer services environment. This discussion has centered around philosophy, mission, and goals, and the means of achieving them—the committee structure, and the participative strategic planning process, and examples of successful projects completed through the planning process. What now appears most appropriate is an assessment of those factors critical to Pepperdine's achievement over the past six years, factors that will be used to refine the role of Computer Services over the next five years. The reader need not infer that factors which have enabled Pepperdine to succeed are those that will necessarily work in a different environment. Rather, these factors suggest how this institution is achieving its own goals.

The first critical success factor[11] is Pepperdine's role in higher education, as defined in the university's mission statement. Computer Services coordinates all of its planning to conform to the larger goals of the university.

The second factor is top administrative support. The president of the university has declared computer literacy to be a goal of the institution. On most other occasions he has been directly involved in systems decisions. The Executive Vice President serves as chair of the Systems and Planning Committee. The value of their support cannot be measured.

The third factor is the integrated committee structure. The SPC directs all major Computer Services efforts. Since vice presidents, the controller, and the Executive Assistant to the President sit on this committee, this group also provides the top administrative support listed as the second factor. The other committees, DAG, MAC, and ICC, work in a manner that assures client input and priority, while monitoring the level of service within the Computer Center. These committees ensure involvement from middle management within the university.

The fourth factor is the extensive task force structure. Whenever major projects or tasks are undertaken, with SPC approval, a task force is created, bringing together the best thinking of appropriate client offices and Computer Services. These task forces encourage divergent views and produce a final convergent plan which is always required. As systems and tasks are completed, their ownership belongs to the committee, and thus to the university.

The fifth factor is the ability to establish relationships with vendors. This relationship has proven beneficial to the university in terms of price, service, and product releases, and has been beneficial to the vendor because his product is housed in an outstanding facility. A fine cooperative effort between the educational and private enterprise sectors has thus been created.

The sixth factor is participative strategic and tactical planning. This process is initiated within Computer Services where first drafts and revisions take place in-house. The plan then becomes a public document and receives close scrutiny from SPC, DAG, and ICC. When approved it represents the best thinking of the entire university, and, as such, elicits a commitment from all involved.

The Computer Services Department of Pepperdine University takes pride in being a part of and contributing to the vision first set forth some forty-five years ago which has become Pepperdine. Just as the size, the scope, and the location of the university have changed dramatically since the late 1960s, the computer services available now and those soon to come present an awesome contrast with even the very recent past. Visiting the Malibu campus a few years ago, the late Will Durant commented on the "apparently end-less sea" which the university community views from its mountain campus. This striking setting seems unusually appropriate for those engaged in computer technology at Pepperdine; for them, an apparently endless sea of dreams is always becoming reality.

References

1. Pepperdine, George. "Founder's Statement," September 21, 1937. From *Faith Was His Fortune: The Life Story of George Pepperdine*, by Bill Young, (n.p.), p. 209.
2. White, Howard A. "The Mission of Pepperdine University." Mimeographed. Malibu, California: Pepperdine University, September, 1981.
3. White, Howard A. "Statement on Information Technology Literacy." Mimeographed. Malibu, California: March 1982.
4. Academic Computing Advisory Subcommittee. Recommendation on computer literacy. Presented to the Systems and Planning Committee, November 17, 1981.
5. Carver, Fred D. and Sergiovanni, Thomas J. *Organizations and Human Behavior: Focus on Schools.* New York: McGraw Hill, 1969, pp. 167–182.
6. Likert, Rensis. *The Human Organization: Its Management and Value.* New York: McGraw-Hill, 1967. Likert, Rensis and Likert, Jane Gibson. *New Ways of Managing Conflict.* New York: McGraw-Hill, 1976.
7. Warford, Stu. "The Systems Analyst Role Reviewed: An Alternative Approach." *CAUSE/EFFECT*, No. 3. May 1982, pp. 20–23.
8. Penrod, James I. and McManus, John F. "Decision Support Systems: Finding the Best Mix of Information, Technology, and People." *Proceedings of the 1981 CAUSE National Conference*, December 1–4, 1981. Boulder, Colorado: CAUSE, pp. 43–56.
9. Nadeau, Michael E. "Canada Turns on Telidon." *Desktop Computing,* March 1982, pp. 48–50.
10. Urrows, Henry and Urrows, Elizabeth. "Videotex for Learning?" *Creative Computing.* May 1982, pp. 50–60.
11. Rockard, John F. "Chief Executives Define Their Own Data Needs," *Harvard Business Review.* March–April 1979, p. 85.

5

Carnegie-Mellon University

DOUGLAS VAN HOUWELING
Vice Provost for Computing and Planning

Introduction—The Past Is Prologue

Two key attitudes underlie planning for computing at Carnegie-Mellon University—an awareness of the large role that computing has historically played at CMU and a conviction that the potential for further applications overwhelms all that has been realized to date. A private institution with approximately 450 faculty and 5500 students (4000 undergraduate, 1500 graduate), Carnegie-Mellon University has traditionally made a major investment in computing. CMU is now contemplating the development of a computing system which could support a personal computer for every student, faculty member, and professional staff person. In September 1981, President Cyert created a Task Force for the Future of Computing at Carnegie-Mellon University. The depth of commitment to computing is demonstrated in his charge to the task force:

I have personally committed myself to a major expansion of the role of computing at CMU ... This commitment has grown from

95

my sense that CMU has already taken this direction by [a] quarter century of decisions and also from my own belief that it offers us an immensely exciting future.

The task force responded to this charge in a report which included the following conclusion:

By advocating a substantial increase in computation at CMU, we are advocating that CMU lead universities into a world saturated with computation.[1]

This high level of commitment and involvement in computing leads to a somewhat idiosyncratic set of challenges in planning for and delivery of computing services at CMU. The community is comparatively computer-literate, has a detailed understanding of the potential of computing, and has very high expectations. The basic issues of planning, financing, staffing, and space allocation for computing are not, however, eliminated by commitment. In other words, while computing at CMU is supported by an impressive consensus, it is also expected to be well-planned, available, reliable, and technologically advanced. The combination of commitment and expectation at CMU places a substantial premium on planning for computing and its role in the university.

University Goals and Computing

Carnegie-Mellon's commitment to computing has not been accidental or casual, but reflects a set of strategic assumptions about CMU and its role in society. The broadest goal of education and research at Carnegie-Mellon University is excellence. Computing is clearly providing CMU with a margin of excellence in its research program and is demonstrating increasing capability to support student learning. Since information processing is an important component of the teaching/learning process, computing can increase the effectiveness of CMU education by enhancing the information-processing capabilities of our students.

This concern with the quality of education was emphasized during a major strategic planning effort which Carnegie-Mellon completed in October 1981. General agreement was reached on the proposition that computing technology is becoming ubiquitous and that all students should have some understanding of the technology and its potential. Even more important, though, were the recurring presentations and discussions which stressed the need to reduce the pressure on student time so students could pursue education in fields complementary to their major, participate in a broader range of cultural activities, and develop more intellectual breadth.

As the costs of tuition, on-campus living, and foregone earnings continue to rise, student time is becoming increasingly valuable. The cost of higher education now ranges between $15,000 and $25,000 per year. Universities should now provide students with more support for the routine aspects of their university work, such as writing, information retrieval, and communication with their colleagues and teachers. This support is especially important at CMU, where a strong emphasis is placed on professionally relevant skills such as high-quality writing, presentations, laboratory work, and design.

The planning effort also reaffirmed the importance of the basic mission of the university—the creation and dissemination of knowledge. More convenient and comprehensive access to information, decreased costs for creating and disseminating the written word, and enhanced collegial communication which includes both faculty and students are all vital to the future of the university.

Carnegie-Mellon is making a substantial investment to improve its computing facilities to support these needs. CMU is convinced that computer technology has the potential to improve qualitatively the university's effectiveness and output. For the next five years, the major potential impact of computing will be to increase the effectiveness of student efforts outside the classroom. In short, our goal is increasing the effectiveness of students working on their own. Strikingly, success in this area would carry over to most professional uses of computing. While increased use of computing may eventually contribute to the effectiveness of faculty in their instructional role, this result is more difficult to achieve and less general in its applicability.

While this overall institutional strategy has been evolving for at least a decade, a series of trends and events has recently motivated CMU to undertake a comprehensive review of its computing strategy. In particular, realization of the above educational goals does not seem feasible with existing timesharing systems. As a result, this chapter details a process of strategic planning which has led Carnegie-Mellon to a plan for a distributed computing environment.

Definitions

The concept of strategic planning is the subject of substantial recent scholarship and debate. There is an evolving consensus, however, regarding the fact that strategic planning is directed at change, not maintaining the status quo. It facilitates moving forward. Drucker capsulized the strategic planning concept especially well when he wrote:

> The pertinent question is not how to do things right, but how to find the right things to do, and to concentrate resources and efforts on them.[2]

In other words, strategic planning focuses on making choices rather than on implementing them. As Schendel and Hatton point out:

> Strategic planning is adaptive planning and suited to coping with change; long range planning is inertial and implicitly assumes a future that will duplicate the past.[3]

In fact, strategic planning should be designed to create change, to create a new future. Attaining CMU's goals in computing requires strategic as well as long-range planning. This chapter will describe computing at Carnegie-Mellon from a strategic planning perspective.

Approaches

The literature on strategic planning identifies several approaches to strategic planning.[4] All of these approaches are better characterized as attempts to describe the strategic planning process than as prescriptions for its accomplishment. The reality of the strategic planning process is a mix of intuition and initiative. At Carnegie-Mellon, the institutional and computing leadership are well acquainted with the various approaches to strategic planning. The perspectives underlying these approaches have been the foundation for most of the strategic planning for computing, even when the approaches themselves were not explicitly applied. Strategic planning at CMU has not, in the main, been done through a systematic implementation of methodologies, but through the simultaneous and implicit application of the approaches described below. Since strategic considerations have been fundamental to planning for computing at Carnegie-Mellon, this chapter explores the CMU computing plan in the context of a number of approaches to strategic planning. In particular, the chapter is organized around the following approaches to strategic planning:

- situation audit
- WOTS-up analysis
- market niche location evaluation
- service life cycles
- service portfolio analysis
- synergy
- gap analysis

Each approach will be examined in the CMU context and illustrated by describing the approach's contribution to the computing plan which has been adopted at CMU. The chapter should thereby provide an example to assist others in utilizing these approaches on their campuses while also providing the reader with information on Carnegie-Mellon's strategic plan for computing.

Situation Audit

The situation audit is essentially a careful assessment of the current situation of an organization. It should include an examination of history, an assessment of current status, an analysis of expectations, and a projection of future status based on the extrapolation of current trends.

History

Carnegie-Mellon established a Computation Center in 1956, and established the first university computer science department in 1965. The Computation Center was an early proponent of convenient access to modern computing equipment. The first machine, acquired in 1956, was an IBM 650. In 1961, the Computation Center acquired several Bendix G-21 computers and implemented a conversational remote job entry system on them. As a result, users were able to submit work to the computer from terminals in close proximity to their normal workplace. In 1966 the large demand for scientific computation and the enormous scale economies provided by large batch processing systems led to the acquisition of a UNIVAC 1108. Increasing need for timesharing facilities led to the 1967 lease and 1971 purchase of an IBM 360/67 running TSS.

During the two decades between 1956 and 1976 the CMU Computation Center pursued the policy of acquiring a new large computer every five years. This policy was dropped in 1976 in favor of making "smaller purchases every year or two to take advantage of reductions in system price/performance ratios."[5] At the same time CMU made a major commitment to timesharing based on Digital Equipment Corporation (DEC) TOPS-20 systems. Since 1976 computing capacity has been growing at a compound rate of at least 30 percent annually. This rapid growth in computing capacity has been funded partly through a concomitant decision to reduce computing support personnel. Recently, the growth in Computation Center facilities has been augmented by an even more rapid growth of departmental computing facilities.

Current Status

Facilities

Carnegie-Mellon University has pursued the goal of providing its students and faculty with easy access to high-quality timesharing computing facilities. At present, approximately 75 percent of the student body uses computing during any given semester, and these students utilize approximately two hours per week of terminal time. Computing is provided mainly through user-friendly timesharing systems.

In the Fall of 1982, Carnegie-Mellon users will have access to a Computation Center equipped with six DECSYSTEM-2060 medium-scale timesharing systems, two DEC VAX-11/780 systems for computer science education, a VAX-11/780 for general and scientific computation, a VAX-11/780 machine for office automation and support functions, two DEC PDP-11/45 minicomputers devoted to elementary timesharing and word processing, and a Data General Eclipse system supporting the Integrated Library System. These Computation Center machines are connected to more than seven hundred terminals through a terminal-oriented data communications network that utilizes a combination of fiber optic trunks, statistical multiplexors, and a MICOM port contention/selection switch. CMU also is a major university center on EDUNET, the facilitating computer network that links more than one hundred and fifty universities and colleges across the country.

In addition to the central facilities, a number of academic groups have dedicated facilities. Four groups, Nuclear Chemistry, Medium Energy Physics, the Institute of Building Science, and Psychology have VAX-11/780 timesharing systems. Astonishingly, the computing facilities of the Computer Science Department and the Robotics Institute are at least equal in total power to all the other computing facilities in the university.

The Carnegie-Mellon library system is installing an on-line catalog and circulation system which will be available for patron access in late 1982. The system is based on the Integrated Library System (ILS) developed by the National Library of Medicine. ILS is supported by a staff drawn from the library, Administrative Systems, and an external vendor that is assisting with the adaptation of ILS to the CMU environment. In the administrative computing area, an increasingly large number of systems support on-line access to administrative data. Administrative departments hold full responsibility for data entry and significant responsibility for program execution.

While it is difficult to apply general measures, the power of the total CMU computing inventory totals at least 40 million instruc-

Table 1. *Summary of computer facilities at CMU, Fall 1981*

Computation Center
  User community: more than 3500 users from entire campus (except CSD).
  5 DECSYSTEM-2060/TOPS-20 Systems as follows:
    TOPSA (2400 megabytes) for Administration, CC development.
    TOPSB (1400 megabytes) for GSIA and SUPA research, and graduate education, external.
    TOPSC (1400 megabytes) for CIT research and graduate education.
    TOPSD (800 megabytes) for undergrads, H&SS research, and graduate education.
    TOPSE (600 megabytes) for undergrads, MCS & CFA research, and graduate education.
  1 DEC VAX-11/780 (300 megabytes) for research and graduate ed.
  2 DEC PDP-11/45/RSTS systems (80 megabytes each) for word processing.
  All systems networked together via DECnet (1 megabaud link) with connections to the Psychology, Chemistry, and Physics VAXes, and the CSD DECSYSTEM-2060 (also 1 magabaud).
  Over 550 terminals (most hardwired, some dialup; most 1200, 2400 baud).
  1 XEROX 9700 Multifont printer (2 pages/sec max)

Computer Science Department and Robotics Institute
  User community: 400 in CSD, RI, Psychology, EE, Math for research and graduate education.
    1 DECsystem-1080 (similar to a 2060) (1400 Megabytes)
    1 DECSYSTEM-2060 (1060 megabytes)

---

tions per second. Because of the widespread acceptance of the importance of computing and administrative support for its expansion, faculty and staff are increasingly integrating computing into their teaching, research, and administration. As a result, demand for computing services is growing more than 30 percent per year, and use would be even higher if the university could fund a more rapid expansion of capacity. Furthermore, a number of research projects are using increasing amounts of off-campus computing services, to accomplish large-scale computation because the on-campus facilities are not well-suited to these problems. Despite the comparatively large amount of computing services available, the most frequently expressed complaint about computing at CMU is lack of capacity. The fact that expectations for computing continue to exceed available resources is one of the key issues that a CMU strategic plan must accommodate.

Table 1. *Summary of computer facilities at CMU, Fall 1981 (cont.)*

---

1 DECsystem-KA10 (40 megabytes)
5 VAX-11/780s (600 megabytes each)
6 VAX-11/750s (half 11/780) (400 megabytes each)
All systems networked together via Ethernet (3 megabaud)
Personal computers: 18 Altos, 44 Perqs
1 Dover multifont XEROX printer (half XEROX 9700)
Terminals (half 1200, half 9600; most with access to
all systems): 250

Departmental systems
    Architecture: VAX-11/780 (600 megabytes)
        User community: 25 for research & graduate ed., jointly with CSD
    Chemistry: VAX-11/780 (500 megabytes)
        User community: 40 for research & graduate ed.
    Electrical Engineering: VAX-11/780 (160 megabytes)
        User community: 70 for undergrad & graduate ed.
    Mechanical Engineering: VAX-11/750 (120 megabytes)
        User community: 20 for research & graduate ed.
    Mellon Institute: Computer Engineering Center VAX-11/750 (180
    megabytes)
        User community: 25 for research
    Physics: VAX-11/780 (1700 megabytes)
        User community: 60 for research & graduate ed.
    Psychology: 1 VAX-11/780 (400 megabytes) and 2 VAX-11/750s (120
    megabytes)
        Total user community: 50 for research & graduate ed.
    All systems connected to DECnet or to Ethernet

Table 1 summarizes the computational situation as of fall 1982 in terms of the hardware facilities and the numbers of users. It does not reveal the number and diversity of operating systems, programming environments, programming languages, and software tools.

While all of these installations are networked together, the difficulty of operating and using such a complex facility can hardly be overestimated. Carnegie-Mellon has a distributed computing environment which has grown with little design. Operation and administration are difficult and few users are fully knowledgeable of the range of services that could assist with their work.

Budget

CMU's 1982-83 operating expense budget totals approximately $108 million. University research income for 1982-83 is expected to be $42 million. The total 1982-83 computing budget at Carnegie-Mellon can be usefully lumped into three parts: Computation Center ($3.2 million), Computer Science and Robotics ($2.7 million), and departmental systems (Administrative Systems, Library, Chemistry, Physics, Psychology, etc.) ($1.3 million). The addition of the ILS system for the library to its existing automation activities will lead to an annual library computing budget of over $0.2 million in 1982-83. Amortized equipment costs are included in these figures. However, departmental minicomputers are not included, nor is the small amount spent by individuals and individual research grants on terminals and consumer-oriented personal computers. Most important, the extensive support for departmental systems provided by graduate students and faculty is not included.

For the Computation Center, averaging over the past several years, about 35 percent of the budget per year is spent for capital acquisition and 65 percent for operations and support. Roughly, 30 percent of their service goes to undergraduate education, 40 percent to research and graduate education (which cannot be separated), 20 percent to administration and 10 percent to external and commercial uses. Almost all of the Computer Science, Robotics and departmental budgets go to research and graduate education. Putting it all together yields a total annual budget of $7.2 million, with 14 percent for undergraduate education, 62 percent for research and graduate education, 17 percent for administration and 6 percent for external and commercial. This provides about $250 per undergraduate student per year and $2,250 per faculty/graduate student per year. Average figures for computer usage must, however, be interpreted with special caution, since usage is always distributed very unevenly, with about 90 percent of the computing being done by about 10 percent of the users.

Organization

The organization of computing at Carnegie-Mellon is shown in Figure 1. The Vice Provost for Computing and Planning is responsible for coordinating all computing on campus. He directly supervises the Computation Center and Administrative Systems.

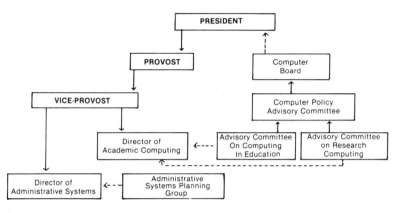

Figure 1. *The organizational structure of Carnegie-Mellon's computing and information services.*

Administrative Systems has responsibility for all administrative computing on campus; it is a software organization, working entirely on Computation Center systems. Major decisions about computing are made by the Computer Board, composed of the president, the provosts, the Vice President for Business Affairs, the chairman of the Computer Policy Advisory Committee, and the Vice Provost for Computing. The Computer Policy Advisory Committee is broadly representative of the whole campus. The Advisory Committee on Computing in Education is charged with exploring the educational use of computers in the CMU environment. The Advisory Committee on Research Computing provides policy guidance on research computation and facilitates coordination among CMU's many research-oriented computing facilities.

The departmental facilities are administratively separate from the above organization, though their acquisition decisions must be approved by the Computer Board, and several of them have their machines maintained by the Computation Center. They are mostly too small to have distinct organizational structures. The exceptions are the Computer Science Department and the Robotics Institute, which run a joint facility. There are about 45 full-time equivalent people in the Computation Center, 15 in the Computer Science-Robotics facility, and 20 in the departmental facilities (including Administrative Systems), for a total of about 80 people.

Expectations

Perhaps the best summation of the expectations of the Carnegie-Mellon community regarding computing is provided by the report of its Task Force for the Future of Computing:

> The starting point for analysis might be whether there should be any increase in computing. But the neutral assumption is, in fact, that computing will continue to increase substantially, with or without comprehensive planning. Both growth of computation in the external world and the already deep involvement of the university drive CMU along this path. The important issues are then how to shape this growth and whether to seize the moment to make a dramatic move to accelerate the increase in computational facility to attain some worthwhile goals.

> We take the position that a substantial increase in computing at CMU is fundamentally good. By a substantial increase we mean that most of the community would no longer find computing a scarce resource; terminals would be available when needed, response times adequate to most tasks, storage sufficient, and printing quick and convenient.

> We believe in the potential of this increased computation not only to help all manner of separate activities, each in their own way, but also to support new modes of integration and community. Although the ongoing computer revolution has often failed to achieve these goals, and we share with many in the CMU community concerns about the effects of letting the computer seep further into our lives, withal, we believe the promise is great and the benefits clearly outweigh the dangers. We believe our energies should go into finding the right way to proceed and to do a high-quality job.[6]

The university administration also expects very high-quality computing facilities at CMU, and the university's national reputation is partially based on the quality of its computing. The Computation Center staff is aware that CMU provides its users with a comparatively large amount of computing power, but past decisions to reduce staff levels in order to fund computing facilities have resulted in low expectations regarding the university's willingness to provide staff levels adequate to fully support that power.

Forecast

A forecast of computing trends at Carnegie-Mellon is most unsettling. Despite the fact that the real budget of the Computation Center has been rising modestly for several years and that departmental investment in computing facilities has been rising faster yet, the university community continues to be dissatisfied with the quantity and quality of computing it is receiving. In fact, an expansion of facilities adequate to fulfill the expectations outlined above would require an equipment investment of roughly $50 million using currently available timesharing technology. The resulting system would fragment the community into at least several dozen groups and would be extraordinarily difficult to maintain and manage.

Even without a decision to finance such an expansion, continued rapid growth of CMU timesharing facilities will create large technological and service problems. As a result of the steadily larger number of students coming to CMU with their own personal computers, and the increasing rate of growth in departmental computing facilities, a substantially increased amount will be invested in computing even if central fund growth remains constant. The result of this growth would, however, be a highly fragmented and inefficient computing environment which would make inefficient use of user time and would waste a large amount of support personnel resources. Users would have to become competent in the use of several different computing environments and would constantly have to deal with the complexity of finding the environment best suited to the task at hand and of moving their work to it. Support personnel would have to be dedicated to the computing activity in each of the facilities and scale economies that might be achieved through a consolidated support group would be lost.

Summary

In summary, the situation audit of computing at Carnegie-Mellon reveals that CMU's high level of computing service is likely to lead to steadily increasing demand for computing in the foreseeable future. This analysis is based on historic trends, the current status of computing at CMU, and the expectations of the user community. As a result, user expectations will have to be scaled down, and expenditures for computing increased at a much faster rate, or a new approach found.

WOTS-Up Analysis

WOTS is an acronym for Weaknesses, Opportunities, Threats, and Strengths. Based on the situation audit, it is possible to systematically assess the strengths, weaknesses, threats, and future opportunities for CMU computing services thereby gaining a deeper analytic understanding of the strategic alternatives.

Strengths

The central computing facility at Carnegie-Mellon has many strengths. Most computing services are provided in an interactive mode which greatly enhances user productivity. The services are very widely used and are provided at low cost. The Computation Center has been a pioneer in providing state-of-the-art text processing facilities, including powerful editors such as EMACS, document formatting facilities such as Scribe, and multifont output devices such as the XEROX 9700. The staff of the Computation Center, although small, is highly expert in the hardware and systems software areas. Finally, the Computation Center has a national reputation for supplying high-quality computing to the university.

The CMU community also contributes substantially to the quality of computing. The community is highly computer-literate and includes one of the strongest computer science departments in the nation.

Weaknesses

Despite these strengths, improvements are needed at CMU in the areas of student services, access, capacity, reliability, user support, large-scale computation, and user satisfaction.

- Undergraduate and professional students have too little computing power available to realize its full potential for enhancing their effectiveness. This is true even though CMU's commitment to more effective use of student time has led to the provision of more computing power than is available to students at most other colleges and universities.

- Access to the Computation Center's facilities is not adequate. It has not been possible to expand the number of terminal connections rapidly enough to keep pace with user demand.

- Despite the fact that the Computation Center has been rapidly adding computing capacity over the past two years, demand has grown even more rapidly. Service to timesharing users is often inadequate during heavy use periods, leading to a substantial loss of student, faculty, and staff productivity.

- Despite steady improvement in the reliability of computing services provided by the Computation Center, the demands for reliability imposed by the timesharing environment have increased even more rapidly.

- While CMU has a comparatively large amount of computing power per capita, it lags behind many institutions in the provision of user-support services. In the past, this shortfall has been largely ameliorated by the nature of Carnegie-Mellon users—they are predominantly computer-literate and technically educated people. As computing continues to expand outside the engineering and science disciplines into management, social sciences, and fine arts areas, the Computation Center will be able to depend less on the computer literacy of its users.

- While the strategy of employing multiple medium-scale timesharing systems provides a cost-effective and user-friendly environment for most applications, it does not provide good service for all applications. Several science and engineering disciplines require large-scale computations that cannot be broken into concurrently executing jobs. Machines are available that can provide ten to twenty times the numerical computing power of CMU's VAX-11/780s. While the great majority of applications do not need computing power on this scale, some do, and CMU has no on-campus facilities to support such applications.

All of these weaknesses are partially caused by the high level of demand and expectation for computing. Every improvement in quality raises the level of demand and expectation. Users continually discover more uses for computing, and they become more dependent on access to computing services. The users therefore have an increasing need for stable service to carry out their everyday affairs. The weaknesses in service which impact each user are well recognized by that user. As a result there is substantial dissatisfaction with the current level and quality of computing service.

Threats

Reduced levels of support for basic research, student financial aid, and a decreasing number of college-age individuals in the population are clouding the financial horizon for universities. The resulting difficulty of financing and implementing university-wide solutions to the weaknesses cited above generates a threat of local solutions which may reduce the coherence and increase the overall cost of obtaining any given level of computing service. This threat is made more serious by the very high expectations of the community for computing and the community's commitment to its importance. If university solutions fail to materialize at CMU, local solutions will.

Opportunities

Opportunities for the future development of computing at CMU are based on the university's commitment to high-quality computing and the strengths outlined above. A strategy for capitalizing on this opportunity becomes more apparent when viewed in light of the other approaches for strategic planning. In particular, an analysis of the market niche for central computing and services now offered by the Computation Center reveals a substantial opportunity to move towards a distributed personal computing strategy.

Market Niche Evaluation

A key aspect of strategic planning for any organization is deciding the services it can best supply. The services should be picked to allow the organization to take advantage of its strengths and should be targeted at areas where other organizations do not or cannot effectively fill the community's needs. Carnegie-Mellon University has chosen to stress a commitment to a combined liberal and professional education for its students, an emphasis on basic research and graduate education, and pursuit of innovative and interdisciplinary approaches to education and research. All of these directions require high-quality information-processing facilities, and CMU's strong cognitive psychology/artificial intelligence/computer science community provides the foundation for the application of computing in support of the university's mission.

As pointed out above, computing services at Carnegie-Mellon are provided by a variety of sources. The two main categories are the quasi-independent departmental facilities and the Computation Center. The Task Force for the Future of Computing stressed the important strategic role of the Computation Center while simultaneously recognizing the rapid growth of the departmental facilities. Since the departmental facilities are largely independent, they contribute to the institution's strategic computing plan only in an indirect fashion. The Computation Center is important not only for the services it directly supplies, but also because it creates the climate for development of other services. Therefore, the Computation Center should seek out service areas in which it has substantial leverage on the computing activities of the university, and should concentrate on services which it can perform more effectively than the departmental units. Because the Computation Center plays such a key role in implementing the university's computing strategy, this chapter is oriented primarily towards describing plans for centrally-supplied services.

Perhaps the most important service the Computation Center can provide in the foreseeable future is data networking. The capital investment and required coordination make this area a natural campus-wide service. Furthermore, appropriate standards in networking will stimulate the interconnection and complementarity of the many computing service groups that develop on the campus.

Another service that can be provided especially well by a computing center is large-scale computation. The cost of such facilities is still beyond the reach of most research groups and departments and the Computation Center can aggregate the total need for such computing. In some cases the appropriate response is acquisition of specialized computing equipment or program libraries. In other cases the best approach is facilitation of network linkage to appropriate off-campus facilities.

In addition, the numerous and diverse small computing users on the campus usually can be supported only through a central organization which can achieve some scale economies. In any case, the appropriate market niche for the Computation Center changes across time. For instance, improvements in networking and communications have caused most large-scale computation activity to migrate to specialized national or regional facilities.

A potentially important market niche for the central computing facility at CMU is the development of a network-oriented distributed computing software system. One of the major impediments to the full realization of the potential of distributed computing technology is the lack of an operating system that allows users of networked computers to view the total campus computing facility as a single system. At present, the user has to think of the computer he or she is using as a separate machine which can be connected to other computers to access additional services. The user therefore has to be constantly aware of the nuances of interacting with more than one computer. The central computing facility is uniquely able to develop and support a single-system-image computing facility that incorporates a hierarchy of computers.

Service Life Cycle Analysis

Another approach to strategic planning is an analysis of the life cycle status of each service provided. As Figure 2 shows, it is possible to track each service through five identifiable stages based on the service's use and the cash flow it generates:

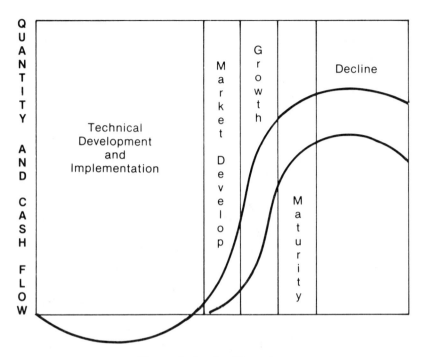

Figure 2. *Service life cycle.*

1. Technical development and implementation—During this period investment is made to enable the addition of a new service to the service portfolio. Since investment is being made and the service is not available to users during this stage, there is a negative cash flow. At present the CMU Computation Center has no major service in the technical development and implementation phase, although the Computer Science department is developing a system of integrated distributed computing.

2. Market development—For some time after the service is first introduced use grows relatively slowly and the cash flow at an even slower pace since a new service often has to be subsidized during its introductory period. The Computation Center is in the market development stage with support of secretarial and clerically oriented word processing facilities.

3. Growth—If the service is really needed and supplied in an attractive enough fashion, a point is reached where it really "takes off." During this stage the cash flow increase just about matches the increase in consumption since the rates can be increased to cover full cost. Decentralized computing, via departmental computers, is very much in the growth stage at the present time; it's well through the market development area and will start reaching maturity in the next year or two. Interestingly, this growth is occurring external to the Computation Center. On the other hand, the growth of data communications service is supported by the Computation Center, and is very rapid.

4. Maturity—In a service's mature stage the growth continues at a slower pace and scale economies combined with movement down the learning curve allow cash flow to increase faster than the quantity of service provided. Timesharing computing is in a mature state at CMU. It is still growing, and growing substantially, but people are looking beyond it, and the development work is no longer oriented toward timesharing.

5. Decline—In its declining stage, a service is consumed in decreasing quantities and starts to yield an even more rapidly declining cash flow. It may need to be continued, however, to provide for continuity of service. At Carnegie-Mellon batch computing service is clearly declining relative to other services. While batch computing is used for large scientific calculations and administrative computing, even those jobs are submitted and controlled through interactive computing interfaces.

The service life cycle analysis reveals that most of the services now offered by the Computation Center are in the mature or declining phases of their life. There is very little now under way in technical development and implementation. There is a substantial opportunity for decentralized growth of word processing facilities, and decentralized computing is already growing with little centralized support.

Only five years ago, the picture was very different. Timesharing was in a market development phase, and substantial technical development and innovation were focused on facilities to better utilize timesharing technology. The rapid pace of technological development in computing has led to a situation which threatens the future viability of the central computing organization. While an increasingly distributed and decentralized computing facility is probably desirable in the 1980s, the central facility needs to provide the foundation for this expansion and its integration. If the CMU Computation Center is to provide this foundation, it must focus more attention on developing services in the earlier stages of their life cycle. This conclusion is reinforced through an analysis of the Computation Center's service portfolio.

Service Portfolio Analysis

The service portfolio analysis is closely related to the service life cycle analysis. An approach similar to this has been used extensively by the Boston Consulting Group to analyze products. Rather than emphasizing the temporal stages through which a service passes, the portfolio analysis emphasizes each service's relative position in the market. The service portfolio analysis categorizes services along two dimensions: growth rate and market share. As shown in Figure 3, by dichotomizing each dimension (i.e., low and high growth and low and high market share), portfolio analysis yields four categories of service.

1. A service with high market share and high growth is called a star. If a service has high growth and a very large portion of the market share for such computing on campus, the service is probably very important. Chances are that it is either in the growth or mature period of its life cycle, and is vital to users. At Carnegie-Mellon, the Computation Center's star is probably document production by faculty and students.

2. A service with a high market share and a low growth rate might be called a foundation service. If a service is not growing rapidly and the computing facility has a large portion of the market, then it's probably a service which has been heavily depended on in the past and is into the mature or even declining stage of its life cycle. Such a foundation service needs to be carefully analyzed to

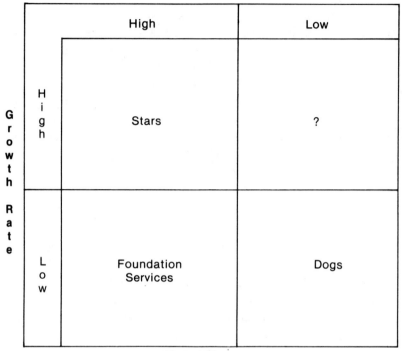

Figure 3. *Service portfolio matrix.*

determine how long it will remain an attractive service. The Computation Center's foundation service is probably timesharing support of numeric computation.

3. A service with a high growth rate and small market share can be best characterized as a questionable service and requires careful assessment. The small market share may simply be a result of the fact that other organizations have a natural advantage in the provision of the service. On the other hand, the service could be a potential star for the computing organization. Specialized timesharing is a service that is growing rapidly, but the Computation Center provides only a small portion of this service. There are a large number of departmental facilities running medium-scale timesharing facilities utilizing operating systems such as UNIX. The Computation Center has concentrated mainly on TOPS-20 services. The specialized services are growing rapidly. The interesting question is whether or not the Computation Center should make an effort in this new area.

4. A service which is not growing and in which market share is small is often referred to as a dog. Services in which both the market shares and growth rate are low often need to be trimmed away to make room for new services. The Computation Center's dog is undoubtedly specialized batch computing. Relatively little is done at CMU and much of what does get done is supplied by departmental machines.

Combining the outcomes of service life cycle and service portfolio analyses reveals that the university needs to concentrate more effort on new services which have a rapidly growing demand. Important areas include distributed computing and document production. While timesharing and batch computing are still needed by the community, even these services are being increasingly provided by specialized departmental and external facilities.

Synergy

The final and perhaps least tangible approach is to search out opportunities for synergy. What elements can be combined to produce more than their sum? In some cases, such opportunities are obvious. At Carnegie-Mellon, one of the most important arises from the strong Computer Science Department and its research effort in personal computing and user-friendly systems. Even when such obvious synergisms exist it may be difficult to realize them. The useful and non-disruptive coupling of research and delivery of production computing is a difficult task.

The search for synergy should include not only opportunities to develop and supply services, but also for complementary strengths in the service provider and the consumer. Carnegie-Mellon University, with its commitment to a liberal-professional education, places very heavy demands on the time of its students and faculty. Perhaps as a result, CMU is very conscious of the need to make efficient use of student time. The result has been the development of a computer-intensive environment for students and faculty.

The very existence of such an environment, however, has resulted in an explosive growth of demand for service. The university and its Computation Center have reacted by providing steadily increased levels of timesharing computing service, and have stressed the use of computing facilities for new uses such as document preparation. It is now becoming clear that a continued expansion of timesharing computing is not alone adequate to maintain high-quality computing at CMU, and substantial growth has begun to develop in distributed computing facilities. The above analyses show that the Computation Center has a substantial responsibility and opportunity to provide services which coordinate and integrate this growth.

The Strategy—Networked Personal Computing

While much has been accomplished at Carnegie-Mellon University through the use of timeshared computing, a number of factors lead to the conclusion that the most prudent approach to future utilization of computing at CMU will use networked personal computers in a gradual evolution from timesharing. Economic trends, advantages of personal computers over timesharing computing, and the steadily increasing popularity of home personal computers have all led to this conclusion. The conclusion is reinforced by observation of the trend towards distributed computing already in evidence at CMU.

Economic Trends

There has been an extraordinary increase in the cost-effectiveness of computing hardware. Based on technology trends over the past two decades, computing equipment has exhibited a cost-effectiveness improvement of approximately 25 percent annually.

A second and perhaps more revolutionary change over the past five years is that small computers have become as cost-effective in providing computing power as large computers. This cost pattern is a fundamental change from the previous decade when scale economies provided a powerful impetus to the sharing of one large computer.

As a result of these two trends, distribution of computing power through an increasingly large number of comparatively small computers has become attractive. CMU's computer acquisition strategy has taken advantage of this situation for several years through the acquisition of multiple medium-scale systems. Furthermore, a proliferation of specialized departmental computing facilities has already resulted from these economic trends.

Unfortunately, the economies that have been gained in computing equipment are now being diminished by the problems of supporting and managing a large multi-machine complex. It is difficult to distribute load equally, to take advantage of economies in large-scale, on-line storage, and to control software costs. In addition, the difficulty of system integration encourages groups to develop independent systems which often do not have effective facilities for communicating with other systems in the university. As a result, the community finds itself partitioned into a number of somewhat isolated groups.

None of these problems are inherent in a distributed machine environment if software support is available to provide the user with a single-system image of the facility. Unfortunately, there is little experience in the management of such facilities and little software and expertise available. A major investment is warranted by the great potential of a distributed computing environment including personal computers. When the economic trends are combined with the explosion of demand for computing at CMU, it becomes imperative that future expansion of computing be undertaken through the more economical distributed computing facility. Indeed, even if such a facility provided no better service to users, it would be desirable on economic grounds alone.

Advantages of Personal Computers

The CMU community has developed an understanding of both the utility and the limitations of timesharing. Access to an interactive computing resource with good human factors has increased substantially the effectiveness of CMU students and faculty. The faculty and students have also gained an acute appreciation of the obstacles which impede further contributions of computing to the educational and scholarly process and believe that these obstacles can be surmounted through the use of networked personal computers.

Reducing Contention

Resource contention poses a major barrier to more intensive use of timeshared computing. Contention results in difficulty in gaining access and/or adequate responsiveness after access has been gained. Students and faculty will not rely on computing in any fundamental way until these obstacles are removed. Contention for a computing resource limits the ways in which computing can enhance education and scholarship in the CMU environment since the applications which have the greatest potential are fundamental to the scholarly process (writing, information retrieval, data analysis, correspondence, and modeling). A personal computing environment can provide each user with computing power independent of the demands of others and greatly diminish contention as a barrier to user effectiveness. Ultimately each user needs access to a dedicated machine, and only the personal computing approach fulfills that need.

Simplicity

Despite recent improvements in the interface between the computer and user, all users still must master a large and complex system before being able to use parts of the system for their own limited purposes. The individual who wishes to use the data analysis capabilities of the computer must first learn how to use the computer's file system, editor, job submission language, and user-access control commands, and then master the user interface to the data analysis program. Furthermore, the need to accommodate a number of different types of computer equipment in the central facility often requires a user to understand more than one such environment.

A timesharing computer serves a diverse set of users by providing a general set of tools embedded in a complex operating system.

The requirement that a user master the resulting complexity is a significant impediment to wider use of computing throughout the university community. A personal computer customized through microcode and software can efficiently provide the specific environment(s) needed by each user, thereby reducing the apparent complexity of the system.

User Interface

Increased applicability of computing technology has depended on a steadily improving interface between the computer and the user. In the early days, this interface consisted of switches and plug boards which were set and wired specifically for each application. As computing progressed, the interface advanced to include a typewriter-like device called a keypunch and a set of programming aids which reduced the user's need to understand the detailed operation of the computer.

At present, almost all computer use at Carnegie-Mellon is carried out through interactive terminals. The user is now able to type commands to the computer and the computer responds to the command in a relatively short period of time. Advanced programming aids further enhance this interactive environment.

Despite these advances, the fundamental mode of user interaction with the computer remains one in which the user defines the task to be performed through a typewriter-like device and receives written responses. The use of audio and graphic interfaces remains almost nonexistent, and the computer provides the user with minimal assistance in solving a particular problem. In summary, true "conversational" computing remains rare indeed.

Two key technological constraints limit further development in this area. The first, and perhaps more important, is the limited capacity of the data communications circuits connecting the time-sharing system to the user terminal. The speed of these circuits often is barely adequate for the presentation of written text and is clearly inadequate for effective transmission of graphic or audio information.

Second, providing a more "conversational" interface between the user and the computer requires the instant availability of substantial computing power. Timesharing systems typically do not have adequate computing power to provide such an interface to their users except during periods of relatively light system load. During periods of heavy load, delays in response from a timesharing system make the use of such a "conversational" interface an impediment rather than an assist. Including a substantial portion of computing power in the display unit will enable high-quality graphic and audio interfaces to assist the man/machine interaction. Adequate distributed computing power also could support a more conversational user interface.

Dependability

Before faculty and students are willing to rely on computing, they need to be confident that it will operate when needed. Timesharing computing systems disable a large number of terminals whenever a failure occurs. Furthermore, without careful attention to design and substantial extra cost, it is difficult to back-up one timesharing system with another in the case of failure. Finally, the complexity of equipment and software in timesharing systems makes it difficult to attain and maintain high levels of reliability. Where a large number of personal computers are available, the breakdown of any one machine can be corrected by simply exchanging it with a working machine. The less complex software in these systems also should contribute to a higher level of reliability.

Home Personal Computers

The declining price of computing equipment and increasing cost-effectiveness of small computers is causing an explosion of activity in the personal computer area. Apple, Atari, and Radio Shack microcomputers are selling by the thousands for home, professional, and small business use. Personal computers are becoming common in the homes from which CMU is likely to draw students. We also are beginning to see a substantial increase in the students' willingness to invest in personal computing equipment. A recent survey showed that approximately 18 percent of the student body at CMU now has access to a personal terminal or computer. Technological forecasts predict that by 1985 at least 40 percent of the incoming students at an institution like CMU will come with some type of personal computer of their own, and that the penetration of these personal computers will continue to increase rapidly. To take advantage of this new technology CMU must have a structured and planned approach.

Unfortunately, the personal computers being marketed to the general public now and in the immediate future are almost certain to have computing power, display technology, file storage, reliability, and software support below the level needed to provide CMU with the gains that potentially are available.

Description of the Planned Environment

The trends and opportunities detailed above make it possible to describe a computing environment which should support a significant improvement in user effectiveness. Any such description is speculative, depending as it does on uncertain projections of future technology. The pace of development is especially difficult to predict. The following sections describe a reasonable end-state for the development of a personal computing environment. Most of these goals appear to be feasible in the decade of the eighties, some within a few years and some substantially later.

The computing environment at CMU will consist of four system elements: the central computing facility, the communications facility, the local clusters, and finally the personal computers. At successive stages in the evolution of the environment, function will migrate from one system element to another. For instance, during the early period, color graphics capabilities may have to be provided at local clusters but they can be provided by the personal computers as soon as technological advance reduces their cost.

The Central Computing Facility

The central computing facility almost certainly will grow over the entire development period of the personal computing environment. The growth will be smaller and more specialized than it would be if the central facility were to continue to provide the majority of the computing capability. It should be noted that the "central" facility may not be provided by a co-located concentration of large computers. Technology may dictate a centrally managed facility which consists of a geographically distributed group of hardware installations. Areas which may continue to require substantial central capacity are large-scale, on-line, and archival storage; large-scale computation; and costly specialized devices.

Large-Scale On-Line and Archival Storage

Current experience with professionals who have unconstrained access to computing facilities indicates that they easily can utilize three million characters of on-line storage in support of their writing, administrative, and research activities. For Carnegie-Mellon University to achieve this standard, 20 billion characters of storage are required. Approximately 10 percent of the work done each month will be archived for possible reference months or even years later, which necessitates an archival system capable of growing at the rate of approximately 20 billion characters per year. As access to the bibliographic resources grows, the library will require an increasingly large amount of on-line storage.

Large-Scale Computing

Despite the fact that the personal computers are expected to meet most of their users' computational needs, a minority of tasks will require the capability to execute a single instruction stream at a rate which exceeds the capabilities of the personal machines. In addition, substantial computing power will be required to manage the large body of on-line and archival storage and distribute it to the local clusters and the personal computers. The personal machines will also make substantial use of the central facility to acquire, develop, distribute, and store software. Finally, a minority of users may need special purpose computing facilities to support large-scale numerical computation.

The central facility must be highly reliable because it will play a small but critical role in the functioning of the overall environment. As a result it should contain a fully duplexed set of equipment designed so that loss of some element will cause only a temporary interruption in service. Based on current usage projections, it appears that the facility will need a processing capability of at least 20 million instructions per second if it is to support the volume of use expected at Carnegie-Mellon University. The needs of users with large-scale numerical tasks indicate that a floating point processor which can execute about 20 million floating point operations per second will also be desirable.

Specialized Devices

The anticipated heavy use of graphics and text processing facilities requires that facilities be available to produce high-quality final output. In addition, facilities will be needed to input data from the printed page, from various types of magnetic media, and probably from the new video disk technology. In particular, the following equipment will be needed:

1. Multifont and graphics-capable laser printer
2. Phototypesetter
3. Color graphics printer
4. Color graphics transparency camera
5. Color, high-resolution, large-format plotter
6. Microform printer
7. Character page reader
8. Tape, floppy disk, and video disk drives for media conversion.

Many of these central facilities will be especially needed to expand access to library resources through the network of distributed computers. As technology advances and costs change, it is likely that additional devices will be needed at the central facility and that some of the devices will be low enough in cost to migrate to local clusters or into the personal computers themselves.

The Communication Facility

The computing environment must be knit together with a high-performance communications network. Because the network will be shared by many computers—those at the central site, those in the clusters, and all of the personal computers—total bandwidth must be high to assure that the communications facility will not become a bottleneck. This requirement is heightened by the projected use of the network to transmit audio and video media as well as support a distributed file system and software library. Data rates in excess of a million characters per second are desirable. Lower data rates combined with larger capacity on-line storage in the local clusters and/or the personal computers would be acceptable.

The communication facility must support not only on-campus connections, but will also need to provide moderately high-rate communications to the surrounding community and gateways to other networks. Such communications capabilities are now being provided by Bell Telephone, but the data rates are inadequate and the expense is too great for the networked personal computing application. The cable television system now being installed in Pittsburgh is being evaluated as a source for communications in the city, and packet radio needs to be investigated. CMU already has a Telenet node and an ARPANET node, and is investigating satellite communication facilities. Access to national bibliographic search systems will become increasingly important, and the network must easily accommodate this access.

Local Clusters

Local clusters of personal computers will provide facilities which are too expensive to include in each personal machine. For instance, the transition to a full personal computing environment is likely to be made by replacing the current clusters of terminals with clusters of personal computers which can be shared by many users. It is also likely that the expense of on-line storage may require a period in which ten to twenty personal machines share access to a relatively large and fast local disk storage facility. It appears that hard copy output and color graphics display facilities will not be available at a cost which allows their inclusion in the standard personal machine so they will probably be provided in a shared-access mode in a local cluster. We expect that these local clusters will vary in size and capacity and will be located at a large number of strategic locations on and off the campus (academic buildings, dormitories, storefronts, etc.)

Personal Computers

The technological characteristics of the personal computer will depend on the rate of technological development and costs. The following capabilities would be desirable:

1. The display should include capabilities which enable the support of graphics and multiple contexts. (Bit-mapped, high-resolution display with an unencoded keyboard and graphic pointing device.) This type of display and user interface will allow interaction through graphics as well as character interfaces and can accommodate the presentation of a printed page with special characters exactly as it will be printed or typeset.

2. Machine architecture which enables the development of large applications without substantial constraints on program and data structure size. (Virtual address range and paging facilities to support an address space of at least one billion characters.) While these facilities do not need to be available at the outset, the system software should support it to avoid the need to undertake later revisions.

3. Execution speed in the vicinity of one million instructions per second. This specification can obviously evolve over the life of the system, but implementation of a user interface which includes graphics and some of the results from current cognitive science research will require a substantial processor.

4. Capabilities to interface to audio input and output devices. It may be that provisions for audio input will be critical to support of users lacking typing skills.

5. Capability to accept static video input. It is likely that some applications will be greatly assisted by interfacing to video disk technology.

Current technology can provide most of these characteristics at a cost of approximately $20,000 per unit. CMU does not expect personal machines of this capability to be available for much less than $6,000 per unit by 1984-85. As a result, we expect that the 1985 environment at CMU will consist of shared personal computers and/or personal computers with more limited capability.

Implementation Planning

Full implementation of the personal computing environment probably will take the remainder of the decade. During that period evolution will take place along three dimensions:

1. An increasingly large portion of the user community will have a dedicated device to provide computing and/or access to computing.
2. The actual computing power will become more widely distributed throughout the user community.
3. Software will be developed which provides an increasingly seamless migration of computing activity throughout the distributed facility.

Carnegie-Mellon University's objective is to deliver service to the general campus community which is very close to the state of the art. The development schedule must also provide for a steadily improving set of computing facilities. A period of poor service during development and conversion would not be acceptable to the CMU community. The actual schedule for movement along any of the dimensions will depend both on the technology's capability to support advancement and on CMU's ability to finance the acquisition of the required equipment.

Implementation Strategies

While it is premature to outline a specific timetable for the project, we anticipate the following strategies will aid in rapid development:

1. Use timesharing systems to do the initial development and testing of some of the software. For instance, software could be developed in a machine environment which closely matched the environment chosen as the design specifications for the personal computer.

2. Acquire personal computers for development and cluster use before they become cost-effective for wide distribution. While it will not be possible to pay $10,000 for a personal computer for each user, it may be quite cost-effective to pay that sum for a personal computer which would be shared by a number of users. Furthermore, it is prudent to acquire a few machines which provide facilities comparable to those specified for the goal machine even if a premium must be paid.

3. Provide function that is ultimately to be provided by the personal computer through the central facility or cluster until it can be provided in a personal computer. As pointed out above, color graphics may initially be available only on a comparatively small number of personal computers in clusters.

4. Deploy a personal computing environment which does not meet all of the goals to a subset of the community on a trial basis. If it is judged that a sufficiently large subset of the capabilities which are to be supported at the end of the project can be provided to make a useful and cost-effective contribution to user productivity, a decision could be made to deploy an interim personal computer.

5. Undertake the development of the distributed software system in an incremental fashion which allows some elements to be in use very early in the development period. For instance, it may be that implementation of a distributed full screen editor and a command language interface on intelligent terminals will provide a migration path from the current TOPS-20 environment to the new environment under development.

6. Begin the deployment of personal computers with small pilot groups. While the ultimate goal may be the provision of a personal machine to every student, faculty member, and professional staff member, the first set might be provided to a few faculty and stu-

dents actively involved in the development effort. A couple of academic departments could be chosen to participate in a pilot study, then the entering classes in one or two colleges, and finally all entering students. In the early stages, the personal machines could be substantially more expensive than would be tolerable in the later stages.

Gap Analysis

The last step in the development of a strategic plan is Gap Analysis. The procedure requires that the selected strategy be used as the basis of a long-range plan and has the goal of isolating areas in which it appears a gap will result between the strategy's objectives and the institution's capability to reach those objectives. We have been testing the personal computing strategy in this fashion and have identified the following possible gaps and tentative solutions.

1. Will it be possible to develop the required software? Careful discussions with the Computer Science Department and several large computing manufacturers have led to a guardedly affirmative conclusion.

2. Will it be possible to finance the required facilities? An assessment of the life-cycle costs of the networked personal computing environment leads to the conclusion that it will be the most cost-effective means of providing high-quality computing. CMU is hoping to realize substantial outside support for the venture in view of its pioneering nature.

3. Will the implementation change the institution's character in undesirable ways? The Task Force on the Future of Computing carefully considered this issue and recommended a number of ways in which the possible negative effects could be ameliorated. The plan provides for a continuous evaluation of the impact of networked personal computing on the campus, and allows for corrective actions if the impacts appear to be negative.

4. Will CMU be faced with the long-term maintenance of an idiosyncratic software environment? A central tenet of the plan is that a large computing manufacturer pursue this strategy with CMU in a joint venture. The result is hoped to be the adoption of the CMU-developed system as a product by the manufacturer. If this goal is reached, the long-term maintenance and support costs will be shared among many users.

In summary, a number of such items have been evaluated, and solutions developed. It is too early to predict confidently the gaps will all be overcome, but Carnegie-Mellon is hopeful and proceeding vigorously with the plan.

Summary

Carnegie-Mellon University is committed to the importance of computing as an integral part of the university. This commitment has been responded to by a very rapid growth in the demand for and use of computing for a broad spectrum of activities. The result has been an increasing level of dependence on computing for activities increasingly central to the academic enterprise. Computers support the writing process; facilitate communications between students, faculty, and staff; enhance access to the library; support real and simulated laboratory work; and generally provide much of the thread for the fabric of the institution.

This computer-intensive environment has stimulated the faculty, staff, and students to develop additional applications for computing. As a result, even though CMU already ranks high on computing use per student, demand for additional computing power is increasing more rapidly now than at any time in the past. The future will almost certainly reward a significant investment in computing facilities for student use. Furthermore, since computing is now playing a central role in the university, extraordinarily high demands are placed on the Computation Center for reliable and easy-to-use facilities. In fact, the commitment of the administration and the existing high level of computing has led to a steadily increasing demand for a large quantity of high-quality computing service.

An evaluation of Carnegie-Mellon's resource base indicates insufficient funding to continue expansion of computing at the required pace utilizing timesharing technology. Furthermore, time-sharing technology has been revealed to have significant deficiencies as a source for computing power. The CMU Computer Science Department has been addressing these problems with an effort to develop the software base for a network of powerful personal computers, and a strong trend towards distributing computing power has already become evident on the campus. As a result, Carnegie-Mellon has made the strategic choice to develop, in partnership with a commercial vendor, a software system to support a network of personal computers designed to enable every student and faculty member to have their own computer.

The result should be an environment in which computing can be used as easily as a telephone. It is our conviction that such an environment will provide our students with a more productive learning environment and our faculty with better facilities to support their teaching and research.

Acknowledgement

This chapter embodies the ideas of a very large number of people, both within and outside of Carnegie-Mellon University. The basic elements of the computing strategy outlined herein preceded the author's arrival at CMU. Key contributions to the development of the strategy have come from the Task Force for the Future of Computing at CMU, Richard Cyert, Horace Flatt, Nico Haberman, Michael Levine, Jack McCredie, Raj Reddy, Richard Van Horn, Howard Wactlar, and others too numerous to recall here. Daniel Updegrove, Richard Van Horn, and Andrea Van Houweling were all instrumental in assisting me with the task of organizing and writing this chapter. Despite all of the help I have received, infelicities and mistakes remain—for those I take responsibility.

References

1. The Task Force for the Future of Computing at Carnegie-Mellon University, Allen Newell, chmn. *The Future of Computing at Carnegie-Mellon University*. February 28, 1982, page 13.
2. Drucker, Peter F. *Managing for Results*. New York: Harper and Row, 1964, page 5.
3. Schendel, Dan E. and Hatton, Kenneth J. "Strategic Planning and Higher Education: Some Concepts, Problems and Opportunities." *Proceedings of the Fourth Annual Meeting of the American Institute for Decision Sciences*, November 1–4, 1972.
4. A particularly good review is given in Steiner, George A. and Miner, John B. *Management Policy and Strategy*, New York: Macmillan, 1977, chapters 7–9.
5. A full explanation of this policy change can be found in McCredie, John W. "Computer Acquisition: The Carnegie-Mellon Strategy." *EDUCOM Bulletin*, Fall 1979, pp. 10–14.
6. The Task Force for the Future of Computing at Carnegie-Mellon University, Allen Newell, chmn. *The Future of Computing at Carnegie-Mellon University*. February 28, 1982, page 7.

6

Rensselaer Polytechnic Institute

JAMES MOSS
Director, Office of Computer Services

Introduction

Planning for future information technology at an academic institution should be integrated with other strategic planning activities. To be most effective, long-range plans in this important area should be derived from overall institutional goals and should be consistent with both previous campus information-processing developments and future technological trends. Historical circumstances and past decisions of both administrators and faculty shape the physical realities of an existing campus, and more importantly, its academic programs, traditions, management, and faculty. The latter, in turn, provide the ongoing stimuli to shape students and influence the attitudes and support of alumni.

At RPI, the basis for the present computing environment and plans for future computing and information technology are deeply rooted in on-going processes and historical circumstances. It is in this context that two documents, both integral to the RPI planning process, have evolved. The first, called "Rensselaer 2000," is the institute's overall long-range plan for development by the year 2000. A specific goal for RPI is to be one of a small number of first-rank, internationally-renowned, technological universities. To accomplish this goal, Rensselaer must provide students, faculty, researchers,

135

and administrators with the support and capabilities necessary for a leadership role in the use of information technology in all aspects of university life and in the high-technology society where its graduates will continue to make major contributions.

The second document specifies RPI's objectives for computing and information technology in support of the broad goals of "Rensselaer 2000." It has been approved by the Provost as the description of the general framework for RPI's future information-technology environment. The objectives presented in this plan are included in the "Future Computing Environment" section of this chapter.

To provide a context for the planning and implementation processes taking place at RPI, the following section presents a brief outline of the university's traditional historical perspective. The next section describes the current state of computing and information support facilities at the university.

An Historical Perspective

The present position of RPI in the educational establishment derives in large part from the original goal of Stephen Van Rensselaer, who founded the school in Troy, New York, in 1824. He wrote, "I have established a school . . . for the purpose of instructing persons who may choose to apply themselves in the application of science to the common purposes of life." He established a tradition of instructing students to be practical, hands-on engineers with inquisitive, problem-solving inclinations. Since 1824, RPI has continued to grow at a slow and controlled rate, resisting the pressures to become a large, public institution or a "research factory."

However, it became clear to some of the more perceptive alumni and trustees in the late 1960s that RPI should become more aggressive in developing new academic programs, new research, imaginative faculty, and better management techniques. To reestablish a national and international reputation for excellence, and to compete successfully for outstanding students, changes had to be made. The transition years of the early 1970s were turbulent ones.

During this period there was recognition of the need for major improvements to many academic services, including RPI's computing capability. Until 1974, support for computational activities was provided by an IBM 360/50 and a small, underpaid staff. In the transitional period, an IBM 360/67 was acquired. However, computing continued to be a source of frustration to most users and of acrimony among faculty, students, and administrators.

When George M. Low became RPI's president in the summer of 1976, he was aware that computing had been a problem on campus and that a strong technological university must have excellent computing support. He immediately formed, and participated in, a Computer Study Task Force composed of faculty, staff, and administrators. The charter of the group was to study and report on future computing needs in terms of university policy, hardware, physical facilities, staffing, and external and research use. There was wide campus participation in subcommittees that submitted reports on several issues related to the computing environment at RPI.

Throughout this planning stage there were no specific fiscal constraints placed on the task force. The group was to develop several long-range plans that would meet campus computing needs and to compare the costs of alternative solutions. Established in September 1976, the task force was directed to have alternative plans developed for presentation to the Board of Trustees in May 1977. At this time, the Board and senior management made an important strategic decision: RPI should move into an academic leadership role in the application of computing technology to the social, instructional, research, and administrative needs of the university and of the greater society of which it is a part. Specifically, the Board approved the following actions having a total cost exceeding $7 million:

- Procurement of a large centralized computer (an IBM 3033).
- Development of a campus network to support 180 terminals available to students, with an equal number for research, faculty, and administrative use. (With 180 terminals RPI could allow students a 30-minute terminal session daily.)
- Renovation of an existing building (a beautiful old church) to become a new computer center.
- Staff increases necessary for high-quality service.
- Implementation of several policies to serve as guidelines for managing computing activities.
- Funding to support necessary peripheral improvements as requirements increase over a five-year period.

The Present Computing Environment

General Campus Computing

In the years since these recommendations were approved, the nature of computing at RPI has changed dramatically. Virtually all of RPI's 5500 students use the computer. The number of timesharing sessions has increased from 1000 per month to 100,000 per month. The "average" student is now taking three courses per semester that require use of the computer and is using the system every day. Computer literacy has been achieved for all students, and computing now is used routinely as an important tool in all professional degree areas. A parallel effort in the Engineering School has resulted in the development of an Interactive Graphics Center, supported by two PRIME 750 computers and currently used by about 3000 students each semester.

Under the organizational structure of RPI, the Academic Computing Services department reports to the vice provost, who reports to the provost (Academic Vice President). The administrative computer support group reports to a Senior Director for Finance and Administration, who reports to the Administrative Vice President. This group is responsible for administrative systems analysis, programming, documentation, production control, and data entry. Administrative software is acquired primarily by purchase of software packages which are run on the IBM 3033 in the Academic Center. Each group has separate advisory committees, consisting of faculty members, administrators, and students.

RPI uses the MTS (Michigan Terminal System) operating system on its central IBM 3033. This software was designed by a group at the University of Michigan in the late 1960s to provide high-quality, user-friendly, interactive computing in an academic environment. There are eight universities throughout the world using MTS. These universities have a close working relationship and share software developments. Representatives of universities in the MTS group are also working jointly on local network development.

Departmental Systems

Schools and departments within RPI have a wide variety of mini-computer equipment including several systems manufactured by Prime Computer Corporation and Digital Equipment Corporation.

The primary acquisition criterion is that systems should be complementary; special computing needs should be met by equipment of appropriate size and location. With this philosophy, computing is gradually becoming a distributed function. The same philosophy applies to word processing equipment, where both the central computer and stand-alone systems are being used more and more. There is a standard review of computing and hardware procurements.

A unique program to investigate the effectiveness of personal computers as part of a sophisticated computing environment was initiated at RPI in the fall of 1981. The Provost Scholar's Program awards to approximately 20 outstanding RPI freshmen a financial grant-in-aid of $2,500 per year. They are also provided with a personal microcomputer to use in academic, research, or personal projects at their own initiative with asistance from a faculty mentor. This program is expected to provide data about how students will actually use personal computers. It will also explore many related issues such as maintenance, security, documentation, staff support, software distribution, and network-loading implications. There is also ongoing research on social and psychological implications of computer use including such issues as: how students learn to use personal systems; how ownership affects use of student time; how personal computer ownership impacts academic achievement, social life, and campus activities; and what human factors are important in the student/personal computer interaction. These data will be very important in decisions which must be made in anticipation of the time, probably mid-decade, when substantially all RPI students will have, and may be required to have, personal computers on campus.

The RPI library is moving rapidly to the use of computing to support its information-related mission. It presently has in place both an acquisitions/accounting system and a serials system, two elements of an overall plan to automate all phases of the library's operation. These systems are based on SPIRES (a general data base package written by Stanford University) and are being designed in the library as an integrated set of routines in which information entered for one application is shared with other systems as required.

The next phase, the on-line catalog, is currently under design with an anticipated completion date in the summer of 1982. Concurrent with this activity, and continuing through the summer of 1983, is a retrospective conversion project. Drawing from the On-line Computer Library Center (OCLC) data base in Dublin, Ohio, records for all pre-1974 holdings are being converted to machine-readable form. RPI holdings acquired since 1974 can already be processed by computer.

All of the library's programs are implemented on the institute's IBM 3033 mainframe. This design allows the library's information systems to be accessed through the network of terminals already in place throughout the campus. Some local data back-up and pre-processing will be handled in the library, using one or more micro-processors. For the future, the library is investigating alternatives of receiving full-text material on-line upon demand. The role of the library is expected to increase as a searching and screening operation, but will diminish as a storage facility.

Guiding Principles

Thus, RPI's Board of Trustees has made a strategic commitment to create an intensive information-processing environment and to do so in a relatively short period of time. The following lessons, learned during this process, will guide future planning efforts at RPI:

1. Top administrative commitment and participation are essential to obtain the cooperation of varied elements on campus and to arrive at decisions acceptable to these various groups.

2. The computing function is integral to the overall goals and objectives of the university, and a computing plan is essential for systematic improvement. The plan must be consistent with the financial, academic and administrative needs of the university.

3. Computing is expensive, and, if computing resources are available, growth in usage is inevitable. Computing is an essential ingredient of the college educational process and there is no viable alternative to spending the money necessary for adequate facilities and services. While research and other external sources may pay a share of computing expenses, the major costs of instructional and student use must be accepted as normal university operating costs.

4. The computing center staff must be highly professional and able to relate to the needs of students, faculty, research, and administrative users. Today and for the foreseeable future, computing professionals are expensive, and universities must be willing to compete for them in the job market.

5. The computing needs of an academic institution are diverse. It is unlikely that a single simple answer could meet all needs. Different styles of software and hardware systems have a place in education and should be considered complementary. The responsibility of the computer center is not just to provide computing service, but also, where appropriate, to assist others on campus in the selection of micros, minis, terminals, packages or other appropriate computing services. Avoiding undue waste, duplication, and misuse of computing are management responsibilities that should involve recommendations from computing professionals. However, there is every reason to believe that many types of computers, from very small to very large, will have a place on university campuses for many years to come. The challenges are to make all campus computing systems complementary and to meet diverse computing needs in the most cost-effective way.

6. Computer-based pictorial display techniques, such as plotting and interactive graphics, and techniques that save student, faculty or staff time, such as timesharing, word processing, and personal computing, are extremely popular with members of the campus community. The demand for these facilities is expected to grow dramatically in the next few years.

7. There are few absolutes in meeting computing needs at a university, and there are no permanent solutions. Computing requirements will continue to grow and to change. New solutions in terms of hardware, software, staff, university policies, and physical facilities must be provided to meet the changing circumstances of a dynamic technology. Unfortunately, these changes also require continuing financial support.

The Future Computing Environment at RPI

Over the past five years, RPI has made dramatic progress in developing computer services appropriate for a leading technological university. It is a continuing goal of the institute to maintain and improve the information-processing facilities available to faculty, students, and administrators. During this same time period the planning process at RPI has evolved. Computing and information-technology goals have been defined in support of "Rensselaer 2000," the long-range plan for the university. Five-year plans are now developed each year by computing center staff with the first year directly tied to budget guidelines. This plan is reviewed and approved by the provost. The five-year plan is intended to describe the programmatic and financial implications of moving systematically toward the goals enunciated in "Rensselaer 2000." In practice this process is not rigid. The planning and decision-making process at RPI can best be described as budgeting, programming, and planning with flexibility to take advantage of new academic or social needs and opportunities. The flexibility to search for "targets of opportunity" is an advantage of relatively small private universities.

As a result of this strategy, RPI is developing 1100 acres into a high-technology park which could transform the upper Hudson Valley into an eastern "Silicon Valley" of the 1990s. Another example is the Center for Manufacturing Productivity, which has developed a close working relationship with many large companies. The center uses faculty, staff, and students to provide solutions to manufacturing and productivity problems in industry on a tightly scheduled, project-management basis. A Center for Integrated Electronics is also under development, which, in conjuction with computer-aided design and computer-aided manufacturing capabilities already developed in the Center for Interactive Graphics, will provide a full range of support, from research through design and manufacturing, in areas related to the use of very large-scale integration (VLSI) technology.

These examples demonstrate some of the innovative activities taking place at RPI within an overall framework of long-range goals, intermediate-range plans, and programs related to the annual budget process. The institute's management style is flexible, but it is guided by a well-publicized, long-range plan. This style encourages administrators to evaluate special programs and projects within a broad context and to select those that appear to have the best combination of short- and long-range benefits for RPI.

"Computing and Information Technology in Support of Rensse-laer 2000" describes the specific objectives to be achieved in the information-technology area. Like "Rensselaer 2000," it is designed to provide overall guidelines for future developments while encouraging flexible responses to rapidly changing developments in mini-computers, personal computers, interactive graphics, communications and networking techniques, text processing, videodisc storage, electronic mail, large data base storage and retrieval methods, photocomposition and publishing techniques, and data collection and analysis equipment.

To support the overall goals of "Rensselaer 2000," RPI has set forth the following information-processing and communications objectives to be reached by the year 2000:

1. Students, faculty, and administrators will (a) become proficient in the use of computing and information technology as appropriate to their professional development, research interests, and administrative responsibilities, and (b) understand how information technology can be utilized to increase productivitiy in these areas of endeavor.

2. An integrated, university-wide system will provide easy access to local, national, and international communications networks. Facilities that are expected to be available on the various networks include:

- World-wide access to a variety of computer networks to support rapid communications for faculty and staff to exchange information of mutual interest with colleagues. This will be especially important to increase the productivity of faculty in a research university.

- Access to computing hardware located at Rensselaer, at other universities, and at research locations around the world. This will provide a broad range of computing capabilities to meet specialized computing requirements for research, instruction, or information retrieval.

- A wide variety of computer applications software that will enhance Rensselaer's instructional, research, or administrative needs.

- Software especially appropriate to scientific and mathematical computing in statistics, simulation and modeling, linear programming, and other mathematical techniques for data analysis. It will also include applied scientific software in structural analysis, computer-aided design, process control, and other applied problem-solving areas.

3. A full range and variety of equipment, software and services appropriate for the instructional, research, and administrative requirements of an outstanding high-technology university will be maintained.

4. Students and faculty will have access to personal computers for individual projects that will be connected to a campus network for access to other large-scale, mini-, and personal computers and other elements of integrated information technology.

5. Electronic mail services will be available for use by members of the RPI community, including on-line notices and information systems, consulting, counseling and advisement scheduling, and paper-independent administration. These services, including electronic conferencing, will be available on local, national, and international levels.

6. Scientific document preparation and text-processing capabilities and equipment, including photocomposition and printing, will be available to faculty, students, and administrators. These capabilities will facilitate the development of research proposals and high-quality research reports for publication.

7. Data collection and analysis capabilities will be available for faculty and student research use on a real-time basis.

8. Computer-aided design techniques will be available to improve both faculty productivity and the dissemination of knowledge to university students. These techniques will be utilized to assist in training of the handicapped.

9. Local university data bases and retrieval software will improve the availability of information. There will be easy access to public data bases world-wide to permit faculty researchers to contri-

bute data to these data bases and to draw on this information for research and instructional purposes.

10. There will be full technical staff capabilities for the procurement and support of a wide variety of large-scale, mini-, and personal computers, communications equipment, software, and other components of emerging information technology.

11. Computer graphics hardware and software will be distributed over various RPI computing systems for instruction, research, and university administration. Rensselaer is committed to pioneering efforts and a leadership role in the development of graphics software and the teaching of computer graphics in appropriate university curricula to ensure that graduates will be literate in this new and important technology.

12. The university environment will be oriented to full exploitation of computing and information technology, which will prepare students to live and prosper in a high-technology society.

13. Full telecommunications and networking capabilities will permit off-campus faculty and students to function effectively in the telecommuting society that is expected to evolve in the last decade of this century.

All of the objectives described in this section are integral to the accomplishment of goals in "Rensselaer 2000." Computer and information technology are seen as a means to provide greater productivity in the research, instructional, and administrative functions of the university. The utilization of this technology is not an end in itself and is viable only within the total university environment in which RPI is able to achieve the goals contained in "Rensselaer 2000."

The realization of these objectives will require a continuing commitment of personnel, equipment, top management support, and creativity. Campus-wide participation and cost-effective management considerations are essential to establish priorities and redirect existing resources to phase in appropriate technological developments as new capabilties become available. RPI is dedicated to a position of leadership in computing and information technology in order to maintain an international reputation of excellence as a high-technology, academic and research institution.

7

Stanford University

PAUL R. KAUFMAN
Center for Information Technology

Daughter: What do you really do at the university?

Father: I help the school plan.

Daughter: Is planning a good thing?

Father: Absolutely. When people plan they use reason to set a course for their future actions. Planning is our best way of dealing with uncertainty and complexity.

Daughter: Then, everybody must like to plan and you must be quite popular.

Father: Don't you have any homework?

Introduction

Stanford plans for the use of its land, buildings, and facilities and is a leader in the theory and practice of financial forecasting and modeling. Yet, in talks to the trustees and the Academic Council, Stanford President Donald Kennedy noted that there was much in the academic tradition that is antagonistic to formal planning.

147

Does that mean that planning is undesirable in a university? Surely it does not, and we couldn't afford the consequences if that were what it meant. It does suggest, however, that planning cannot gain the status of state religion that it enjoys in many corporate settings, where it is deeply embedded in a cultural consensus. The cultural consensus of the university, by contrast, scarcely includes it; so to plan, or at least to plan comprehensively, we must swim against the current . . . .

It is especially important to emphasize . . . that plans are not necessarily centrally determined and imposed programs for institutional action. Indeed, in our circumstances the most appropriate model will not be a plan in the sense of a blueprint—the complete set of explicit instructions for assembling something—but rather a set of principles and conditions that promote self-assembly through the encouragement of decentralized initiative.[1]

These words fit with the general culture of the university which holds that the best results come about as a result of enterprise and cooperation rather than central edicts. A university culture is hard to describe, but it does offer clues to understanding the university's preferred ways of getting things done, including technology planning. So, at the risk of seeming slightly whimsical, an illustration will be given of a culturally approved scenario for action. The following excerpt is from the campus newspaper.

Fortunately, George Pake of XEROX Palo Alto was standing in line at a gasoline station during the oil shortage of 1979.

There he met a Portola Valley neighbor, John Linvill, then chairman of the Department of Electrical Engineering at Stanford. While they were waiting for gas, Linvill told Pake about a project he was considering. Pake was very interested.

When Pake had accepted the job of establishing the XEROX research facility in Palo Alto in 1970, one of the conditions was that it be set up in association with a major university. What Linvill told him seemed just perfect for fulfilling that condition: Stanford was thinking of setting up the Center for Integrated Systems (CIS) and would want industrial sponsors.

Two years after that conversation, XEROX became one of the first of CIS's 17 sponsors.[2]

The story tells of a casual meeting between a scholar and a corporate officer. Each one turns out to be alert to the potential interests of the other. They both have plans but what emerges is a natural, unforced perception of a common interest which leads to joint planning. The creation of the Center for Integrated Systems (a new engineering facility not to be confused with the campus Center for Information Technology) is the latest variation on the theme of Stanford's partnership with the computer industry. Hewlett, Packard, Varian, Shockley, and Terman are names that symbolize the university's historical links to the growth of information technology. Professor Linvill would appear to be acting in the tradition of Frederick Terman, the Stanford engineer whose vision helped create the Silicon Valley industries around Stanford. (Incidentally, Terman, along with Albert Bowker, head of the Applied Mathematics and Statistics Library, established the first Stanford Computation Center in 1953.) A university publicist has this to say about Terman: "He understood the needs of industry. He climbed down from the ivory tower and drew their support to Stanford in exchange for the kind of support they needed."

As a fragment of the university's culture, the foregoing scenario offers clues to the nature of the environment in which planning takes place. Stanford values enterprising persons who have a vision of what ought to be done and a knowledge of how to do it. Planning, while important, certainly ought not to get in the way of initiative.

The story also reminds us that Stanford is a world center of computing activity. This creates a good environment for continuing innovation in technology use, but it also causes the regular surfacing of what Pogo called "insurmountable opportunities." To know which opportunities are surmountable and which are not is a challenge to the planning process.

Information Technology and Planning

For the purposes of this discussion, information technology means the machines and systematic procedures which help create, collect, process, and disseminate signs and symbols. Included in this definition are computer-based technologies for calculation, text handling, data storage, and communication as well as voice and video technologies. While information technology facilitates the creation and communication of signs and symbols, information itself is the result of a process of interpretation. This crucial act of interpretation is a product of an individual's knowledge, values, and intentions. Information-technology planning then, is concerned with knowledge used toward some end or purpose. This means that values and evaluation are at the heart of the planning process. The planning efforts at Stanford have been a continuing struggle to bring evaluative criteria to bear upon the imperatives of technology.

There is no neat, comprehensive planning process for information-technology development at Stanford. Efforts to create omnibus plans have not met with much success, although the university implements specific recommendations with university-wide scope, e.g., computer networking. It is not easy to describe a planning process. Organization charts are sometimes helpful but these can range from the very stark and sterile to something resembling Pooh's trek to Piglet's house. Figure 1 shows the major actors in the information-technology planning process. Two systems are depicted: an advisory/governance system and a management system.

There is a good deal of communication between members of these systems, as well as top-down and bottom-up flow of information within each system. Most of the people and groups referred to are discussed in the text, where their activities are described in greater detail. The foregoing simplified view of planning entities was offered as little more than a reference point for our discussions. Here are some general observations on how things work.

Stanford is a rambling institution composed of loosely coupled organizations. Each organization, whether academic, administrative, or service, operates within a particular set of political and financial constraints. Their discovery of one another in pursuit of a common cause is often marked by genuine enthusiasm but sometimes tempered by a rather ambiguous collegiality which may be familiar to the reader. Bringing these groups together is an act of planning, although those who perform these catalytic functions are rarely "planners" in an official capacity.

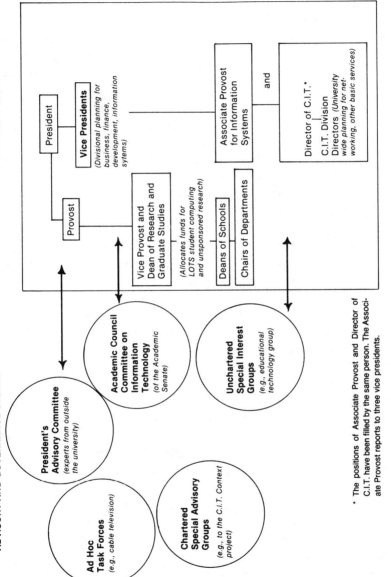

MANAGEMENT SYSTEM

President

Vice Presidents
(Divisional planning for business, finance, development, information systems)

Provost

Associate Provost for Information Systems

and

Director of C.I.T.*

C.I.T. Division Directors *(University wide planning for networking, other basic services)*

Vice Provost and Dean of Research and Graduate Studies

(Allocates funds for LOTS student computing and unsponsored research)

Deans of Schools

Chairs of Departments

ADVISORY AND GOVERNANCE SYSTEM

President's Advisory Committee
(experts from outside the university)

Academic Council Committee on Information Technology
(of the Academic Senate)

Unchartered Special Interest Groups
(e.g., educational technology group)

Ad Hoc Task Forces
(e.g., cable television)

Chartered Special Advisory Groups
(e.g., to the C.I.T. Context project)

* The positions of Associate Provost and Director of C.I.T. have been filled by the same person. The Associate Provost reports to three vice presidents.

Figure 1. *Persons and groups involved in Stanford's planning process.*

Consensus building is important. For example, a new group studying the impact of technology on education has recently been meeting weekly. It is not a formal planning body and its longevity is uncertain. But, it has become the first regular, campus-wide forum for identifying policy and planning issues which bridge both video and computer technology. Meetings have been attended by people who ordinarily might have had little to do with one another: people from medicine, education, business, engineering, psychology, computer science, and campus service centers for computing and television. They share an interest in better faculty access to video facilities and increased university recognition of the creative and economic potential of cable, videodisc, and other technologies. Of course, their interest competes with a lot of other interests. Turning interests into university plans and policies often requires a mixture of internal guerrilla warfare combined with pressures brought on by external events.

One of the most useful images for understanding the planning and use of information technologies at Stanford is a series of spheres of interest, some contained within others, some overlapping, and some not touching at all. Where they touch and overlap, the result can be the identification of a university-wide interest and a call for high-level policy attention. Fundamentally, these spheres derive their legitimacy from their relationship to the university's missions of teaching, research, and public service. To establish this legitimacy or to renew it periodically is a function of the planning and management process. Thus, at the center of all planning activities are "why" or "what for" questions which point to anticipated benefits. Sometimes the benefit is in sight. At other times the pointing is more like a dousing rod—there is a good deal of wriggling in expectation but some uncertainty as to what's really beneath the surface.

These spheres of interest in some cases represent a general technological function, e.g., networking or data base management; or in other cases a specific, substantive interest, e.g., data about students, or teaching computer science. Information technology tends to draw very different political entities together, creating new spheres of interest. The networking sphere of interest has included among others: the Network Development Division of the main computer service center, the Center for Information Technology (C.I.T.), and the Computer Science Department. Each is creating a part of the Stanford University Network. As the network concept has been broadened to include two-way cable television, the Department of Communication has joined in the planning process.

The planning and management of information technology at Stanford is conducted by parties with mutual interests but, often, representing different funding sources, budgetary procedures, managerial style, and positions with respect to the university's missions. Just how much direct, central leadership and faculty guidance ought to be given to this process has been a question to which a variety of answers has been given over the years. There has, however, been a sustained commitment by the university to plan for basic information technologies which are recognized as important to the university's primary missions and to its administration. These general, computer-based services provide the essentials for the creation, communication, and storage of information. Like traditional "common-carrier" services, the telephone networks for example, these basic computer services are university-wide and, in a manner of speaking, indifferent to the data which they carry or organize. They are: networking, data base management, central mainframe computing, and text processing.

Planning and management of the services is done by the Center for Information Technology (C.I.T). A word or two should be said about C.I.T. and financial support of computing in general. The expenses of providing these basic services are met entirely by revenues gained from the use of C.I.T. computing by the university community and by clients outside the university. In 1982, aggregate expenditures by C.I.T. were approximately $22 million, and total revenue slightly more than that. Historically, the largest source of revenue to C.I.T. has been computer use by the university administration, hospital, and non-university clients such as the Research Libraries Group. Despite its imposing budget, C.I.T. has rather limited discretion in developing new products and programs, since these must be financed off the "rate base" of charges to its various clients. C.I.T.'s rates must remain competitive with commercial services readily available to on-campus clients. Further, it is worth noting that less than 10 percent of C.I.T.'s revenue comes from instruction and research activities by Stanford's students and faculty. The bulk of research computing is conducted independently by faculty in their own labs, using specialized computing facilities purchased under projects sponsored by government and business. For its part, student computing is largely supported by operating funds given through the Vice Provost and Dean of Research and Graduate Studies. This money goes to the student computing facility—the Low Overhead Timesharing System (LOTS), operated independently from C.I.T.

Depending upon one's perspective (and mood) a global view of Stanford's information-technology scene can look like an old map of the Balkans or a pluralist's vision of the Golden Age. Either view raises some questions of university-wide governance, leadership, and service. These will be discussed further on.

Planning for Basic Technologies

At this point it is useful to get a picture of what is being planned for the basic university-wide technologies.

Networking

The "Stanford University Network" (SUNet) is currently being developed into a campus-wide, coaxial communications network with base-band and broad-band components.

The broad-band will provide facilities for all of Stanford's academic and administrative buildings. Service will include general-purpose data communications, automated energy management systems, telephone trunk line carriers, fire and intrusion detection systems, other digitized signal transmissions, and a variety of video channels, including conventional CATV channels and experimental/research video channels. In addition, the base-band (Ethernet) component system will be installed for high-speed inter-computer communication.

The high band-width network will form the backbone for the university's software services, a number of which are now in use. One service provides electronic messaging and filing at the desks of several hundred university managers, while another system offers messaging, file transfer, and text-production services tailored to the needs of scholarly publication. Administrative and scholarly users are able to exchange both files and messages. With the installation of the cable network, data and video communication will be university-wide.

Computer networks have also been initiated by departments and schools. The Computer Science Department already operates a network using experimental Ethernet technology. It connects computers used by Computer Science, the Medical Center, Electrical Engineering, the Graduate School of Business, the Center for Integrated Systems, the student timesharing system (LOTS), and the facilities of C.I.T., including the text-handling program, Context. This version of Ethernet is being integrated into the emerging broad-band network.

Data Base Management

Stanford's data base environment includes at least six systems, some of which are general purpose and institutionally supported by C.I.T. Of special note is SPIRES which has been planned and developed by Stanford and used for over a decade. Use of SPIRES has increased from approximately 200 user sessions a day in 1975, to 1,800 sessions a day now. In addition to the Stanford campus, the Stanford Linear Accelerator, and the Research Libraries Group, SPIRES is licensed to 28 educational and governmental institutions and was recently introduced to the commercial market.

Several research projects have also developed their own more specialized data management and analysis programs. A good example is the ARAMIS (American Rheumatism Association Medical Information System) data bank system, which stores information about thousands of arthritis patients for purposes of research, education, and improved treatment.

University projects, such as the widespread provision of terminals for use by managers, have increased the computer skills of many administrators. A planned interrelationship between technology product development and evolving user skills, connects with the university's deep concern with performance effectiveness. Thus, planning of basic information technologies is increasingly drawn into the light (or shadow) cast by the question of productivity.

Text-Handling

Stanford has designed and produced its own text-handling system, Context. Its success depends upon the ability to attract subscribers to the system, and it must compete for the document-production dollar with commercial word processors being used on campus. As a timesharing system, Context faces competition from networked, text-processing workstations and personal computers. Context is really a marketing venture by the university within the university.

Academic use of Context has, in some cases, sparked interest in further automation of departmental administrative work. As the electronic office begins to take root in the academic area, a new sphere of interest is being created, one which includes both administrators and scholars. This is generating the need for some fresh approaches to office systems planning.

Central Computing

Finally, among these basic, university-wide technologies are the large central host computers and smaller computers, linked as remote job entry facilities, which provide daily processing to more than 1,000 terminals on and off campus. Two IBM 3081s and a Digital Equipment Corporation DECSYSTEM-2060 are the main computers operated by C.I.T. Special system software has been developed by Stanford over a number of years. Note should be made of WYLBUR, a command program for text editing, and job control and execution, which has been adopted by 40 other universities and businesses. The companion system, ORVYL, is a highly effective timesharing system supporting interactive languages and the SPIRES data base system. SPIRES, WYLBUR, and ORVYL have helped make Stanford a ready home for new computer-based consortia serving messaging and data base needs of other institutions. For example, the EDUNET data base in SPIRES, and C.I.T.'s electronic mail system, CONTACT/EMS, have more than 150 users around the country. The American Association of Universities has asked its members to join CONTACT/EMS, which already serves as a link between many university public affairs offices.

There is another way of getting a perspective on Stanford's information-technology use, and that is by looking at how the broad university missions are being served.

Instructional and Student Use

Undergraduate students are entitled to free but limited computer use through a timesharing system (LOTS) funded by the provost. Some 4,300 students use LOTS, and about one-third of them are doing so in connection with computer science courses. University-wide planning for instructional uses of information technology is a cooperative venture which involves consultation among: the Center for Information Technology and the Academic Council Committee on Computing and Information Technology, the LOTS Advisory Board, the Vice Provost and Dean of Graduate Studies and Research (to whom the manager of the LOTS student computing system reports), and the Management Advisory Committee, which represents the vice presidents of the university.

One of the important external forces in the development of long-term planning goals is the annual visit of the Advisory Committee on Computer Science and Computing. For several years the committee has urged the university to make a stronger financial and cultural commitment to instructional computing. As one member of the committee put it, instructional computing at Stanford "really hasn't been sold as essential to education." For a world center of computer science, this seems to some, almost paradoxical. The committee suggested that access to the computer is analogous to access to the library. "The assumption is that access to library resources is necessary to all students. Access does not mean that the student is forced to use the library in the middle of the night nor to sign up for a chance to read."[3] To deal with this condition, collaborators in planning are moving to create a mixed service environment which includes four basic elements:

- Direct, central, operating-budget support for general-purpose instructional computing through the timesharing system.
- Use of departmental machines.

- Support of microcomputing, particularly integration of personal computers into the Stanford University Network (SUNet).
- Introduction of a student workstation designed and developed at Stanford.
- Special efforts to fund personal computing for faculty in the humanities.

Research

Research computing is largely funded through projects sponsored by agencies outside the university. There is also a fund for unsponsored research administered by the Vice Provost for Research and allocated to deans and departments. No university-wide planning for research computing exists, although there are efforts made to ensure that research computing resources that can be shared are in fact shared.

There are very large scale, independently managed sources of computing, such as at the Stanford Linear Accelerator, and dozens of smaller labs. A typical pattern of information-technology planning and management for one of these labs would look something like this: with assistance from the Dean of the School and the Vice Provost for Research, the faculty obtains funds for the research project, with computer equipment as part of the budget of the sponsored project. Any joint planning among scientists is done within the lab through an informal "computer committee." The attempt is to optimize at the lab level. The university traditionally has reviewed such computer acquisitions through the procurement process, of which the Center for Information Technology (in this case) is made a part. A university-wide data base is maintained on research computer procurement but no effort is made to control the particular choices of research computing equipment by faculty members.

Aside from the central C.I.T. facility, Stanford has 17 mainframes (IBM 360s, 370s, DECsystem-10s, DECSYSTEM-20s); approximately 250 minicomputers and hundreds of microcomputers and word processors. The Stanford Linear Accelerator also operates its own IBM 3081.

This represents a powerful array of computing resources supporting research. But, computers are also a subject of research. In the Computer Science Department, they are used for work in, among other things, artificial intelligence, the mathematical theory of computation, symbolic computation, semantics of natural languages, and robotics.

Researchers also use the Computer Search Service, available through the libraries, which provides access to on-line searches of over one hundred data bases (like Dialog) produced by learned societies, government agencies, and other organizations.

Information resources and computer technologies are used in the Stanford Medical Center for research, instruction, and medical monitoring systems, as well as hospital administrative systems. Of special note is the Stanford University Medical Experimental Computer for Artificial Intelligence in Medicine (SUMEX-AIM), a national computer resource with a dual mission to provide computing resources and assistance to scientists applying artificial intelligence methodologies to biological and medical problems, and to facilitate scientific communication and collaboration within a national community of health research projects by the use of electronic communications technologies.

Administration

Several general systems support management and administration, including electronic mail, word processing, text formatters, and public data bases. In addition, technical assistance is available so that individual departments and administrative units can have tailored data bases, management-information and decision-support systems, and other administrative systems.

Some of these specialized uses are systems for financial information, physical plan information, accounting, and payroll. A network for student information has been developed to support operational and analytical requirements of the offices charged with maintaining records in admissions, financial aid, graduate studies, undergraduate studies, registration, and student affairs. Other data base systems contain information on gifts and alumni records. Some managers have initiated, quite independently of central planning, striking experimental uses of information technology. The Stanford Lively Arts performance series has developed a computer-based system for forecasting attendance at future events. Its accuracy (to within a few seats) has helped in determining the advertising budgets for concerts.

Individual administrators have complex and continually changing connections to the system of planning and management for information technologies. A typical manager might make use of the electronic messaging system, which was developed by and introduced to managers through the initiative of C.I.T. This electronic messaging system was first introduced to senior managerial officers (about one hundred in all) on a free basis. It rapidly spread downward through the organization so that today it has become a part of most managers' office operations budgets. The manager might also use a computer-based project control system in order to monitor and schedule the work of his staff. Data for this system could be processed on campus. However, the manager could choose to buy any of his information services from a place other than C.I.T., e.g., through a commercial vendor. Or, for that matter, the manager could establish an in-house data system with the computer specialist hired as a member of the office staff. Each manager establishes an information-systems plan which is usually integrated with plans made in his or her vice-presidential area and with C.I.T.

An Administrative Systems Policy and Planning Group has recently been created to coordinate university-wide administrative systems planning. Among policy issues due for consideration are word processing guidelines, data base selection, data security and data sharing, and uniform cost-benefit methodologies as planning tools. Within this effort at coordination individual line officers will still remain responsible for systems planning and accountable for the information and services they provide within the university.

The Evolution of Planning and Management of Information Technology

The planning and management of information technology has evolved as a means of providing the university with knowledge of what is going on, criteria for understanding why certain things should or should not be done, and assistance in how things might actually get done. Since 1967, when the first university-wide officer for computing was appointed, three functions have been performed, although through a variety of institutional forms. *The knowledge function* helps the university know what kinds of uses are being made of information technologies, what is being spent and by whom. The knowledge function also includes creating the language, the models, and the images that help the university community to understand the trends in information technology. *The value function* assists the university in weighing expenditures in the information area against demands elsewhere, e.g., for physical plant or salaries. The value function provides standards of measuring the contributions made by information technology to work productivity and to the effectiveness of the university's missions of teaching and research. *The action function* is represented by efforts to organize and implement technologies and services, for example, the development of an electronic mail or text-handling network, or the creation of a financial information system.

The institutional style by which these functions have been conducted has varied considerably over the years. During some periods, all three functions appear to be centralized. At other times this centralization has given way to loose confederations of cooperating and occasionally competing agencies. Here is a brief history.

In 1973, administrative, hospital, and research computing were centralized to form the Stanford Center for Information Processing (SCIP). Links were established between the development of computer use on campus and automation in the library. Stanford pursued a course of in-house software development and production, thereby enlarging the resident technical staff. In the 1970s Stanford helped form the Research Libraries Group and became the technical home for bibliographic data base use by more than 27 major libraries and by another 150 or so special libraries.

In 1978 the provost, a computer scientist, created the Task Force on the Future of Libraries and the Task Force on the Future of Computing. The goal was to create a long-term Stanford agenda in each area. Academics and administrators collaborated to produce the final reports. The computing task force called for:

... a transition in Stanford's computing environment from independent, centrally shared computing facilities that support isolated communities to an interconnected set of distributed computing facilities that provides faculty, staff, and students with access to a wide variety of computer resources and services.[4]

In their report of April 1980, the library task force also proposed a major transition; from an emphasis on collecting and storing to an emphasis on selecting and sharing. The two task forces share a common goal; to support the creation of, access to, and distribution of information required by the university's instruction, research, and administrative processes.

The task force offered this perspective:

We caution readers not to underestimate the impact this technology will have on university operations or the efforts and resources required to adopt and manage the new technologies. The effectiveness with which we manage computer-based information technology will, in large measure, determine the future strength of our instructional, research, and administrative programs.[5]

The thrust of the task force was development of a linked environment for the creation of, access to, and distribution of information. A high-speed, campus-wide, digital data communications network, enabling rapid communications and sharing, was seen as the foundation for direct use of computer tools by faculty, students, and staff. The task force recommended that the university support a network text-handling system and limit the purchase of stand-alone word processors. Data base use was foreseen as the dominant means of storing information used by scholars and administrators.

While the task force report was in preparation, the university created the Center for Information Technology (C.I.T.). This signaled the university's "determination that Stanford will have the capacity to provide the information-systems support required by its academic and administrative programs." The memo (from the Stanford vice presidents to deans, university offices, and faculty) that announced the creation of C.I.T. noted the increasing development costs of computing and networking and called for regular planning efforts "in those instances in which the university assumes institutional responsibility (as distinct from faculty initiatives)."

The Director of C.I.T. would also serve as Associate Provost for Information Systems. C.I.T. and the Associate Provost were charged "to become a highly competent and objective source of analyses about options in information technologies—regardless of which university department or unit plans, develops, or operates the particular technology." The Associate Provost was to report to three vice presidents. Thus, while he was given line management authority over the campus computing center, he was also asked to become an honest broker and planner at the highest administrative institutional levels. Management of C.I.T. within the university was to be conducted through regular meetings between center directors and advisory groups of administrators and scholars.

By 1982, C.I.T. had a staff of 230 full-time employees with divisions for data base management, instruction and research, networking information systems, text-handling, basic computer services, and administrative information systems. Stanford had created a large and complex organization for the central management and development of information technology, certainly one of the largest single concentrations in a university environment.

Despite its organizational size, C.I.T. does not centrally control information-technology development at Stanford. However, C.I.T.'s directors do serve as catalysts for university-wide planning in instruction, administration, and basic technologies such as networking.

Planning for the network is one example of current procedures. As noted earlier, three functions are embodied in the overall planning process. A knowledge function lets the university know what is going on or what might be desirable. The value function helps the university weigh the benefits. The action function provides a model for getting things done. To a greater or lesser degree, each function is present in all phases of planning.

Thus far, there have been four general phases of network planning. Phase one was represented by the task force's detailed description of networking trends and technical alternatives open to Stanford.

The value of the network was tied to university objectives by the task force's assertion that information technology would "in large measure, determine the future strength of our instruction, research and administrative program." The vice presidents in 1981 agreed to:

1. The development and implementation of an integrated high-speed, digital data communications network.
2. The provision for campus-wide access to that network.
3. The development and installation of software to support data transfer across the network.
4. The attachment of other computer facilities and personal computers to the network as capacities permit.
5. The provision via the network of access to external networks and computers and specifically to large-scale computing resources at other locations.

Phase two of the planning process consisted of an intensive technical and economic study, which resulted in a commitment to networking by cable broad-band technology which could support both digital and video communications and certain portions of voice traffic. During this phase, network planning became linked administratively into the overall university management processes by budget and management review of the Center for Information Technology. Thus, networking became subject to regular processes of evaluation and cost-benefit analysis. Plans for action were reviewed by the vice presidents.

Phase three consisted of the formation of the Cable Communications Task Force among those beginning to constitute a new sphere of interest in cable networking. They included university managers and scholars interested in the programming potential of cable television, e.g., the performing arts and public events; those responsible for utilities, such as telephone, energy management, and delivery; and others concerned with physical plant construction, or responsible for carrying out data transmission among research and instructional facilities. The Cable Communications Task Force reported to the wider Stanford community on the merits and feasibility of broad-band networking.

Phase four is now in progress. It consists of giving networking and cable communications additional staff resources and a more precise point for focusing management and policy decisions.

This style of planning and development, an evolutionary process based upon interest and consensus, attempts to maintain a delicate balance between top-down leadership and local initiative. As might be expected, it occasionally results in some wasted effort and a slow growth to the stage when that which has been planned is finally in business.

Planning Policy and Philosophy

The question of leadership has been a puzzling one since it was determined that the positions of Associate Provost and Director of C.I.T. should be filled by a single person. The original intent was to create the strongest link between the knowledge of what ought to be done and the ability to get it done. Perhaps more important was a belief in the university-wide nature of information-technology issues. These issues appeared to cut across somewhat rigid institutional boundaries and therefore required brokerage at a very high political level. However, by remaining Director of C.I.T. the Associate Provost role has not quite escaped the stigma of favoring the central computer shop. On the other hand, without the line relationship to C.I.T. the Associate Provost position could appear to be limited to declamatory exercises unconnected to operational realities. Then there is the question of whether there should even be a large central computing organization; a question of whether the institutional form of C.I.T. really fits with the evolution of Stanford as a dispersed computing environment dominated by the new realities of networked communications.

In 1982, some of these questions came under high-level management review and study. They are part of the continuing search for a style of technological growth suitable to the university.

Planning not only has political and financial realities, but psychological and philosophical dimensions as well. Information technology development is increasingly user- or client-centered. The user community is hardly uniform in its response to technology. Planning depends on good communication among users of technology, and this communication is conditioned by the different kinds of awareness that attend technology use.

The use of information technology at Stanford is shaped by three levels of awareness or sensitivity through which both individuals and institutions tend to pass. The first level of awareness or sensitivity is largely dominated by the concern for machines and hardware. The computing tool is new and has not become "transparent" to the user. Planning and management are looked upon as the care and feeding of machines, with attention to their efficiency and cost.

The second level of awareness is of applications, programs, and software. There is less need to be concerned about the machines, with the result that more attention is paid to the applications of technology. All sorts of new uses are cooked up, some of questionable necessity.

Third, there is awareness of knowledge generated by the technology. Concerns with hardware and software are encompassed within a higher-order view that focuses attention on the ways in which information can serve creativity and productivity. Members of the community are distributed unevenly over the kinds of awareness, creating a kind of mosaic. Some persons are just getting to know about information technology and others are deeply immersed in questions about knowledge productivity or the effect of electronic communications on the decision structures of their organizations.

Each level of awareness calls for and creates different approaches to planning and management as well as different models for evaluating benefits or measuring progress. Each kind of awareness has its own language, frames of reference, and values. These differences can affect how questions, such as those about productivity, are asked and answered.

At Stanford and elsewhere, there is considerable concern with the relationship of information technology to productivity. Productivity is an industrial age concept, which cannot readily be applied to information work. We may take efficiency to be a measure of the relationship between an organization's efforts and its outputs. But, as the National Science Foundation has pointed out, "information technology is neutral with respect to efficiency. It can just as readily intensify as ameliorate problems of productivity because it is a producer as well as a processor of information." An organization's increase of horizontal information flows (made easy by electronic mail and copiers) is done for the sake of "information" and "accountability." But such an increase may, in fact, disrupt the organization's ability to function decisively. "In this sense," writes the NSF, "information technology has made new modes of productivity loss possible." [6] Paul Strassmann, Vice President of XEROX, writes:

> The overall volume of information is growing at a rate far exceeding the growth of our labor force, so we are experiencing exponential growth in information overload . . . Instead of increasing efficiency, (information workers) are contributing to today's information overload by helping generate redundant information in increasing quantities.[7]

Strassmann's view suggests that "the new technology has been used to increase the information (or computational) complexity of bureaucracies and other organizations in a way that has offset the dramatic reductions in unit processing costs made possible by the technology, with the net result that information sector productivity is declining and may accelerate its decline as it becomes increasingly capitalized."[8]

This thesis is only one of the many warnings against applying "neat" but naive guidelines for measuring benefits of information technology. Planning at Stanford will be hard-pressed to bridge the gap between measurable efficiencies and a more subtle understanding of how the university's effectiveness is mediated by information technologies.

Of course, the university is not simply a collection of individuals using technology but rather a collection of working groups, offices, departments, divisions, and schools—each one part of the hierarchical structure. As parts, they are, to use Arthur Koestler's metaphor, Janus-faced. That is, every part has a self-assertive tendency to preserve individual autonomy, and every part has an integrative tendency to function as part of a larger whole. The information-technology planning process works best when it recognizes these dual tendencies. Information then, is more clearly seen as human communication that is continually transforming both the "wholes" and the "parts." Information, in this view, does not travel around inside an organization: information shapes the organization. This is why information-technology planning touches so many nerve endings.

Planning seems to be about what is most uniquely human—our extraordinary capacity to reflect, model, and forecast; to bring the future into the present. But this effort to predetermine and shape the world, which we individually find so natural, can on a collective level be quite troublesome. The reason for this is that planning is an exercise of freedom, carving out some future space, a commitment. Very often we see exercise of freedom by one person as arbitrary control over another. This is why so much effort goes into achieving joint agreement to abide by the constraints which can result from having made choices.

To date, no master plan for information technology has been created for Stanford. One supposes that such a plan would require, speaking metaphorically, a spot from which one could get a spectacular overview. But the university has not yet found such a spot. Perhaps this is due to the even lay of the land at Stanford, as well as the fact that many influential persons here are inclined to believe that no such spot ought to exist. Short of a grand design, Stanford does have a way of recognizing and dealing with the fact that a major dimension of the university's life is represented by individual and collective work with information technologies.

To have gotten this far is no small accomplishment. However, the future may test planning and management in some interesting new ways. Stanford's move to develop cable communications raises issues far beyond the traditional scope of computing. Faculty and staff homes are likely to have two-way, interactive communications with university offices and laboratories. Access to local and national databases, "on-line" collaboration with colleagues and students, transmissions to remote, book-quality printers will be some of the services readily available from home or office. It seems that just as the university has begun to understand how to manage computing, a different set of questions is being posed. These have more to do with human communications than computing, more to do with the essential shape of the knowledge community than with the technology of data processing.

While universities have their peculiar responsibilities as both generators and conservators of knowledge, they are subject to the same pressures as society at large. It is difficult to resist the daily blitz of the information society. Commercials advise "If your family (or your boss) asks what you did all day . . . tell them you managed information." Happy secretaries, sprouting arms like Shiva, do magical things with computerized typewriters. Sweaty loggers and thirsty fishermen share the TV screen with a new breed of Americans: the data wranglers. Having taken from nature all that she could give, it is time now to turn to the ultimate frontier, the mind.

Untethered in the hard-driving climate of computerization, the futurists are running wild among the chips and wafers, promising the book on a chip, the doctor on a chip, even the politician on a chip. A headline occasionally spells out relief: "Human Intuition Irreplaceable, Clinician Says."

Not only is intuition irreplaceable, it may prove to be the saving grace of planning.

References

1. *Campus Report*, October 7, 1981. Stanford, CA: Stanford University, pp. 20 and 21.
2. *The Stanford Observer*, February 1982. Stanford, CA: Stanford University.
3. "Report of the Advisory Committee on Computer Service and Computing." Stanford, CA: February 1982, p. 4.
4. "The Future of Computing at Stanford: Report of the Task Force," January 1981. Stanford, CA: Stanford University, pp. 1 and 2.
5. "The Future of Computing at Stanford: Report of the Task Force" January 1981. Stanford, CA: Stanford University, pp. 1 and 2.
6. Resnikoff, Howard L. and Weiss, Edward C. "Adapting Use of Information and Knowledge to Enhance Productivity." Presented at Conference of Productivity Research, American Productivity Center, Houston, TX, April 21, 1980, pp. 39, 41, 42.
7. Strassmann, Paul. "The Office of the Future: Information Management for the New Age." *Technology Review*, December–January 1980, pp. 54–65.
8. Resnikoff, Howard L. and Weiss, Edward C. "Adapting Use of Information and Knowledge to Enhance Productivity." Presented at Conference of Productivity Research, American Productivity Center, Houston, TX, April 21, 1980, p. 42.

8

Cornell University

KENNETH M. KING
Vice Provost for Computing

Cornell University is a private university and it is also the land grant institution of New York State. Four of its eleven colleges are administered by the Cornell Board of Trustees under contract as units of the State University of New York. These four statutory colleges are the New York State College of Agriculture and Life Sciences; the New York State College of Human Ecology; the New York State School of Industrial and Labor Relations; and the New York State College of Veterinary Medicine. There are six endowed schools or colleges and a medical college in New York City. The endowed colleges are the College of Architecture, Art, and Planning; the College of Arts and Sciences; the Graduate School of Business and Public Administration; the College of Engineering; the School of Hotel Administration; and the Law School. In addition, a substantial number of divisions, centers, laboratories, institutes, and programs are units of research and advanced studies. The co-existence of privately and publicly funded components under a single administration results in some administrative complexity.

The main campus is located in the Finger Lakes region of upstate New York in Ithaca. There are about 12,000 undergraduate students and 5,000 graduate and professional students. Instruction and research at Cornell cover a very wide range of disciplines. Students can simultaneously be studying nuclear physics and learning to milk cows. The university competes for students and faculty with the premier academic and research institutions in the country. The deans of the individual colleges enjoy considerable autonomy and the 1,800 faculty members actively participate in defining academic directions and goals.

The research budget at Cornell is currently about $130 million. Research is broadly distributed with heavy concentrations in agriculture, engineering, life sciences, and medical and physical sciences, as well as substantial activities in economics, social sciences, environmental science, computer science, and astronomy. The importance of computing in research and instruction has been a relatively recent discovery.

Support for developing and maintaining a first-rate computing environment is now widespread. A position at the level of a vice provost was created in 1980 to coordinate the development of computer facilities in support of instruction, research, and administration. The university has an active Computer Board that advises the provost on computer-related issues. The board meets often and its members are unusually well informed by virtue of their backgrounds and the time they have devoted to computer issues. The board has played a major role in pushing the university to improve computer facilities and has developed the following goals for computing at Cornell:

1. To provide ready access to modern computing facilities and services for all students who require such access for purposes of: acquiring computing skills and a fundamental understanding of computing necessary to achieve their career objectives and to fulfill their societal roles; developing such skills to a high degree of proficiency as appropriate to their interest and disciplines.

2. To provide access to essential computing facilities and services to support faculty, student, and staff research and extension services and to achieve and maintain quality consistent with the high academic goals of Cornell University.

3. To provide the facilities needed for the operation of modern, efficient administrative support systems.

4. To further the growth of computing awareness throughout the University to the point where faculty, students, and staff determine the extent of their involvement by informed choice.

5. To progress toward the above goals in a fiscally sound manner consistent with overall institutional requirements, and in a fully accountable manner.

The university has an excellent but small Computer Science Department. Faculty members in this department provide a large part of the computer-related instruction on campus. Enrollment in courses offered by the department has been growing at 15 percent per year. Several faculty members in the department have research interests directed toward improving computer-related instructional tools. The department is also a laboratory in which new facilities and software are tested and later disseminated.

Current Status of Computing Facilities

Instructional computing is supported by 65 microcomputers, a DECSYSTEM-2060, and an IBM 4341-II. The microcomputers consist of 50 Teraks which are DEC LSI-11s, and 15 Apples. The Teraks are used to support introductory computer science courses and the Apples support a variety of courses in the School of Agriculture. The Teraks run special software developed by Professor Tim Teitelbaum of Computer Science. This software, called a program synthesizer, is extraordinarily user friendly and provides a set of tools for program development and debugging which enables students to ensure that their programs are structurally and syntactically correct at each stage of development and allows them to test program fragments as they are developed.

Approximately 160 ASCII terminals are available to students. These terminals are connected through a Develcon switch to the DECSYSTEM-2060 and IBM 4341-II. The DECSYSTEM-2060 runs

TOPS-20 and is used extensively by students in the School of Business and Public Administration and by a growing number of students from other schools. The 4341-II runs VM/CMS and supports students taking advanced computer science courses and students in courses that require software like SAS. In addition, the School of Engineering supports an advanced interactive high-resolution graphical computer facility which is available to students taking design courses in the School of Engineering. This facility is a clone of a facility developed by Professor Donald Greenberg to support research activities in the School of Architecture.

Research activities are supported by a large number of laboratory medium-scale and minicomputers, a central IBM 370/168 and two array processors. The laboratory computers are primarily PRIMEs, and Digital's VAXs, DECsystem-10s, and PDP-11s. The array processors are an FPS 190L and an FPS 164. The array processors are fast, cheap FORTRAN engines which support large-scale computations in physics, chemistry, astronomy, and engineering. The 190L and 164 are attached to a channel on the IBM 370/168. The 370/168 runs VM/CMS for interactive support and OS/MVT for batch support. Conversion to MVS for batch support is in progress. The 370/168 is shared by research and administrative users.

Administrative computing is supported by an IBM 4341-II and the previously mentioned shared support on the IBM 370/168. The 4341 supports on-line users during the day with MVS batch available at night. The 370/168 is used for batch systems still running under OS/MVT. New administrative systems being developed use ADABAS as the data base management system and NATURAL as the transaction processor and report writer. Both systems are marketed by Software AG.

Since the central computing facility is located four miles from the Ithaca campus, the Medical College is located in New York City, and laboratories and agricultural extension centers are distributed all over New York State, communications has been a major problem for a long time.

Clusters of remote ASCII terminals are connected to the IBM computers in Ithaca via statistical multiplexors over leased lines. Ithaca campus terminal clusters are connected by locally installed twisted pair to a Develcon switch with statistical multiplexors behind the switch providing connection to the IBM 3705 communication controllers over leased lines. The DECSYSTEM-2060 is located on campus adjacent to the switch so the 2060 communication is enabled by wiring from the switch to ports on the 2060 communication controller. An experimental broad-band cable network has been established using SYTEK equipment. At the present time, it is used primarily by staff.

The Ithaca campus consists of more than 400 buildings distributed over an area of 740 acres. There are no steam tunnels. Buildings are connected by wire in conduits which are buried in the ground. Since it is possible to amortize local wire connecting major terminal clusters in under three years, local wire has been run to the ten buildings with major public terminal clusters. The wire pulled through the conduit consists of about 300 twisted pair, 3 coaxial cables, and an empty subduct with a fish wire in it for pulling fiber optical cables if this is required. This wiring plant was designed to have the capacity to support computer, video, and voice communications over at least the next decade. Since Computer Services owns several hundred pair of line drivers, we expect to use twisted pair for some communications for some time into the future. Most of the campus terminals run at 9600 baud. Broad-band communication over coaxial cable is a technology that is emerging and we expect to use it as it proves reliable, particularly for connection of laboratory computers into a local network.

A consultant has been retained to investigate alternative plans for upgrading the Cornell telephone system. Among the possibilities being evaluated is a Cornell-owned system. At the present time, putting voice and data through a common switch does not appear to be as economical as separate voice and data networks. These networks can, however, share a common wiring plant. When the telephone system is upgraded, a major opportunity may exist to expand the local computer network to all of the buildings on the Ithaca campus.

Communication from outside Ithaca is provided via links to TYMNET and Telenet and via leased and dial-up lines. Cornell is a sustaining member and supplier institution in EDUNET. EDUNET gives Cornell users access to computing facilities of 15 major universities across the country, and assists Cornell in fulfilling its extension and public service mission by providing outside access to Cornell computing facilities. In early 1978 EDUCOM chose Cornell as the host for development to the EDUCOM Financial Planning Model (EFPM). EFPM has matured into a generalized model building system used by over 120 colleges and universities nationwide.

A leased line has been installed from Cornell to Penn State providing access to BITNET. BITNET is a network which includes 30 colleges connected by leased lines. Network membership is growing. Through this network, scholars can exchange messages, mail, and files. Current members include Brown, Boston University, Yale, the 20 colleges of City University, Columbia University, Rockefeller University, New Jersey Educational Computer Network, Rutgers, Princeton, Penn State, Cornell University, MIT, Harvard, the University of California—Berkeley, University of California—San Francisco, Rochester University, and the State University of New York at Binghamton.

Current Status of Computing Activities

About 50 percent of Cornell's 12,000 undergraduate students have had significant contact with computers and are competent to write a computer program of some complexity. Virtually 100 percent of the 2,250 students in the School of Engineering enjoy this competence, while only approximately 20 percent of the 3,700 students in the College of Arts and Sciences and the 3000 students in the College of Agriculture possess this skill. In the four other undergraduate colleges less than 50 percent of the students have had significant computer contact. Among the 5,000 graduate students at Cornell, students in Engineering and Business and Public Administration use computers routinely in course work and research. Graduate students in other disciplines vary in their level of access and facility with computers.

Researchers in well-funded disciplines have managed to equip themselves with laboratory computers that meet their basic requirements or are able to purchase central support. Researchers in disciplines that are not well-funded and researchers who do large-scale computations have serious problems. The research funding problem and the student computer literacy problem are connected, in that faculty computer literacy is an important precondition to infusing computing into the curriculum. Faculty have an additional strong incentive to learn to compute if a computer is an essential tool in their research. Major current research computing needs exist in the areas of text processing support, interactive social science support, data archive support, graphical support, and support for large-scale computations. Research expenditures for laboratory and departmental computers have been growing rapidly.

As a matter of policy, Cornell has encouraged the acquisition of laboratory micro- and minicomputers. A Decentralized Academic Computer Support Group has been established in Computer Services to provide advice and assistance to faculty acquiring laboratory computers and microcomputers. This group has the ability to support special electronic interfacing requirements, and provides special support for software and hardware that is particularly popular. This group is also responsible for developing software for linking microcomputers and laboratory computers into the local network.

Computer Services also has a new group dedicated to word and text processing support. This group provides support for three word processors (the IBM Displaywriter, the MICOM 2001, and the XEROX 860) and is responsible for developing a campus mail system that will link local computers and word processors and provide for links to national networks. The group has benefited from advice and assistance from the Computer Science Department and from discussions with colleagues on BITNET. Members of the group act as technical and administrative liaison to the MAILNET effort.

Cornell is a member of the Research Libraries Information Network so that support for its libraries is currently provided primarily via a leased-line link to Stanford University. Access to special bibliographic files for retrieval purposes is provided through campus links to national vendors over Telenet and TYMNET.

Administrative systems at Cornell have evolved over 20 years to support the operations of individual offices. These systems were designed for second-generation computing equipment and run very inefficiently on fourth-generation equipment. They are clerically intensive, expensive to maintain, prone to error, and difficult to adapt to changing requirements of individual offices. It is frequently impossible to relate data across offices in a manner which meets the requirements of top-level administrators. These systems provide generally poor services to students, faculty, and staff.

A plan to replace major administrative systems at Cornell over five years is in place. A design for a new student system, the principal components of which are an admissions, registrars, financial aid, and bursar system has been developed, and the admissions and registrars components are in development. A package has been acquired to meet 90 percent of the requirements of the financial aid component. All of these systems will use ADABAS as the data base manager, NATURAL as the transaction processor (with a few components written in PL/l), and NATURAL and MARK IV as the report writers. A new alumni affairs system has been designed and implementation will begin shortly. A new financial system is in the process of being designed.

The Planning Process at Cornell

Cornell has recently initiated an institutional planning process which requires that each unit of the university maintain a rolling three-year plan defining goals, objectives, and resource requirements. These plans will be reviewed and refined by the administration and by committees representing the constituencies with a stake in the plan. This planning process will result in the development of institutional priorities and a tentative commitment of resources over the planning horizon. The Computer Services plan has three major thrusts: to improve significantly student computer literacy; to maintain state-of-the-art facilities in support of research; and to replace obsolete administrative systems. The University Computing Board is in the process of filling in the details of this plan by providing functional requirements for computing over the next three years and reviewing alternative strategies for meeting these requirements. As of this writing, many components of the plan are tentative but are expected to be fully developed over the next six months.

Planning Assumptions with Respect to Requirements

Over the next three to five years we expect computing will infuse the curriculum at a rate which will require support for an additional 1,500 students per year. This support will have to be provided by clusters of microcomputers or terminals in instructional buildings, libraries, and dormitories. In the latter half of the decade, we expect personal computers will be cheap enough so that a significant number of students will acquire them and facilities will be required to connect them into the campus network. Text processing support, graphical support, and user-friendly computing will be required to support new students entering the computer-literate population. In addition, faculty offering new courses in many disciplines will require significant course development support. Ideally, the faculty will be able to offer courses on a computer with the same software they use for research.

The area where support requirements are most difficult to project is research. Some federally supported research budgets are currently being cut by 12 percent or more and the combined impact of these cuts and inflation could result in little or no growth in research computing over the next few years. It is important in this area to maintain maximum flexibility. Emerging requirements include:

1. Support for professional workstations that provide text and graphic support
2. Electronic Mail
3. General access to national networks for scholarly interchange, collaborative research, and access to special computing resources
4. Interactive social science support
5. Data archive support
6. Support for large-scale computations
7. Bibliographic search capabilities.

Although the trend toward private faculty terminals in offices and laboratories is growing, there will continue to be a need over the next three to five years to provide special facilities for scholars with common interests. These facilities will contain devices such as plotters, laser printers, and high-resolution graphical terminals. Special consulting support and documentation should also be available at these sites. It is desirable that facilities serving faculty and their graduate students be separate from facilities serving the general undergraduate population.

Over the next five years we expect to implement a new student system, a new alumni affairs system, a new financial system, and a new facilities and business system, as well as a number of small systems. These systems will permit individuals in administrative offices to enter data, retrieve data, and generate ad hoc reports. Offices will, in addition, require support for electronic mail, for graphical presentations, and for links between computer files and word processors.

Parallel with the creation of operational administrative data bases, it will be necessary to create an institutional data base. This data base is formed by taking a snap shot of operational data bases at appropriate points in time. For example, financial data needs to be captured at the end of each quarter and student data needs to be captured at appropriate times at the beginning and end of each semester. This data base is necessary to meet internal and external reporting requirements and to produce projections showing trends over time.

Because computing resources are distributed, it is essential to further develop the local communications network. This network must support shared use of peripheral devices such as printers, tapes, disks and phototypesetters and permit terminals to talk to each other and to computing resources on the network. This local network requires gateways to national networks for access to special external computing resources and to permit information exchange between scholars at Cornell and at other institutions. The network needs to permit terminal interconnections at speeds of at least 9600 baud and have data file transfer capabilities at speeds significantly higher. In addition we believe that it is important that the communication network support video communications.

Facilities will have to exist in this network to do accounting, to provide security, to solve terminal interface problems (perhaps in the manner of the Yale Series 1 support for ASCII terminal emulation of IBM 3270's), and to simplify the problems associated with accessing multiple systems with different operating systems and software capabilities (that is, a network help facility is required).

Elements of the Plan for Meeting These Requirements

The basic strategic concept in instructional computing is to move as much of the computing load as possible onto microcomputers. Meeting instructional requirements is, however, complicated by the fact that the university instructional community is partitioned into three major groups. The Computer Science Department faculty run UNIX on their in-house research computers and would prefer to teach advanced computer science courses using UNIX. There is currently no instructional UNIX support provided. A growing community of users has discovered the user friendliness of TOPS-20 on the DECSYSTEM-2060 and we expect support requirements to grow. The largest community of faculty uses VM/CMS because of the availability of a great range of software and because this style of computing has been available at Cornell for the longest time. Introductory computing courses are taught on microcomputers, but no special support for micros exists on our mainframes except for a file transfer package and the ability of the micro to emulate an ASCII terminal.

Since the economics of providing word and text processing support and graphical support on micros is significantly more favorable than on mainframes, it would be very attractive to have packages which are compatible running on both micros and mainframes. This would largely eliminate the requirement to have separate software development and maintenance activities for our micros and simplify life for users with an interest in using both. From several viewpoints, UNIX would appear to be the logical framework for integrating facilities across a range of hardware. This is because UNIX has been ported to a wide range of computers and because it is a small operating system that will run on small computers. It also appears to be the operating system of choice for computer scientists working on systems such as professional workstations. Its major disadvantage is that it is an orphan with no support from a major vendor. It is also too early to conclude whether or not the implementations for IBM computers or the DECSYSTEM-2060 will be efficient and be essentially compatible with versions used in the Computer Science Department. We are actively exploring a UNIX-based approach to integrating microcomputers into a university system for support of professional workstations. It is too early to determine the ultimate feasibility of this approach.

Building support for the DECSYSTEM-2060 community is complicated by the fact that this technology is more than five years old; it is not on the current price-performance curve and Digital Equipment Corporation (DEC) has not, as of this writing, announced a follow-on system with better price performance. The expectation is that the next system DEC announces will be a high-end system which implies that the price of expansion may be too high. Our plans for this area await an announcement from DEC.

The problems associated with building support to meet growing IBM-compatible requirements involve choosing among a large number of alternatives. Hardware is available for lease or purchase and it is possible to upgrade in a fairly modular way from a small computer to a large computer. A basic problem in this area is to decide whether or not to meet instructional, research, and administrative requirements on one or several large computers, or to provide separate facilities in each area. The latter decision can lead to expensive replication of software and difficulties in load balancing; the former to loss of flexibility and scheduling problems. Which path to follow is currently the subject of analysis with opinion leaning toward acquiring medium-scale computers and separating academic and administrative facilities.

The major problem in planning to meet research requirements is the uncertainty of research funding over the next few years. As in the instructional area, there are major groupings of faculty with common interests and our efforts have been directed to meeting their separate needs while finding as much opportunity for commonality across these groups as possible. Support for laboratory computers that are owned and operated by an individual researcher or research group will continue to grow. Efforts here are directed at standardization of approaches in dealing with common problems, with the carrot being the availability of help and sometimes special discounts. Another inducement is the probability that popular laboratory computers will be interfaced with the local network first which will enable file exchange and access to shared devices.

Over the next few years support for large-scale computations will be met on local array processors and connections to class 6 computers at national laboratories or other universities. There is interest in emerging technologies built around array processors that promise to provide growth capabilities in computational power of several orders of magnitude. These technologies are not expected until the latter part of the decade or later. We are also looking at the feasibility of a UNIX interface to the array processors as a part of an activity which would link professional workstations into a UNIX-compatible support network.

Support for social science research at Cornell has been facilitated by the recent formation of a Cornell Institute for Social and Economic Research (CISER). A special computer facility for social scientists has been established in cooperation with CISER. This facility will contain terminals and other devices connecting into the local network. Plans are evolving for support of interactive social science computing and for support of data archives in cooperation with this consortium.

Support for humanists is largely linked to plans for text processing support and library support. Two text processing paths are being explored, one involving Teraks and one involving shared logic support on a mainframe. It is possible that these approaches can be integrated through UNIX. Non-UNIX shared logic alternatives are also being explored. As a major experiment, over 200 students are using SCRIPT support on the IBM 4341-II for thesis writing. A decision as to which direction will have the longest term pay-off has not been made. Competition between various approaches will, with any luck, determine the most acceptable of the alternatives available. An approach to local support of a library data base for bibliographic retrieval is being planned by the Research Libraries Network consortium. It is expected that local support will be feasible in the next few years although the cost may delay implementation.

Over the next five years the basic administrative systems of the university will be replaced. We have developed the following steps in getting systems designed, approved, and implemented.

1. A broadly based user team is formed to specify requirements and to identify policy issues. To date teams have been formed to design a registration system, an admissions system, a financial aid system, a bursar system, a financial system, and an alumni affairs system.

2. These teams attempt to meet with all segments of the community with an interest in the system and review their proposed design with these segments of the community.

3. The design team produces a report which defines the goals of the system, defines a conceptual design, identifies policy issues, and estimates cost and benefits.

4. A policy advisory committee is formed to develop recommendations designed to resolve policy questions. These recommendations are referred to an appropriate administrative officer or forum for action.

5. An Administrative Priorities Committee allocates development resources among competing petitioners consistent with university priorities.

6. Systems are implemented in a phased way. Ordinarily in Phase l, current data is put on-line with reports produced by the old system. Some new forms may be introduced for data entry but basic information flow patterns are unchanged. In Phase 2, existing reports are modified to meet requirements and in subsequent phases of development, new elements of the system are added one at a time.

7. Contact is maintained with users during implementation so that systems can be modified as experience with use dictates.

In order to distribute the cost of development and operating the new systems in an equitable way, charges for use will be developed when systems are fully operational and users are realizing system benefits. During the development period, offices acquiring terminals pay only for the cost of their terminals and communications. No computer use charges or development costs are assessed. When the system is operational, development costs will be capitalized and amortized over the projected life of the system, and these costs as well as operating costs will be distributed to system users proportional to use and benefits.

Basic tools in developing the new administrative systems will be VM/CMS with XEDIT for program creation and NATURAL as the transaction processor. We use ADABAS as the data base manager and NATURAL and MARK IV as report writers. Batch programs will run under MVS. We expect to upgrade on-line support hardware to meet a response time goal of average response time plus standard deviation of about five seconds.

The local network development plan will be based on broadband cable communication. Over the next year we expect to have about 100 ports using this technology. Major unsolved problems include the protocols to be used in transmitting messages, mail, and files among computers, word processors, and terminals; access control, security, and accounting procedures; devices to be on the network; and economical ways to link the network to channels on computers. Early resolution of these problems is hoped for so that the network can grow with limited retro-fitting necessary. We hope to be able to accommodate television channels on our cable sometime during the next year. An early experiment will include an attempt to equip several classrooms with data and video channels so that instructors can use our sophisticated graphical computer system to teach computer-aided design with real-time computer interaction and display in the classroom.

9

University of Iowa

JAMES W. JOHNSON
Director of the Weeg Computing Center

Forces for Planning

Like computing, formal planning is a relatively new phenomenon in most colleges and universities. Indeed, in many ways the relationship between computing and planning is more than casual. Forces that encourage some sort of formal planning include rapid growth in computer use requiring planned changes every few years, large investments in capital equipment, the need to coordinate plans across several units—for example, computer science enrollment and instructional computing capacity—and converging technologies so that telephone, television, and computer decisions offer potential for resource sharing.

While such forces are common throughout society, it is not to be expected that planning at a university will be the same as that at a steel company. Nor is it to be expected that planning at large state-supported universities will be the same as planning at a privately funded technical institution. Nor should one expect planning to be the same at all major state universities.

So planning for computing at a university must be considered first in light of the institution's ethos. Institutional character defines planning objectives, style, and effectiveness.

Planning Context

Institutional Character

The University of Iowa's statement of mission says that "It will be characterized by a general orientation toward human growth, the health sciences, the humanities, the fine arts and the social sciences. It will continue to maintain strong programs in the physical and biological sciences and engineering." Since similar statements abound at universities, it is helpful to examine institutional character. The keys to the University of Iowa's character are its role among Iowa's public institutions, its place as a major research institution, its tradition in the arts, its growing commitment to health sciences, its pleasant ambience, and its collegiality. Each has an important effect on planning for computing.

A Public Institution

The university occupies 900 acres of rolling hills overlooking the Iowa River in Iowa City, a town of 50,000. It is the principal liberal arts and science public institution for the state of Iowa, enrolling 26,000 students in undergraduate, graduate, and professional studies. The people of Iowa, among the most literate in the country, support two other major universities: Iowa State University at Ames, a major land-grant university known for its engineering and agriculture departments, which serves 25,000 students; and the University of Northern Iowa, with 12,000 predominantly undergraduate students, which has evolved from a teacher education college.

A Major Research University

The university's early (1909) membership in the Association of American Universities and its graduate college classification by the American Council on Education as a "top-ranked institution," reflect its research tradition. In 1981, the university accepted $43 million in grants and contracts for research into such diverse, but non-secret, areas as aging, solar radiation, bladder cancer and saccharin, wool economics, archaeological surveys, and coronary risk factors in children.

While Iowa is a major research institution, it emphasizes teaching—all faculty are expected to teach and some of the best researchers are also the best teachers.

An Arts Tradition

The university has a long, proud tradition in the liberal and fine arts. Its original nine departments in 1855 were ancient and modern languages; natural, intellectual, and moral philosophies; history and natural history; mathematics; and chemistry. Today it has nationally recognized programs in creative writing (The Writers Workshop), communication and theatre arts, psychology, educational testing (The Iowa Testing Programs), speech pathology, and space physics (James Van Allen). The fine arts occupy a prominent position at Iowa; the immediate past president, Willard L. Boyd, once commented, "Due to the foresight and imagination of earlier generations, the arts are at both the physical and intellectual center of the University of Iowa." Significantly, journalism, communication and theatre arts, art and art history, psychology, and English appear among the most popular eleven undergraduate majors, along with business administration, engineering, education, pharmacy, nursing, and computer science.

Health Sciences Growth

The growth of health services at the university parallels the growing importance of this sector of our society. Iowa was a midwest pioneer in creating a university-based medical center that has become the country's largest university-owned teaching hospital. The university developed the first Pharmacology-Toxicology Center and the Institute of Agricultural Medicine. Medical teaching and research occupy a central position at Iowa; the basic sciences underlying health care, such as biophysics, anatomy, biochemistry, physiology, and microbiology, have a high priority.

Pleasant Ambience

Located in what is to many an isolated part of this country, ambience has a special meaning at the university. The university actively works to provide scholars and staff with a pleasant setting for their work: free bus service, art displays in most buildings, recreational activities, unparalleled cultural programs, and accessible computing. A recent review team found that people, almost without exception, "like it here" and "like to work here."

Collegiality

Highly autonomous colleges and departments, a small central administration, and a management style that was reported by the North Central Accrediting Association to be informal and trusting contribute to collegiality. An amazing amount of business is transacted on the telephone; the administration tries to decentralize and avoid formal coordinating bureaucracies. The net effect creates an environment where individuals, small groups, and entrepreneurial departments can flourish.

Institutional Planning

The university's formal planning process reflects its decentralized style. The current system, established in 1971, formalized overall institutional practice and tradition and built on practice in the medical college.

Review System

The heart of long-range planning is a review system that begins with departmental self-studies. Self-study guidelines stress reviewing program objectives; each unit is charged to "identify and reassess its goals, examine functions in terms of quality and continuing need, establish priorities for programmatic development, review the financial structure with regard to sources of funds and amounts required to support essential missions and objectives, and establish a base for future planning and development."

The self-study is submitted to an ad hoc review committee, consisting of discipline experts from outside the discipline and the university. The ad hoc group conducts interviews, evaluates quality, and receives reactions from external sources.

Collegiate reviews build on departmental reviews to articulate collegiate priorities and directions. As with departmental reviews, the collegiate review focuses on teaching, research, and service program missions and priorities. In addition, this review includes evaluating collegiate organization, administration, and fiscal structure. The collective results of department and collegiate reviews, the University Mission Statement, and various social and economic trends are considered in determining the future direction of the university.

Recently, university-wide offices such as Academic Affairs and Student Services have been included in the review process.

While departments, colleges, and support units are reviewed every five years, and the university as a whole every ten years, plans are continuously updated, with formal reports to the Board of Regents every two years.

Ad Hoc Coordination

University-wide issues and directions are typically handled by standing and ad hoc committees. The university administration supports the departments and colleges and provides a university-wide perspective; it does not make educational and research decisions for these centers. However, university administration does increasingly provide information such as employment and enrollment trends to colleges and departments to aid in their planning and it does set overall priorities.

Few university-wide planning groups exist outside of standing committees and existing collegiate structures. An exception is a facilities planning group that allocates and plans physical space and equipment. There is no similar technology planning group. This style of planning and decentralized organization, while contributing to collegiality and ambience, creates some problems for university-wide or rapidly changing units such as computing. It also leads to differing planning styles within different computing organizations.

Place of Information Technology

Currently, the university seeks to be highly competitive (upper third) with other major research public institutions in the overall use of computer-based information technology. University-provided resources since 1979 have become easy to use, accessible, reliable, and only moderately overloaded. Funds for unsponsored research and instruction are easy to get. In Iowa's decentralized way, one department may be in the top 10 percent of competing universities, while another may be in the lowest quartile. Leadership positions emerge in departments with strength, interest, opportunity, and administrative support. Innovative and intensive applications of information technology are found in hospital patient care, political science, electronic music, theatre design, materials engineering, speech pathology, instructional computing across the university, and medical areas such as biochemistry and physiology.

During 1981-82, the director of Academic Computing, acting as a special assistant to the president, is conducting a broad-based study on future information technology uses at Iowa. Ad hoc advisory group views on a university-wide strategy have ranged from, "An intensive strategy putting us in the upper quartile is the only reasonable course," to "We cannot afford anything but a keep-up, lower quartile approach." (A pioneering, upper five percentile approach, has been rejected.) In Iowa's context, an intensive university strategy would provide resources for those who choose to use them. Whatever strategy is selected, Iowa will likely continue to reward excellence and seek to support worthy ideas—whether outside funds are forthcoming or not.

At first glance, one would suspect that administrative support for information technology would have few takers at an arts-oriented university. But initial indications are that if resources were available, use would be widespread throughout the university. A 1982 Academic Computer Services Committee report noted that "The largest increases in computing may come from areas that have not been large users in the past." Nevertheless, for the foreseeable future, intense information technology use here is likely to be significantly less than at a more technologically oriented institution.

Computing Organization at Iowa

Organizational Evolution

Early Roots

The roots of computing at Iowa go back to 1935 when the statistical services center was established. Initially, the center used tabulating equipment to score and analyze tests for the nationwide Iowa Testing Programs. In time, the record processing equipment was also used for university administrative functions such as grade reporting and class scheduling. By 1958 the two functions—test scoring and analysis, and administrative data processing—were large enough and different enough to be split. Administrative processing went the data processing route of an IBM 1401 and 1460, and testing went the scientific route of an IBM 650, UNIVAC SS80, and IBM 7044.

The Iowa Testing Programs facility became the academic computing center and offered its services to other academic units—most significantly physics and psychology. While still using the academic computing center, Iowa Testing Programs acquired specialized equipment and developed considerable local expertise for test scoring and analysis. This capability became the Measurement Research Corporation which was ultimately purchased by Westinghouse Corporation.

Combined or Separate?

By 1966, the separate administrative and academic routes seemed to be converging on IBM 360 series equipment and serious thought turned to consolidating operations. (It is almost axiomatic that separate facilities will consider consolidating and combined facilities will consider separating.) A detailed 1966 ad hoc review, instigated by the president and conducted by IBM, concluded that savings from consolidation were much less than expected and any benefits were overwhelmed by administrative difficulties. It also noted that on-line data acquisition and experimental control systems did not lend themselves to combination. However, the report mentioned the need to prevent further fragmentation of computing facilities that had resulted in 18 different computers on campus.

The direct results of the 1966 study were (1) support for acquiring an IBM 360/67 timesharing system for academic work, (2) continued separation of administrative, general purpose academic, and laboratory computing, and (3) renewed efforts by the computer advisory committee, consisting of key academic center users, to nurture a strong academic center.

While the early 1970s saw the shrinking of several small, obsolete computing facilities, it also saw the splitting off of two key users: the physics department from the academic center, and the university's hospital data processing from the administrative center. The IBM 360/67 never came, and the 360/65 that arrived in its stead was overloaded and out of date by 1972.

Coordination

In 1977, confronted with an obsolete IBM 370/155 for administrative data processing, an outmoded IBM 360/65 and Cyber 70/71 in academic computing, and a growing hospital complex consisting of an IBM 370/158, the university again reviewed the organization of computing. An ad hoc review committee, chaired by Professor James Van Allen of the Department of Physics and Astronomy, recommended continued separation of facilities, but suggested enhanced coordination between academic and administrative centers and liaison with the hospital center. Computing coordination was to be provided by a director of university computing reporting to the Vice President for Finance and University Services, and responsible to the vice presidents for Educational Development and Research, Academic Affairs, and Finance. A search was conducted and candidates interviewed, but changes in vice-presidential personnel and in directorships of the centers caused this realignment plan to be suspended.

Current Organization

Major Centers

General-purpose computing at Iowa currently is centralized in three major centers: Hospital Information Systems, Administrative Data Processing, and the Weeg Computing Center (academic). The academic center serves the medical faculty's research and instructional computing needs. In addition, dozens of smaller facilities handle special tasks in laboratories and clinics.

Hospital Information Systems has an annual budget including equipment amortization of $3.9 million (about 3.5 percent of the total hospital budget), employs 45 full-time staff, and reports to the deputy director of University Hospitals. Administrative Data Processing has an annual budget of $3 million (slightly less than 1 percent of the university, less hospital, budget), employs 59 full-time equivalents, and reports to the Vice President for Finance and University Services. The Weeg Computing Center has an annual budget of $3.5 million (about 1 percent of the university, less hospital budget), employs 70 full-time equivalents and reports to the Vice President for Educational Development and Research. Installed equipment includes dual IBM 3033Ns at the hospital supporting 375 terminals; an IBM 3031 at Administrative Data Processing supporting 180 terminals; and an IBM 370/168 connected to a PRIME 850, four PRIME 750s, four HP-2000s, an HP-1000, and a DEC VAX 11/780 at the academic center supporting over 800 terminals.

The seeming disparities between budget, people, equipment, and terminals at the three centers is most easily explained by differing clientele and strategies. The administrative center does all the programming for its clients, operates 24 hours a day (five days a week), and supports on-line systems from 8:00 a.m. to 5:00 p.m. The Hospital Information System places some programming in user hands, maintains a large, integrated data base, operates 24 hours a day, and provides considerable security, back up, and redundancy. The Weeg Center places almost all programming in user hands and operates 24 hours a day, 365 days a year, with limited redundancy. All three centers emphasize production and isolate development efforts from day-to-day operations.

Decentralized Computing

In addition to the large centers, several departments operate computers ranging from laboratory microcomputers to word processors doing record keeping and computation. In sum, they represent an investment and annual cost equal to one of the major centers. General purpose departmental facilities are less prominent at Iowa than at other universities. The physics facility consists of substantial, but fairly old, equipment; most departmental laboratories have nothing larger than a Digital Equipment Corporation (DEC) PDP-11/44; PDP-11/23s, and PDP-11/34s prevail in laboratories and clinics. The largest departmental facility is engineering's PRIME 750 for computer-aided design research; it is connected to the Weeg Center's PRIME network. The computer science department has a Burroughs 1700 for researching systems design, but it depends on the academic center for its instructional and research computing.

Planning for Computing

At Iowa planning for computing is no different than planning for other resources. Typically, requests are incremental and must compete with other university needs. Departmental requests begin in departments and pass through collegiate and vice-presidential review. University-wide support center requests also pass through vice-presidential review. Plans help justify requests, but seldom are long-term plans automatically supported without annual review.

Contrasting Planning Styles

Since planning is decentralized at the University of Iowa, planning for computing is also decentralized. Hospital Information Systems, Administrative Data Processing, and the Weeg Center each have unique planning styles reflecting their constituencies. Examination of each provides interesting contrasts.

Hospital Information Systems

Information is an important resource for improving patient care at university hospitals. Planning for computing may be characterized as:

Strategic. The university hospital's strategy develops a total hospital information system based on patient records being accessible where needed and in a format that is useful to the entire hospital staff. While new information-processing applications are added one at a time, each must be part of, and contribute to, the total system. The hospital has also adopted development strategies to speed design and enhance flexibility. These strategies include using available application packages and giving users "screen painting" capabilities, resulting in an impressive new development to maintenance ratio of nine to one.

Professional. Consultants, collaborating with hospital staff, have been heavily used to develop computing plans. In 1968, Cresop, McCormick, and Paget Company developed the overall strategy. In 1974, Compucare, Incorporated, studied progress to date and reconfirmed the basic strategy of a total information system. The Information Systems Advisory Committee, within the hospital's governance structure, reviews all changes in the information system. All planning is professional in approach and results in high-quality published documents.

Goal-oriented. All new development projects must clearly contribute to patient care, improve cost effectiveness, or reduce staff load. New projects must include specific goals that use information to improve management. For example, an infection control system must help reduce the infection rate, benefiting patients and reducing costs. Similarly, a monitoring and scheduling system for operating rooms should actually improve their use. Plans also reflect hospital concerns; a major one is patient record security.

Collaborative. Planning is open and collaborative. Broad objectives are agreed upon and active review committees, including heads of clinical services and staff members, evaluate and rank all projects. Typical of medical and hospital practice, professionals and governmental authorities review all plans involving major acquisitions. Units design specific projects and must commit staff time to design, develop, and implement those plans. Nevertheless, Hospital Information Systems must provide the leadership to harness technology and identify key issues.

These computing planning characteristics reflect the hospital's management style of careful planning in a strategic, professional, goal-oriented, collaborative fashion.

Opportunistic. Long-term plans are set to take advantage of opportunities as they present themselves. Plans are entrepreneurial; they answer what kind of business the center is in, and what opportunities it will accept or reject. The center also makes assumptions about university goals when setting its own goals; for example, significant center effort has resulted in use of graphics, intelligent videodisc players, and sound generators for teaching art, dance, theatre, and music. Opportunistic planning requires knowing where the next dollar will be spent or where it will be cut. All such plans are made with full user participation.

Policy-oriented. Policies are a type of strategy to deal with rapid change and a large array of choices. Three general policies based on experience are: first, use of available, vendor-supported, standards-oriented software and hardware; second, purchase of tested, in-place systems; and third, internal standards that permit all terminals to talk to all systems and all systems to transfer files to all other systems. Other strategies include using several vendors' systems tailored to specific needs but only one large mainframe system. New policies are set by frequent use of pilot projects and experiments. Examples of pilot projects are the terminals for humanists in the English Department, the department terminal clusters program, and Political Science's experiment of putting a microcomputer in every office.

Frequently reviewed. Academic center plans are frequently reviewed by committees. Typically, plans and objectives are set by the computing center in consultation with users and reviewed by three advisory committees dealing with instruction, operations, and overall computing policy. Yearly plans are published in the center's newsletter. Ad hoc review committees have been appointed to study major plans. For example, the 1976 self-study identifying a computing crisis on campus was reviewed by an ad hoc computing committee appointed by the president, the Educational Directions Committee, and the North Central Accrediting Association visitation team. This process is consistent with the university-wide academic review process.

Evolving. Different elements have been put into the planning process as experience highlights their importance. A special appropriation of $400,000 emphasized the need for long-term plans. A period of low staff morale and high turnover revealed the internal importance of visionary plans that contributed to the greater goals of the university; and the loss of user confidence highlighted the importance of leadership. The need to plan for obsolescence and replacement required an equipment amortization reserve. Finally, a sudden and unexpected doubling of computer science use stimulated constant monitoring of projected enrollment and curricular changes.

In addition to internal planning, the Weeg Center has worked with other state regent institutions to prepare plans for academic computing. These plans serve immediate needs to demonstrate coordination and answer legislative questions such as, "Why not have one computer for all the universities?" They have been amazingly accurate projections of academic needs.

Common Strategies

Amid differing missions and contrasting planning styles, several strategies common to all three centers are emerging.

Software Development

Each center has decided to buy rather than write most software. Versatile, high-quality software packages have been a boon to speeding applications implementation. Each center has installed a data base management system, and the hospital and Weeg centers have installed report generators. The hospital center is completely on the data base path, while the administrative center is beginning such a pilot project. At the academic center, users can pick their own approach, but the center provides a rich array of packages, and all internal and custom-design applications use packages. Only in cases of compelling need and package inadequacy is low-level coding done locally. One example is the hospital's development of an innovative module, called the "Iowa Bridge," which extends traditional functional security by added patient record control.

Administrative Data Processing

Iowa's administrative computing facility pioneered applying data processing equipment to university administrative tasks beginning with tabulating equipment in 1933. Formalized long-range planning has not been part of center management. Planning can be characterized as:

Reactive. Historically the department has reacted to user demands for new applications and changes, often resulting from state, federal, and university regulations. Nevertheless, two key strategies have been a move to interactive systems and a self-supporting charge-back system for all services including development. Since the department operates on a full charge-back system, there has been little pure development and overall conceptualization. The department now is seeking to anticipate rather than react to changes and to engage in development projects.

Client-driven. Established department customers control priorities and planning to a high degree. Each customer is assigned a liaison person by the center who suggests changes and plans for new systems. All development must be funded by the client. In theory, a department with the funds could order any application, but in practice, funds usually come to the department from the central administration and are subject to vice presidential-level review. Also, the data-processing staff works with groups of clients to standardize multi-user files such as student records, alumni records, and payroll records.

Task-oriented. Lacking strategic or visionary plans, the administrative center's direction is task oriented. Projects are very well planned and monitored by a project management system. Regulatory guidelines often dictate the selection of new tasks. There are no explicit criteria to measure the importance of tasks; rather, there is an informal understanding of university priorities.

Informal. A three-level internal review is used to set the center's application development plans, but most priorities are reviewed externally before they get to the center, either through funding decisions or regulatory guidelines. There are no formal advisory committees. Informal relationships, common at the university, make the absence of advisory committees less surprising; Administrative Data Processing is located in the same building as its major clients and interaction is frequent and amiable.

Changing. Since it has the longest, most centralized tradition, changes such as providing access, distributing capability, and installing advanced security protection will have a large impact on Administrative Data Processing's planning. As new constituencies from throughout the campus seek to access administrative records, unwritten goals and conversations in the hall will likely be replaced by more formal processes.

In sum, the university's informal management style is demonstrated in the administrative computing planning style. But technological pressures of increased use by relative novices and the need to coordinate different data files in a data base approach will likely force more rigorous long-range planning.

Academic Computing

The Weeg Computing Center (the academic center) has always engaged in visionary planning. However, formal planning involving projections, performance monitoring, contingency options, and regular equipment replacement has evolved over the last four years. Academic computing planning is characterized as:

Visionary. Long-range academic computing plans project a vision of computing in the academic community. The 1966 IBM report stressed the importance of interactive computing in intellectual work. A 1972 ad hoc committee developed "A Proposal to Make Iowa a Leader in the Use of the Emerging Educational Technology," resulting in distributed clusters of terminals, three HP-2000 interactive systems, and a Computer-Assisted Instruction Laboratory. A 1976 self-study projected growth at a 30 percent rate per year over the next decade, and set forth a plan to keep up with that demand. The 1978 refinement of the plan stressed interactive resources (eliminating punched cards), ease of use, standard high-quality software, and joint ventures with departments.

Innovation

Each center seeks innovations that are meaningful to the university's mission. The hospital group has developed avant-garde applications that are being marketed by IBM. The academic center leads in the arts, videodisc application, and instructional software for microcomputers (CONDUIT). The administrative center initiated interactive applications particularly in business and registration operations. Each group seeks to separate development from production to protect existing systems that people depend upon.

Professional Staffs

The three centers rely on full-time professionals to support their operation. Staff turnover is fairly low across the centers, a situation that can become a problem for young people seeking advancement. The relatively few students employed are programmers, clerks, and operators, or developers of special applications.

Word Processing

As part of an overall strategy to give their users more capability, each group recognizes the importance of word processing and has installed software and laser printers to enhance their capability to perform this function. Each is focusing on those word processing uses that merge word processing with traditional data processing functions. The hospital has installed an IBM 8100 that ties patient information to a letter writing system; physicians receive reminders and basic information for the required letters. The academic center has installed office automation software including electronic mail, word processing, scheduling, and calendar management to be used with an information-retrieval system allowing access to university records. It is also exploring scholarly oriented word processing with multiple character fonts and layouts. The political science microcomputer and terminals for humanists pilot projects have a heavy word processing component, and funds are provided to all master's and doctoral candidates for using word processing for their theses. Administrative processing is testing word processors to access their system and augment their outmoded text-processing facility.

User Programming

One way to reduce the backlog of projects and time spent on changes is to give users the tools to write their own applications and make their own changes. This approach, well established in the academic area, is being aggressively pursued in the hospital. Users of the hospital system now design their own screens, including content and layout. This method emphasizes ease of use, training, and security. The administrative center is beginning to look at this strategy, but has felt resistance from users who are now well served and do not want to get into the programming business.

Guiding Decentralized Computing

A large amount of computing capacity in academic and clinical units exists apart from the major centers. This decentralized computing takes the form of microcomputers, word processors, on-line data acquisition and experiment control systems, and terminal access. While detailed university-wide plans for decentralized computing do not exist, several centralized planning strategies do exist.

Planning Strategies

Strategies for dealing with laboratory and clinical computing equipment and terminals are well established. Those for microcomputers and word processing are likely to be similar to those for other equipment, but have not yet been set. Strategies now in place involve questions of standardization, communication, financial and technical support, and acquisition review.

Standardization. Benefits of standardization include reduced training, better communication possibilities, and sharing of equipment and software. Difficulties include selecting equipment that may not be adequate for all tasks, decision-making removed from those closest to the activity, and creating an image of lack of choice. Iowa's overall standardization policy encourages and supports recommended systems. Recommended systems either result from detailed review, such as is done every two years for terminals, or because one vendor dominates the market, such as Digital Equipment Corporation in laboratory support.

Communication. The academic center emphasizes communication between decentralized units and the center. A laboratory support group supports and develops communication facilities such as DEC-net for DEC computers, a Hewlett-Packard system for HP computers, and WCCNET for small laboratory and personal computers. Major barriers to this strategy are the cost and low speed of telephone lines, and the cost of installing communication devices and software on existing systems. Currently these costs are borne by the user.

Financial and technical support. Before acquiring equipment, departments are asked to consider and plan for continuing financial and technical support for their systems, including maintenance contracts and equipment replacement reserves. Such planning attempts to assure long-term financial support. Facilities management agreements between departments and the academic center are one result of this plan.

Review. The academic and hospital centers advise departments on equipment selection by writing specifications and evaluating alternatives. Acquisitions are also reviewed by computer advisory committees; their recommendations are passed to appropriate administrative officials. Initially the advisory committees served to prevent fragmentation and nurture a strong academic center, but today reviews are more to assure adequacy of choice and support, compatability with existing equipment, and competitive bidding where possible.

Pilot projects. Pilot projects allow departments to develop a technology that may have wide applicability. Typically, pilot projects are joint ventures with selected academic units. One noteworthy project involves putting a few large clusters of interactive terminals in departments that use instructional computing heavily. Other projects include: placing communicating personal computers on every faculty member's desk in Political Science, providing an office-automation system for a major administrative office, placing a jointly owned and managed DEC VAX-11/780 in the Physiology department, and installing a dedicated system for alumni records and fund raising information.

This decentralized computing strategy seeks to balance departmental decision making with university-wide interest. The balance is evident in word processing, microcomputer, and terminal plans.

Word Processing

Word processing is either a special case of decentralized computing or an extension of office equipment such as the typewriter, depending on one's point of view. The strategy for dealing with word processing equipment has been consciously laissez faire.

During 1979-80, an informal ad hoc committee investigated and reviewed the potential of word processing and office automation. Vendors and consultants provided information and insight. The group concluded that:

1. Word processing was part of the broader issue of office technology.
2. Training and staff support for acquisitions were important and should be added to existing offices such as purchasing.
3. Standardization and communication were crucial issues.
4. Because of rapid changes, the university should monitor activity but adopt a wait-and-see attitude.

Since 1979 the base of word processing equipment has grown to about $3 million, with about $1 million being electronic typewriters. About ten different equipment vendors are represented on campus. IBM Displaywriters and NBI systems are emerging as the models of choice. Recent installations of departmental or college-wide shared-logic systems have renewed interest in using word processors as entry points for a campus-wide records access and electronic mail network.

Because of interest in tying offices together, as of December 1, 1981, all purchases of word processing equipment must be reviewed by the president's special assistant for communication and information planning. (This review is a temporary situation pending a full report by that assistant.) Requests for word processing equipment must justify its use, prove its ability to communicate with existing centers, and include an analysis of office functions and alternatives.

Microcomputers

Several hundred microcomputer systems handle tasks from experimental control to word processing. Departments purchasing these units must receive approval based on review by computer committees. Because of existing populations and associated expertise, recommended systems are Apple, TRS-80, and Commodore Pet as appliance microcomputers; and CP/M, S-100-based systems for laboratory areas.

The academic center supports standard microcomputers and development of networking capabilities. (Microcomputer support is one of the center's three major development areas, others being scholarly word processing and graphics.) Support includes: a directory of microcomputer owners and those willing to consult, a rental pool of Apples, partial pilot project financing, sales of software and supplies, maintenance, and training sessions. Network capabilities include the ability to move files from small machines to larger systems and back.

Current work focuses on using communicating microcomputer-based systems in place of terminals for general purpose use. Recent Weeg analyses indicate that the total cost of a terminal connected to a timesharing computer is about equal to the cost of a communicating microcomputer. A terminal connected to a timesharing computer offers more software, less expensive storage, greater peak power, and less user-management responsibility. A microcomputer system offers consistent response time, better display and sound facilities, user control, and portability. A communicating microcomputer-based system offers the best of microcomputer and larger-system features.

A standard microcomputer to replace terminals will soon be selected. Ideally it should act as an excellent stand-alone device and as a high-performance terminal. It should be expandable, from a low-cost, single-use, non-disk-based system to a highly intelligent, multipurpose, disk-based system. It should be capable of being configured as a word processing, data-oriented machine or as a full color graphics and sound generating system. In 1982-83 microcomputers will replace terminals in selected sites; use will be carefully monitored.

Terminals

Terminal and workstation acquisition and location decisions are partly centralized and partly decentralized. Accessible computing requires careful placement of terminals or work stations. Terminals are commonplace in faculty and staff offices, work areas, departmental offices, departmental or collegiate instructional clusters, and homes.

Currently, terminals are dedicated to administrative, academic, or hospital applications. Administrative or hospital terminals are installed as part of the application and are directly connected to the host system. At the academic center, standard ASCII terminals use a switch that allows access to any system resource in the network.

Planning for terminal growth is difficult. Departments or individuals are responsible for purchasing or leasing their own terminals and communication equipment. If standard terminals are used, the academic center guarantees they will be supported for five years. The academic center has grossly underestimated department and individual propensity to install terminals, a situation that will become more unpredictable with a new wave of $300-$450 terminals. A major barrier to growth is communications cost.

Iowa's instructional terminal cluster program is unique. Essentially the program is a joint venture between departments or colleges and the academic center. The department supplies space and consultants for at least 55 hours a week; it also pays half of the communication, maintenance, and supplies costs. The center supplies terminals, manuals, communication equipment, and half of the monthly communication, maintenance, and supplies costs.

The current plan is to increase terminals in clusters by 25 percent per year. All requests to establish terminal clusters (a cluster must have at least four terminals, none has fewer than eight) are reviewed by the Computer-Based Education Committee. Existing cluster configurations are also reviewed to determine whether the number of terminals should be increased. There are currently 13 instructional terminal clusters on campus. The center will encourage clusters in areas that are likely to be used in off-peak hours, such as dormitories. The instructional terminals cluster program has been quite successful; terminals are brought to the students, and user services are tied to disciplines and departmental courses. Major problems are the cost of keeping the facilities staffed and increases in terminal line costs.

Current Issues

The popular and technical press have given considerable attention to the "information revolution." But without such publicity, increased use of computing and of associated technology at Iowa has called attention to several issues and problems: coping with growth, converging technologies, access, and security.

Coping with Growth

The high visibility of information technology creates high expectations in the academic community: scholars wish to publish in Greek, teachers want access to student records, physicians want patient laboratory results, and students see computing courses as the key to employment. All three centers have doubled the number of terminals during the past three years.

However, the increase in terminals is significantly less than other growth measures, such as on-line data storage, connect hours, or central processor time. And user expectations have grown more.

All three centers, as well as academic departments, have used falling hardware prices to meet increased demand. For example, computer use has doubled during the past two to three years but center staff sizes have remained relatively stable. Nevertheless, one can only take advantage of technological improvements by installing new equipment, so in general, budgets for equipment and equipment maintenance have increased. The Hospital Information Systems group has seen its budget increase from about 2.5 percent to 3.5 percent of the total hospital budget in recent years, while the administrative and academic centers have increased a few tenths of a percent to slightly over 1 percent each. At an institution where 65 percent of the total budget is for salaries and wages, these equipment-related increases have been highly visible. Microcomputers and word processors in decentralized units are an increasing portion of department expenses, often funded out of decreased personnel costs.

The 1981 State Board of Regents' *Academic Computing Services Report* suggests the magnitude of growth in noting:

> In the next ten years, Regents institutions will be faced with providing ten times the current computing activity for faculty and staff and fifty times the computing activity for students ... Increases in the efficiency of computing equipment will absorb perhaps one-half of the increases in the quantity of computing while the additional one-half will require an increase in real expenditure of funds.[1]

This growing activity, along with increases in user expectations, raises questions about university priorities.

Setting Priorities

The first issue in computing and technology priorities is how much money should be directed toward computing. Essentially, there is no answer, no benchmark, for computing. Computing decisions compete with all other incremental budget requests from departments, colleges, and university-wide support services. Priorities are set according to complex overall strategies, individual choices, personal biases, and external forces. However, it is safe to say that requests without departmental, collegiate, or vice-presidential support are doomed. Advocates are important!

Market vs. Planning Systems

Identifying priorities is particularly difficult at Iowa because of a dual-track system supporting computing, roughly akin to market and planned economies. The market system gives all departments (consumers) money to spend on all resources, including computing, as they see fit. The total demand for computing is the aggregate of individual decisions. A difficulty is deciding how much money to give each department, that is, how do departments "earn" money? Also, is the university willing to live with independent decisions?

The planned system allocates a total sum for computing consistent with an overall strategy and parcels out computing resources according to centrally set criteria. At Iowa administrative computing comes closest to the market approach with the important caveat that departmental requests for funds explicitly mention their need for data processing—funds are not "earned" in a classical sense. The hospital system comes closest to a planned approach, but here again, individual departmental needs and judgments are important to overall planning. Setting priorities for academic computing is a complex mix of the planned and market approaches.

At a distance, the planned hospital system and the market-based administrative system appear to work quite well, while the academic system appears chaotic. It is difficult to imagine hospital priorities being set in any other way, but the administrative center's full charge-back scheme presents some difficulties. Few would argue against charge back for day-to-day operations, but the philosophy of charge back for development has led to a short-run view and lack of coordination. As users demand flexible data bases and increased access, issues of charge back, development, and planning become significant.

Academic Computing Priority Setting

Academic computing most closely reflects the university's mission and its priority setting is most complex.

Center Funding. Coinciding with state appropriation decisions, funds for the academic center are allocated on a biennial basis, with yearly adjustments. Approximately 70 percent of the center's budget is from state-appropriated funds. Biennial requests reflect a longer-term plan, and large incremental increases are reviewed by several layers of committees. Regardless of long-term plans, biennial appropriation requests must compete with other university needs at the time. Support for requests includes plans, projections, computer advisory committee recommendations, departmental statements, and vice-presidential support. The Vice President for Educational Development and Research has been the chief advocate of academic computing and, indeed, information technology in general.

The total academic computing appropriation is allocated to departments based on their requests and the center's existing capacity. The Academic Computer Services Committee reviews requests, reconciles them with capacity, and makes recommendations to the Vice President for Educational Development and Research, who makes the actual allocation. This process has several difficulties. First, it is expected that departments carefully review requests before they are submitted; in fact, review rigor varies greatly from department to department and from college to college. Second, departments do not estimate their needs well; for example, in 1981-82, the Computer Science Department ran out of funds, expected to last until May, in November. Third, the Academic Computer Services Committee has found it very difficult to discriminate on academic grounds among requests from over 64 units. Increasingly it has relied on the Weeg Computing Center to evaluate quality of work, use of discounts, and availability of other funds.

The process has been more successful in forging compromises; for example, computer science received a large increase in funding in exchange for an agreement to limit their use to one PRIME computer and a fixed amount of other resources. Similarly, word processing for theses and dissertations on central systems has been supported with the expectation that students will use off-peak hours.

But the system has worked for several reasons. First, in the past quality of service, rather than funds, has been a rationing tool. Second, funds have been made available for institutional and unsponsored research. Shortage of funds has been handled by rate reductions. Third, as demand has increased, resources have increased as well. Capacity has doubled over the last two years. Whether the system would stand the test of greatly increased demand and very constrained resources and whether a better system exists is problematic.

Non-center Funding.   Support (usually in the form of equipment) from non-center-oriented computing must compete with all other equipment or program expenses. Such requests must be high on departmental and collegiate request lists. One difficulty is that faculty are not accustomed to advocating computer requests since the center has been the chief advocate. (One reason for creating the position of director of university computing was to provide an advocate who was not associated with a center and, thus, would champion departmental needs.) Another difficulty has been lack of coordination. Unbeknownst to the academic center, a department may request funds for a large number of terminals without thought to the computing resources necessary to serve them. Recently, the director of Academic Computing has played a larger role in recommending non-center-related requests and coordinating plans. However, in the Iowa tradition, this arrangement is more a matter of individual confidence and trust than a formal apparatus.

Communications and Convergence

Data Communication

Over the past decade, data communication costs have increased to become a significant portion of total data processing costs. Rapid growth in terminals and communicating microcomputers in offices, laboratories, residence hall rooms, and homes also promises to overwhelm physical resources such as space for cables in conduits and incoming telephone lines.

Until recently, Iowa's communication facilities have grown independently. Administrative Data Processing runs coaxial cables to its remote communication controllers and locally attached terminals, as does Hospital Information Systems. The Weeg Center uses non-switched telephone lines and center-owned twisted pair cable for most of its terminals. About 10 percent of terminals accessing the Weeg Center are dial-up; the other two centers do not support dial-up access. Besides data communication cable systems, there is a coaxial cable network for energy monitoring; there is no campus-wide television cable.

Telephones

University telephones are served by a Centrex system with Automatic Route Selection for long-distance calls. Telephone system management is decentralized; departments are free to work with Northwestern Bell in designing their telephone arrangement. All telephone orders pass through the business office, which has two people responsible for those orders. However, this responsibility is a small part of their total job: there is no telecommunication manager. The hospital has its own Centrex switch and a full-time telecommunications manager who must approve all installations and changes. The university has about 8,200 telephone stations and the hospital about 3,800; the switches are tied together to allow five-digit dialing between the hospital and the rest of the university. At present the telephone system has adequate capacity, is reliable, and is easy to use. A few departments are interested in enhanced features and a few offices in the medical college (not hospital) have installed Horizon switches with enhancements such as call forwarding, call waiting, and speed calling. The Bell central office in Iowa City has recently installed an ESS #1 switch offering custom calling features.

The major incentive to replace the existing phone system is financial; a secondary interest is combining voice and data networks. Total telephone expenditures exceed $3 million a year, and have grown by 46 percent the past five years and 24 percent in the past year. In addition, some tariff changes threaten to make data communication between campus areas separated by the Iowa River prohibitively expensive. A combined voice and data system could stabilize costs for data and voice communication.

Convergence

The university is well aware that previously separate communication technologies are converging. The centrality of computing and the pervasiveness of digital representations of information promise highly accessible, intelligent information capabilities and reduce duplication. New communication options have raised issues about the management of communication and the need for coordination.

Planning for the Future

A University-Wide Study

Growth in computer use in all the university's missions, the potential impact of the so-called information revolution, and convergence of previously unrelated methods and technologies demand that colleges and universities reexamine information technology's impact on their programs and management.

In August 1981, the university's interim president appointed the director of the Weeg Computing Center to a one-year term as Special Assistant to the President for Communication and Information Planning. The assistant was charged with formulating a general plan by July 1982 and was instructed to "consult widely."

Precepts, Problems, and Products

The study's general approach, reviewed by vice presidents in September 1981, included precepts, problems, and products. The precepts are that organization style ought to dictate appropriate technology rather than vice versa; that decentralization with coordination was the preferred university organization style; that technological changes and the nature of the university mandated flexibility and diversity; and that wide participation and reviews were essential to any plans.

The study will address the rapidly growing use of information technology, the feeling that the university is not taking full advantage of new information technology, the making of independent decisions that could preclude future cooperation, and the converging technologies such as voice, data, image, and text that blur existing organizational distinctions.

The resulting broad-based report will contain detailed recommendations, including administrative, faculty, student, and staff information needs. The plan will include strategies, tactics, and operations for information and communication systems and topics for further study. Also, recommendations will answer existing questions about word processing, campus cables, data access, data entry, telephone, and organization for computing.

Several committees have been put together to attack these problems. They include an overall task force and groups studying administrative needs, student needs, faculty needs, word processing, telephone systems, video communication, non-telephone communication, and technological developments. Each committee includes faculty, staff, and administrators with a balance toward potential users rather than providers of communication and information technology.

Topics Covered

Strategy and Organization

The overall task force is becoming aware of uses for information technology. Other committee reports should help identify issues and opportunities and point out the need for change. Currently, discussion focuses on an appropriate university information-technology strategy: pioneer (top 5 percent), intensive (top 20 percent), competitive (mid-range), or reactive (lower 25 percent). The price tags for these strategies are being worked out by committees, but order of magnitude estimates are:

- Pioneer strategy: $10 to $15 million per year incremental cost.
- Intensive strategy: $5 million per year incremental cost.
- Competitive strategy: $3 million per year incremental cost.
- Reactive strategy: $1 million per year incremental cost.

These figures do not include any compensating off-sets or costs resulting from diminution of quality inherent in a reactive approach.

The task force is also responsible for reviewing computing and technology organization. The need for coordination suggests some task realignment and assignment. The task force will look carefully at other campuses' solutions to provide insight into what may be appropriate at the University of Iowa.

Administrative Needs

The administrative needs committee, composed of information-technology users, has been concentrating on using information to improve management systems at departmental and administrative levels. There is consensus on the following:

1. People need more information about how technology can improve university management. The group knows that cost and productivity trends suggest increased use of equipment.

2. Administrators would like better access to and awareness of existing university information resources, including:

    a. access to existing information
    b. ability to reformat and augment data
    c. ability to interactively create reports
    d. a system to keep departmental files on-line.

3. University systems must include local computing needs. Because the capability to tailor reports and reformat data is not built in, there is considerable effort spent in:

    a. reformatting information to meet local needs
    b. duplicating student and alumni records
    c. maintaining separate personnel files.

As word processor and microcomputer use grows, duplication will grow unless those functions are built into the system.

4. Data security is an important issue. Increased access need not hinder security; indeed, it may clarify security policies.

The group is now interviewing people to better understand their needs. Next it will look for solutions.

Faculty Needs

The faculty needs group is considering faculty use of information technology. They agree that:

1. There is broad current use of computing—about 600 terminals and 200 microcomputers, half of them for general purpose use.

2. The library will move to computerized searches (LEXIS, MEDLINE, ERIC); terminals for searches in branches; a computerized circulation and acquisition system; and on-line materials catalog.

3. Information processing is moving into the humanities and arts such as english, classics, and history, particularly for word processing.

4. Plans should anticipate a terminal on most faculty members' desks to:

a. access both local and national data bases
b. do word processing
c. access student records
d. send messages, and prepare forms and schedules.

5. The incremental cost of providing a terminal for every faculty member is about $2 million a year. This does not include making data bases such as student records and library catalogs accessible.

6. Various efforts need to be coordinated to guarantee faculty access to a wide range of information resources.

7. The group is very concerned about providing resources to help faculty who do not have outside funds.

Student Needs

The student needs group has been examining past and present student trends regarding information technology. They have observed:

1. There are more students in information-technology-oriented areas. While enrollment for the university as a whole has grown 15.4 percent since 1977, engineering is up 67 percent, business administration is up 78 percent, and computer science is up 350 percent. These trends will not continue at the current rate, but they do suggest a move to fields using information technology.

2. More areas are using information technology. Erling Holtsmark of the Department of Classics notes, "It is my perception, for instance, that, other things being equal, a humanities graduate with any kind of background in working with computers will be given preferential treatment in applying for a job over one who has no such experience." Increasingly, students in professional, preprofessional, social science, humanities, and art programs are using computers.

3. Incoming students will have computer experience. In a survey by Ted Sjoerdsma, chairman of the Computer Science Department, only three of 75 area high schools did not have computers; 55 offer formal programming training. About 50 percent of our incoming students have used computers in high school; this will grow to 95 percent in the next few years. By 1985, about 20 percent of incoming students will have their own microcomputer.

4. The group has developed a model for projecting increased student computer use. Iowa needs to increase terminals from one for every 75 students to perhaps one for every eight in the next five years. In two years Iowa will need to provide one terminal for every 40 students.

5. Projections are based on computer use in formal course work. Right now, use for self-directed learning and for tasks such as word processing is relatively small but likely to grow.

In many ways student requirements over the next decade will be crucial. The ability of the university to attract first-rate students will be in part dependent on its ability to provide excellent information processing resources.

Word Processing

The most rapidly growing area of information processing is word processing, which involves faculty and staff in all areas of the university. The total university investment in purchased, dedicated word processing equipment exceeds $2 million. About $750,000 of the total consists of somewhat outmoded memory typewriters. Most equipment, $1.25 million, is in the medical area. About $400,000 more is spent on purchased equipment yearly. Word processing equipment at the major computer centers adds about $1 million to the equipment base, making the total exceed $3 million.

The committee has viewed word processing as one aspect of office automation, leaving scholarly requirements to the faculty needs group. Toward this view they agree on the following:

1. The use of office technology is complex and not well understood by many, including university executives, faculty, and staff.

2. Equipment should be coordinated and standardized to economize on training, communication, maintenance, and acquisition.

3. Word processing equipment should be integrated into university systems to capture data when and where it is created and to provide access to university information resources.

4. A group needs to be responsible for planning, coordinating and conducting pilot projects using office automation.

The group is now reviewing effectiveness of current use and will make specific recommendations based on these observations.

Telephone System

The major pressure to review the university and hospital telephone systems is cost. In the last four years, local service has cost 46 percent more and long distance 61 percent more. Last year local rates increased 24 percent, driving total yearly costs to about $2 million for the university's 8,200 phones (not including residence halls) and $1.2 million for the hospital's 3,800 phones.

The number of telephone lines used for data transmission has increased even more dramatically than voice lines, but does not yet make up a significant portion of total telephone line costs.

A second pressure for review is the opportunity to combine several communication systems in the phone system. Right now several issues exist:

1. Is a combined hospital and university system mutually advantageous?
2. Should the voice and data system be combined, requiring a digital switch?
3. Should Iowa buy time by waiting or look now at alternatives?
4. Should Iowa retain a consultant to study the situation? Should the consultant be shared between the university and the hospital?

There is general agreement that the university should:

1. Look at alternatives now.
2. Review telephone acquisition policies for the university.
3. Hire a manager of telecommunications.
4. Engage a consultant to provide expertise in selecting a telephone strategy.

The committee is investigating alternatives and awaiting hospital decisions to determine future direction.

Video Communication

Television in its various forms (narrow casting, two-way, teletext, videotext, and videodisc) is a potentially important element in any communications plan. Some observations of this group include:

1. It is imperative that video communication be addressed as part of the university plan for information and communication technology.

2. The current university investment in video equipment in the video center and over thirty departments exceeds $4 million.

3. Because the university does not have a television broadcast station or a campus-wide network, its ability to take advantage of new developments is inhibited. In contrast, the radio station has been able to set up a Regents' two-way, conferencing voice system for off-campus use.

4. A university-wide commitment to video communication in the form of equipment and developmental leaves of absence should accompany a strategic plan for using technology.

5. Faculty, staff, and students do not understand the current or potential role of video communication in instruction and research. A committee task will be to broaden their understanding.

Because of the current low level of understanding and demand regarding video communication, the committee wants to study these issues beyond the deadline for the task force report.

Non-Telephone Communications

Several communication systems or links now exist for various types of communication. The Weeg Center has bundles of copper twisted-wire pairs running throughout the east campus; data processing has over 150 coaxial cables running to various buildings. Physical Plant has a coaxial cable network connected to its original energy management system; its new system uses Weeg Center cables.

These systems could be combined in a single network that would also meet some video requirements for security and instruction. The Committee agrees on the following:

1. For high-speed data, video, and voice communication, a broad-band cable is the best choice.
2. A multipurpose cable must be secure and reliable.
3. Cable use must be managed; for example, frequencies must be assigned.
4. The group is now looking at cable installation and equipment.

Common Themes

Three trends cut across all study groups. First is the impact of information and communication technology on the entire academic community. New constituencies are demanding new resources and more capability in non-professional hands. Second is growth and inequities in student computer use resulting from some having had courses in high school and some owning microcomputers. Third is the growing importance of access and communications causing computer centers to become communication and network management centers. While none of these is critical today, they will be critical in the next two to three years.

Topics for Future Study

During the course of work, several gaps requiring further study have come to light. The most glaring are the need for education and training, concern with humane use, the importance of security, and the magnitude of library changes.

Training and Education

A serious difficulty in trying to involve a broad cross section of the university in technology planning is the lack of knowledge. Few people are aware of potential opportunities, particularly outside of their area of research. Thus a major concern of any planning effort must be an educational program to bring people up to date. If this is not done, participation is lost, resulting in lack of support and loss of potentially valuable ideas.

Unfortunately, many technology planning efforts focus on hardware, technique, and organization, and give less attention to human training and development. Training faculty and staff to deal with computer-based technology looms as a monumental task. (Students, other than remedial cases, do appear to be less of a problem.) Faculty members, pushed by student and research demands, will be forced to learn new techniques and methods. Text processing for scholarly literature, information retrieval from document searches, and using computers to manipulate information all require retraining and relearning. Course content changes, new course development, and revised teaching methods will tax instructional development leave programs and staff support. Changes in research methods and topics will require extensive faculty development programs.

As offices use more technology, existing practices will be changed. For many, shifting from a typewriter to a word processor is difficult; for most, electronic mail is hard to envision. Even seemingly small changes, such as using new telephone features, involves adjustment by the entire university.

Solving training problems will require the best minds the university can muster.

Humane Use

Iowa is particularly concerned that technology be guided toward humane ends, preserving human dignity. This element needs to be added to the planning process. Suggestions have ranged from holding a national conference to conducting detailed studies. Iowa's approach has been to start pilot projects among humanists in exchange for their candid reviews of the technologies. Also being considered is putting together an ad hoc group to review technology plans.

Data Security

Information security in a highly accessible system is a major concern in an institution that values privacy and the sanctity of the individual. It is also a practical concern for those who are considering replacing conventional information storage with electronic media. While concerns such as privacy and integrity are often red herrings brought forth by those protecting their domains, information integrity and security are serious and, in some cases, unsolved problems. Fortunately the hospital center is a leader in providing secure yet accessible systems and so supplies valuable local experience. Nevertheless, security requirements will likely involve major changes in existing systems before they become part of a campus-wide network.

Library Planning

As the principle campus information resource, libraries must be a part of information technology planning. While the necessity of automating searches and considering new storage media is widely recognized, library changes are often measured in centuries or decades rather than in years. The University of Iowa libraries have taken steps toward automation by subscribing to information retrieval services and being a member of the Research Libraries Information Network (RLIN). They understand the need to provide a computer-based catalog and different forms of storage and retrieval, but the size of the task is enormous. The current approach, which appears to be sound, is to rely on inter-institutional cooperative ventures to overcome exceedingly large conversion costs. Another possible, but currently unacceptable, approach is to carve out a few departmental libraries for pilot projects in automation. Current estimates are that it will be at least a decade before computer-based catalogs are fully installed. Speeding this process should be considered a university priority.

Where From Here?

Reviewing planning for computing at the University of Iowa brings to mind John Gardner's words:

> ...creative organizations are rarely tidy. Some tolerance for inconsistencies, for profusion of purpose and strategies, and for conflict is the price of freedom and vitality.[2]

In a very real sense planning for computing has been forced upon the university by external events. These include: the need to provide computing, particularly word processing, to departments with few outside funds and small equipment budgets; the necessity of making administrative data processing more accessible and placing more capability in users' hands; an emphasis on communication as the emerging focal point of computing; a growth in student uses and sophistication; and the emergence of training to use technology as a major faculty/staff development effort.

Yet the fact that the university has chosen to question the appropriate role of computing testifies to the special nature of computers as powerful intellectual tools cutting across the entire academic community.

While it is impossible to predict the results of current efforts, it is clear that computing at Iowa has changed. The importance of computing and related information technologies is now recognized. The need to coordinate various technology-based units has also become apparent. Finally, dissemination of information about use of technology will increase collegiate and departmental awareness of technology issues.

Through all planning, one should not underestimate the importance of people and their ideas in the academic community. At the University of Iowa the visions of E. F. Lindquist (Iowa Testing Programs), G. P. Weeg (Computer Science and Academic Computing), and D. C. Spriestersbach (Vice President for Educational Development and Research) have shaped computing at the University of Iowa—the future, in large part, depends on the emergence of new visionaries and new ideas.

University Office of Information Technology

As a first step in addressing the need for on-going coordination, the University of Iowa has decided to create an Office of Information Technology. The stringent financial situation demands planning, coordination and resource sharing. Continuation of the status quo threatens to cost the university in terms of lost opportunities, needless duplication, and wasted efforts. As shown by other chapters in this book, the university is not alone in reaching this conclusion. Nor is the issue new at Iowa. In 1978, a computer task force chaired by James Van Allen recommended enhanced coordination between computer centers and the appointment of a director of university computing. Today, the need for coordination has broadened.

The creation of an Office of Information Technology is an approach uniquely suited to the traditions and people at the University of Iowa. It is to serve the functions of increasing university awareness, planning technology strategies, coordinating and controlling various support services, educating, and supporting decentralized initiatives. It places considerable responsibility backed by some authority in a single office. Since the office is new and the technology is rapidly changing, the exact nature of the office will evolve over time.

Initially, responsibilities of the office will be to:

- Provide advice on developments in information technology and their potential impact on the university.

- Plan and coordinate the development of the communication systems of the university, including telephone, broad-band cable, cable TV, microwave systems, and building management and security systems.

- Be responsible, as designated through the Vice President for Educational Development and Research, and the Vice President for Finance and University Services, for academic and administrative computing (Weeg Computing Center, Administrative Data Processing, and decentralized computing units).

- Maintain an active liaison with units involved in the development of video facilities and their utilization.

- Provide a university-wide resource for information and advice about the use of information technology, particularly word processing and office automation.

- Provide leadership and planning for the use of information technology, and foster creative development projects in this area which are of university-wide benefit.

Acknowledgements

D. C. Spriestersbach, Vice President, Educational Development and Research; Andrew W. Wehde, Director of Administrative Data Processing; and David E. Wood, Director of Hospital Information Systems, have offered valuable suggestions but are not responsible for content. Editing assistance from D. Harris and L. Grandchamp is gratefully acknowledged.

References

1. State Board of Regents. *Academic Computing Services for Instruction, Research and Public Service.* April 1981.

2. Gardner, John W. *Self Renewal.* New York: Harper & Row, 1964, p.21.

See also:
Ad Hoc Committee on Computing. "Computing in Undergraduate Education at the University of Iowa: A Proposal to Make Iowa a Leader in the Use of the Emerging Educational Technology." 1973.
Ad Hoc Computer Review Committee. *Report of the Ad Hoc Computer Review Committee.* March 1978.
Committee on University Educational Directions. *Educational Directions for the University of Iowa: A Report to the President.* February 1978.
IBM Corporation. *A Report to the President: Computing at the University of Iowa: Study and Recommendations.* July 1966.

The University of Iowa. *The University and its Major Units.* Prepared for the Commission on Colleges and Universities of the North Central Association of Colleges and Secondary Schools, February 1978.

The University of Iowa Hospitals and Clinics. *Hospital Systems Profile.* Fall 1979.

The University of Iowa Computer Center Executive Committee. *A Five Year Program for Self Support of the University Computer Center.* October 1977.

Weeg Computing Center. "Growth of Academic Computing: Report to Vice Presidents and Deans." University of Iowa, April 1981.

10

University of Minnesota

CARL ADAMS
School of Management

PETER C. PATTON
University Computer Center

PETER ROLL
Office of Academic Affairs

Introduction

Although it was not recognized so clearly at the beginning of the 1980–1982 period, it has become apparent since then that different levels of planning have been occurring simultaneously at the University of Minnesota. On one level, there has been planning that addressed immediate tactical issues, such as the replacement of the large academic and administrative computing facilities and provision of some support for the large quantity and variety of microcomputer and word processing equipment that was being acquired. At another level, the university clearly needed to address some intermediate-range planning issues, such as the replacement of its telephone system and the continued automation of its library operations and services. Finally, at the institutional strategy level, trends and applications of computing, communications, and information (CCI) technology in business and industry made it clear that the institution needed to:

1. Select long-range goals regarding the type of CCI environment it expected to have.
2. Choose a strategy for funding these goals (a resource strategy) that was realistic and consistent with the chosen goals.
3. Establish an organizational structure for CCI coordination and management.
4. Set in place major operating policies governing CCI activities throughout the institution.

It is important to recognize the legitimacy and necessity of all three types of planning activity and to realize that, though each type marches to its own drummer, they should form a nested set of activities. In the hierarchy from the tactical to the strategic, the more general and longer-range planning should provide the necessary parameters and guidelines for the more immediate and specific issues. Acceptance of the three levels of planning allows for flexibility and a division of labor that is essential to the operation of an institution as large and complex as the University of Minnesota.

The structure of the remainder of this chapter reflects the authors' advocacy of a model of CCI planning that includes three distinct levels. Some background information on relevant characteristics of the University of Minnesota and on the history, present status, and future prospects for CCI technology at this institution is given. The following three sections address immediate tactical planning, intermediate-range planning, and long-range strategic planning. Each of these sections presents one or more case examples of the experience at Minnesota. The final section is a brief commentary on the status and possible future directions of planning and implementation in the spring of 1982.

Background

Characteristics of the University of Minnesota

A few basic pieces of information about the University of Minnesota will help provide a perspective on the planning processes that are taking place. In many ways, the actions taken at each of the planning levels are a reflection of these characteristics.

- The senior executives of the University of Minnesota consist of a president and six roughly co-equal vice presidents for Academic Affairs, Finance and Operations, Health Sciences, Student Affairs, Administration and Planning, and Legislative and Government Relations. While the Vice President for Academic Affairs is a "first among equals" and is chairman of the Budget Executive, there is no senior or executive vice president.

- The seven senior officers preside over a system including one comprehensive campus (the Twin Cities campus, with almost 50,000 FTE students, 20 colleges, 200 departments, and a breadth and number of academic programs in excess of those at most public universities); a campus with some graduate programs (Duluth, 8,000 FTE students); an undergraduate liberal arts college (Morris, 1600 FTE students); and 2 two-year technical agricultural colleges (Crookston and Waseca, about 1,000 FTE students each). The system administration also serves as the campus administration for the Twin Cities campus.

- The Twin Cities campus is the only comprehensive research university in the state of Minnesota; it provides the only four-year and graduate programs in engineering, agriculture, medicine, and dentistry in the state. It is also the only comprehensive public four-year institution in the Twin Cities metropolitan area.

- The geographical configuration of the Twin Cities campus includes Minneapolis campus areas on either side of the Mississippi River; a St. Paul campus (actually in the city of Lauderdale, a St. Paul suburb) about 2.5 miles from the Minneapolis campus; the University Computer Center, between and north of the two campuses astride the boundary between Minneapolis and the city of Lauderdale; and two administrative and service locations separated from the campuses by almost a mile (one of these includes the administrative data processing facility). This geographical distribution strongly influences the university's telephone and telecommunications planning and costs.

- The annual operating budget of the University of Minnesota is currently about $750 million, with a little less than half derived from state appropriations (37 percent) and tuition (8 percent), and the remainder from endowment and other earnings, private gifts and grants, federal sources, and use charges and fees such as room and board.

• Although the university's Board of Regents enjoys constitutional autonomy, its funding is controlled by the state legislature. Tuition is set by the regents and research income is not directly reappropriated by the legislature; however, the legislature does include both of these as offsets to the university budget based on its expectations, so the effect is not much different.

• The Twin Cities campus has a long tradition of strong faculty governance. Compared with institutions such as Ohio State and Michigan State, Minnesota is considerably less centralized and more faculty directed; compared with Michigan and Illinois, it is relatively more centralized and less faculty directed. The Duluth and Waseca campuses have recently adopted collective bargaining under the state's public employees' labor relations law; the Twin Cities campus recently rejected collective bargaining for the second time (the first attempt failed in 1978). The effects of collective bargaining on the nature of the institution and its individual campuses are only speculative at this time.

A Brief Historical Perspective

As in many universities, academic computing at the University of Minnesota grew out of the needs of the programs in the physical sciences and engineering. The first computer center on campus was established in the 1950s with a UNIVAC 1103. In 1961, a CDC 1604 was obtained to meet the growing need for computing capacity, and by the mid-1960s this machine, too, was becoming inadequate. A CDC 6600 was installed as a replacement in 1967. The procurement of this machine, however, led to some concern on the part of government officials that the university was unwisely expending the taxpayer's dollars on a computing facility that was far larger than it could reasonably use; "Buying a Mack truck to do the job of a pickup," is one way this acquisition was described. Furthermore, the CDC 6600, a batch machine, was installed just as the era of timeshared interactive computing was beginning, leading to some concern that the "wrong kind of truck" had been acquired.

As a consequence of these concerns, and of similar concerns about the growing cost and complexity of computing throughout state government and education, the Minnesota legislature and governor began to take an interest in the subject. This led to the appointment of a Governor's Committee on State Information Systems in 1968; an Advisory Committee on Computing of the Minnesota Higher Education Coordinating Commission shortly thereafter; and in 1969 to a legislative moratorium on further acquisitions of computing equipment in higher education, pending a statewide study of information systems in all publicly supported agencies in Minnesota.

This study provided a strategic planning framework for the development of educational and administrative computing services in all of the state's post-secondary institutions.[1] It built upon the very uneven beginning that had been made in the four public systems: the State College (now the State University) System, the State Junior College (now Community College) System, the Area Vocational Technical Institutes, and the University of Minnesota system. The strategic planning goal that was laid out was to provide Minnesota post-secondary students with roughly the same level of computing support that was provided to students at that time by one of the nation's pioneers in educational computing (Dartmouth College). This goal was projected in the 1967 report of the President's Science Advisory Committee—the Pierce Report[2]—as a necessary and desirable level of computing support nationally. From this starting point and strategic goal, the Minnesota study projected the level of expenditures and computing capacity that would be needed over the ten-year period to 1980.

Although they were not called upon to accept or endorse the results of the study directly, state officials tacitly accepted the strategic goal by appropriating the funds to carry it out. The projections for the first five years of the decade included some detail; the projections for the second half-decade were far more general. Despite the hazards of such projections, the plan has served as a remarkably accurate guide and predictor of the development of computing at the University of Minnesota, as well as in the other state higher-education institutions. For instance, major upgrades of the university's CDC 6600 (to a Cyber-74) and the administrative computer (an IBM 360/50 in 1970, replaced by a 370/158 in 1978) occurred at about the times suggested by the study. The study projected that these two facilities, with evolutionary upgrades, would last out the decade, but that no projections could be made beyond that time.

A major recommendation for new development in the 1970 study was the establishment by the university of an educational time-shared computing facility that would provide the only instructional computing service to 17 of the 18 junior colleges and would be available to supplement the batch computing services available at the six state colleges. This facility was established in 1971 with a CDC 6400. Since then, the need for interactive computing has grown. The community colleges now use service from the Cyber-170/720 operated by the Minnesota Educational Computing Consortium (MECC), another indirect outgrowth of the study in 1973.[3] The state universities use service from both MECC and the university's timesharing system. The university's own needs for interactive computing grew to encompass a much enlarged timesharing system (a Cyber-172) and an interactive remote job-entry service (primarily for research) provided from a Cyber-170/730.

Although all of this development and evolution through the 1970s was within the framework of a goal and a plan laid out more than ten years ago, none of it was directly based on and referenced to that plan. All of the development was tactical, based on needs and opportunities as they arose. In this sense the 1970 study of computing in higher education was not a strategic plan; rather, it represented a strategic goal which was generally accepted, plus a prediction of what would happen if efforts were made to achieve that goal.

The Situation in 1980

Although in 1970 no one had the audacity to predict where the institution would be in ten years, it is interesting to compare the University of Minnesota's position in 1980 with the 1970 plan.

Major Computing Facilities

The Cyber-74 academic computer and the 370/158 administrative computer were, in 1980, both saturated. Plans began for the replacement of both. Although interactive computing has continued to grow, the advent of microcomputers and a few laboratory mini-computers, along with the improvement of interactive central computing facilities over the decade, has not caused the same saturation to occur for interactive computing.

Library Automation

An important section of the 1970 study laid out a $13 million development plan for statewide library automation. Wisely, the legislature chose not to fund this proposal. After several years of development effort on a minicomputer-based library automation system, supported substantially with funding from the National Library of Medicine, the University of Minnesota libraries decided in 1980 that the development and maintenance of a local automation system could not be successfully managed by the library, and that affiliation with the Research Libraries Group and use of the Research Libraries Information Network services as a basis for library automation would be more effective. In the meantime, the university libraries and many other libraries throughout Minnesota have been using OCLC for cataloging; a statewide serials data base and inter-library loan service has been operating throughout the decade; and the State University System has implemented an on-line catalog system using OCLC records for all six of their institutions. In summary, the 1970 study did succeed in identifying library automation as an important and costly area for computer application, and one in which considerable activity and progress would occur during the decade; it was not very clairvoyant concerning the nature of that activity and progress.

Telecommunications

Because of the emphasis on timeshared computing and other interactive applications, the 1970 study mapped and costed out some telephone-based communications networks to interconnect institutions, and it included costs for internal institutional data communications as part of the total costs of the service. But the study did not anticipate the enormous impact of electronic technology on telecommunications options and costs. In particular, it did not anticipate that in late 1979 the University of Minnesota would be informed that its current telephone system would cease to provide adequate service within four years, and that replacement of it would involve a capital expense of some $25 million for a digital, computer-controlled telephone system.

Microcomputers and Word Processing

In 1970 some Digital Equipment Corporation (DEC) minicomputers were beginning to appear. Although it was recognized that these would have an influence on computing at universities, they were viewed as just another kind of computer, in competition with large timesharing systems (and not all that cost-effective in 1970). Their impact was not considered separately. Today, microcomputers are able to provide a major fraction of the interactive computing capability that educational institutions need. They are becoming more ubiquitous and are finding their way into the personal possession of students and faculty, and they may comprise the access equipment or terminals to central services in the future. Furthermore, the use of computers as writing tools may eventually exceed their use as calculating tools. Such factors are likely to dominate planning for computing in the 1980's.

The Future: Potential Issues, Opportunities, and Impacts

By late 1980 it had become clear to a number of administrators that, in addition to the major and obvious adaptations of our major computing facilities and computer-based service centers to changing circumstances, the University of Minnesota was facing much more profound changes in its operations and in the demands on its resources during the coming decade. In addition to the circumstances outlined above, the seeds of this realization included the more pioneering efforts of other institutions, most notably:

- Stanford University's extensive planning effort to mobilize its resources to better support its educational programs and operations with technology, and in particular the success of its Terminals-for-Managers program in bringing its senior administrative officers into active participation and productive use of currently available technology. [4]
- Carnegie-Mellon University's announced goal of providing a workstation microcomputer for each student and faculty member by 1985, along with the resources to support the effective use of these devices.[5]

A little thought about the implications of these developments, together with some knowledge of the directions of the information-technology industry and the U.S. economy, suggested that some conscious forethought and planning would put the University of Minnesota in a much more favorable position to take advantage of opportunities in dealing with the impacts of information technology on its programs, operations, and resources, rather than reacting to problems after they have become visible. There was widespread recognition that the university was facing profound impacts in the following areas:

1. *Educational programs.* Impacts will materially affect the nature of some programs and the resources they would require to keep them current with common practices elsewhere in society. For instance, the use of word processing and related technology in the writing process is already beginning to have visible effects on the teaching of writing and on the writing process which is fundamental to scholarship as practiced by faculty members and students.

2. *Operations.* Impacts will alter the ways in which many processes essential to the operations of any large organization will be carried out, especially those related to writing and formal and informal communications among people and offices.

3. *Resources.* The investments of both operating and capital funds implied by these impacts are, at first thought, staggering, especially when viewed in the context of state budget deficits and possible retrenchments of university programs in excess of anything

heretofore experienced in higher education. On second thought, however, the investments are not staggering in comparison with our investments in the human resources of the university; they bring with them opportunities to achieve cost reductions, control costs, and achieve major improvements in educational/scholarly productivity and quality; and finally, if society moves in the directions predicted, they are necessary investments if higher education is to continue to play a signficant role in society.

4. *Personal and institutional attitudes and behavior.* The effects of information technology on people and organizations have been discussed widely in the literature.[6] Universities and the people that inhabit them are no different than other organizations and people in this regard. This fact, and the importance of dealing properly and humanely with the related problems, have been made clearest to the authors of this paper when they have tried to persuade senior university administrators, faculty members, mid-level managers, and clerical and support staff that we must plan for information technology in the university.

5. *Organizational structure.* All of these impacts raise a question of whether the existing organizational structure at the University of Minnesota will prove to be workable and effective in dealing with the kinds of change we are anticipating. Since organizational structures are matters of tradition and evolution, they are particularly difficult to tamper with in universities. Whether and when to make significant organizational changes is a controversial issue on which people of sound judgment can rightly disagree. The proposals for organizational change at Minnesota, resulting from the strategic planning activity, are described later in this chapter.

Immediate Tactical Planning

As mentioned earlier, the major academic and administrative computers at the University of Minnesota were both saturated by 1980, before any serious thought had been given to updating the institution's long-range strategic plans. For several reasons, the computer centers responsible for these facilities—the University Computer

Center (UCC) and the Administrative Data Processing Department (ADPD)—began immediate planning of a tactical nature to upgrade or replace them:

- The importance of these two facilities to university operations was so great that a prolonged period of degraded service would have been intolerable.
- The two centers were relatively compartmentalized within the University of Minnesota structure, and somewhat isolated from other strategic academic program planning under way.
- The time required to develop a consensus to initiate and then complete long-range strategic planning for computer, communications, and information systems was sufficiently long and uncertain that no serious thought was given to delaying the facilities planning until this was done.

Planning for replacement of the IBM 370/158AP administrative computer was a straightforward process common to many large organizations which depend on large IBM systems to support their administrative operations. It led from a bidding process for IBM-compatible systems, through evaluation of several proposals from IBM plug-compatible manufacturers both domestic and foreign, to selection of an IBM 3033 main frame. The scenario is sufficiently common that we will not describe it in greater detail here.

On the other hand, selection of a class 6 supercomputer to replace the Cyber-74 for instruction and research batch computing was a decidedly uncommon result of planning to deal with an immediate problem. This decision, which was the first of its kind in an American university and will dominate the University of Minnesota's academic computing services for many years, was made just prior to the initiation of a long-range strategic planning process and in the face of trends toward proliferation of microcomputers and distributed processing of various kinds. The remainder of this section describes the conditions and reasoning which led to the decision, as an example of a kind of immediate tactical planning which arises frequently out of rapid technological change and development in the computer industry.

The Cyber-74 computer in 1980 was the University Computer Center's workhorse for FORTRAN and FORTRAN-based software packages. Efforts to offload jobs from this machine to the Cyber-172 (timeshared computer), the Cyber-170/730 (interactive research computing and non-FORTRAN-based services), the Cyber-172 in the Health Sciences, or the Cyber-171 at the Duluth Campus could provide only temporary relief because of the difference in scale between the Cyber-74 and the other machines. As the Cyber-74 saturated, it was becoming apparent that, if central FORTRAN-based services were not improved soon, demand would eventually be satisfied by a growing array of departmental macro-minicomputers of the DEC VAX-11/780 class. Hence, planning alternatives to replace the Cyber-74 were constrained by Control Data Corporation compatibility on the one hand, and by the cost-performance target of the VAX-11/780 on the other hand.

To address this problem, the University Computer Center for-med a technical planning committee to identify viable alternative replacement systems for the Cyber-74. The alternatives studied included one (or two) used Cyber-174's; a Cyber-170/750; a Cyber-170/760; and even a battery of VAX-11/780's either centrally clustered or geographically distributed. None of these alternatives was attractive: those with favorable cost-performance characteristics were not operationally viable and vice versa.

During this time, UCC was also engaged in a system software development program with Cray Research, Inc., a local manaufactu-rer of large-scale computers (Cray Research and Control Data Corp., both Minnesota firms, are the only manufacturers of class 6 super-computers). As a result of this program, UCC staff became aware that Cray Research needed additional computer capacity to support software development. UCC proposed that Cray Research install a Cray-1 computer at the University of Minnesota, with UCC acting as a facilities manager in return for a few hours per day of Cray-1 use. By early 1981, UCC had been offering its research clients limited access to class 6 supercomputers. Short-term agreements had been arranged with CYBERNET for use of the STAR-100 and later the Cyber-203, and with United Computing Corporation for Cray-1 use. These arrangements were satisfactory for only a handful of potential users because of problems with access, funding, and user support. There was some evidence of latent demand for larger-scale research computing services than UCC had been able to pro-vide on the Cyber-74, but this fell far short of justifying a university investment in such a machine. It was in this context that discussions were started with Cray Research on mutually-advantageous arrangements.

In November of 1980, results of UCC facilities planning were presented to a long-range planning subcommittee of the University Computer Services Advisory Committee. The subcommittee was advised that the Cyber-74 was saturated; that no further opportunities for relief by offloading were possible; and that the most likely replacement machine, the Cyber-170/750, would not be cost-competitive with departmental VAX-11/780 systems. The possibility of working out some kind of arrangement with Cray Research for computer use was raised, and UCC was encouraged to explore this further.

Although Cray Research had not expressed interest in a facilities management contract, they approached the university early in 1981 with an opportunity to purchase a used Cray-1B (500,000-word memory) with a low residual value. Several funding alternatives were explored and the negotiations finally settled on terms which seemed possible for the university to manage. UCC would provide Cray with software maintenance, training, space, and a block of computer time for development purposes, in return for attractive prices on the machine and its maintenance. Third-party leasing was arranged to finance the acquisition. Technical and business plans were developed and presented to the UCC planning committee, the director of University Computer Services, and his advisory committee, and two of the university's vice presidents. At the request of the vice presidents, a more detailed five-year business plan was prepared, demonstrating that research income would be sufficient to operate and pay off the machine over five years under the terms arranged.

The Cray-1B proposal was endorsed by the various committees and the vice presidents not because it would provide university research users with access to sophisticated computing power which they needed—such a need was far too limited to justify a $4.5 million investment. Rather, it was because the business plan showed that the unit cost of FORTRAN-based computing would be considerably lower for all users than afforded by other alternatives, including VAX-11/780 service. Benchmark tests performed by UCC showed performance improvement factors of nine (scalar mode) to twenty (vector mode) over the Cyber-74. Cyber-74 FORTRAN benchmark programs ran without change on the Cray-1B, thus minimizing the program conversion problem for users who did not need or wish to take advantage of the special scalar and vector architecture of the machine. Finally, the Cray-1B's cost performance was equal to that of the VAX-11/780 at 32-bit precision, and four times better at 64-bit precision.

The research income of UCC has been derived from use charges to sponsored research projects, state agencies, and a very limited base of local research organizations. These charges recover almost the full costs of the service from university projects and state agencies; and they recover an amount well in excess of full costs from the few for-profit clients. The five-year business plan prepared for the Cray-1B was based on the assumptions that UCC research income would continue to grow at a rate somewhat less than that experienced consistently over the previous several years, and that the Cyber-74 could be phased out in the second or third year of the plan. Not surprisingly, the business plan indicated a shortfall between research income on the one hand and operating and lease costs on the other, extending into the second year. The source of this shortfall was a revenue dip resulting from substantially lower unit costs of computing on the Cray-1B. Since its cost-performance is three times that of the Cyber-74, moving the entire workload of the Cyber-74 to the Cray-1B would produce only one-third of the previous revenue. This lower unit cost requires, of course, that the Cray-1B be utilized at a substantial level; that is, it requires continued growth in the volume of revenue-generating business. The expected dip in revenue has, in fact, been exacerbated by the current recession in the economy, which has reduced the level of spending by state and federal agencies.

The expected revenue shortfall was partially compensated in the business plan by lower lease payments during the first two years. The actual situation is being dealt with by offering Cray-1B services to other research universities and to research organizations in government and industry; by an accelerated schedule for deactivating the Cyber-74; and by careful cost control measures within UCC. The income shortfall was seen in the business plan as a localized UCC management problem; it is being dealt with as such, albeit the state of the economy has made it a more severe management problem than was anticipated.

Within the context of the University Computer Center and academic computer services at the University of Minnesota, the decision to acquire the Cray-1B was part of a long-range planning process begun in 1970 and extrapolated in 1980 into the future. It was based on faith (a strategic posture) that large-scale batch computing will continue to be an important and cost-effective service required to support instruction and research at a large university. It was made with full knowledge that such computing will constitute a diminishing fraction of the total computing environment as we move into an era of microcomputers, workstations, and other distributed and interactive resources. One of the likely directions of systems development on the Cray-1B, for this reason, will be toward integrating it with telecommunications systems to facilitate access to its power and low unit cost.

Within the context of university-wide long-range planning for information systems, the Cray-1B decision was the result of a tactical planning process to deal with an immediate problem and to take advantage of an attractive opportunity. The decision was based on assumptions which preceded the recent long-range strategic planning efforts, and it will certainly impose some constraints on the development and implementation of future plans. Although the ultimate wisdom of the decision will be based on developments during the next several years, we believe, at this point, that the tactics it represents should fit well into the strategy to be adopted.

Intermediate Planning—Tactical and Strategic

In between the immediate decisions which must be made on tactical grounds, such as acquisition of the Cray-1 computer, and long-range strategic planning which cannot influence our decisions on immediate problems until it is completed, are a group of problems, issues, or opportunities which do not have to be acted on immediately, but on which decisions must be made in the foreseeable future. These problems are influenced (or driven in some cases) by immediate decisions and circumstances, and they may strongly influence the long-range planning which is going on simultaneously. It is possible neither to halt the long-range planning until these intermediate matters are dealt with, nor to defer action on the intermediate problems until the long-range plans are in place, though either of these options would be more rational. In this section we describe three such intermediate planning problems at the University of Minnesota.

Telecommunications Systems

University Telephone System

In 1979 Northwestern Bell Telephone informed us that they would not be able to ensure that satisfactory telephone service could continue to be delivered to the University of Minnesota through the central office switch that had served us since 1962. The university in 1979 had the largest telephone system in the state of Minnesota (over 16,000 lines) and the number of lines was growing at a level which suggested saturation of the central office serving us by about January 1, 1983. To ensure that a replacement was in place by this time, and to permit us to take advantage of many new features which were not available through our existing telephone system, we were urged to begin planning with Northwestern Bell immediately in 1979. The Vice President for Finance and Operations, who carried responsibility for the university's telephone system, appointed a Telephone Resources Committee consisting of representatives of Support Services (the operating arm of his office), the University Hospitals (the largest concentration of telephones within the university and a user with special needs), the Physical Planning Office, the office of the Vice President for Academic Affairs, the Administrative Data Processing Department, the University Computer Center, and University Telephone Services.

This group began meeting with telephone company representatives and with representatives of independent vendors and manufacturers of telephone equipment to inform and educate itself about telephone technology and the telephone industry, including its applications to data communications, office automation, and other services that might become important in the future. Northwestern Bell began these discussions with the idea of offering us an ESS1A6 central office switch to replace the electromechanical switch which was becoming saturated; they later concluded that a Dimension 2000 system would better and more economically serve our needs. Both of these devices were computer-controlled analog line switches.

As a result of its educational efforts, drawing particularly on the experience of the University of Chicago in selecting an all-digital replacement for its telephone system, the Telephone Resources Committee concluded in the spring of 1981 that the University of Minnesota should replace its telephone system with an all-digital system representing the current state of communications switching technology. This decision led to the conclusion that our existing telephone system could continue to provide the existing level of service for a few more years. It also led to the initiation by Northwestern Bell and Western Electric of a comprehensive study of traffic patterns for voice and written communications, as well as of alternative telephone/data communications system configurations which could meet the future needs of the university.

These studies are still under way. We expect their results to be useful to us in understanding our options; in understanding in particular the tradeoffs between integration of data communications with the switched telephone system and separate local networks for data; in identifying the most promising directions for our future telephone system; and in preparing specifications for open-market proposals for a new telephone system as required by state law.

One of the significant outcomes of this process to date has been the realization that we will have to capitalize our telephone system in the future by one or another means, both in response to changes in the regulation and structure of the telephone industry and to provide some measure of control over the costs of telephone services that would otherwise be delivered under regulated tariffs. The capital investment required—about $25 million ($1,000–$1,300 per line for a 20,000-line system)—is high enough that it has, without the need for any persuasion, captured the attention and serious interest of all university officials.

Broad-band Cable Communications System

During the spring and summer of 1979, a group was established to provide input to the cable television franchising process in the city of Minneapolis concerning the needs and potential uses by the university and other higher education institutions of a metropolitan-area cable television system. Our hope was that such a system could be used effectively and economically for a variety of university purposes, including service to off-campus audiences and accomodation of data communications needs between the academic and administrative computer centers, both of which were located off-campus, requiring expensive telephone line interconnections. Although any of the franchise proposals would have made these things possible, the franchising process became so enmeshed in political controversy that it still is not clear when and whether a system will be franchised in either Minneapolis or St. Paul. The experience of evaluating the franchise proposals in detail, however, made some of us aware of the benefits and cost savings which could be achieved by combining voice, data, and television communications in the same broad-band communications utility.

With the decision to acquire the Cray-1 supercomputer in early 1981, it became apparent to us that considerably higher capacity and higher-speed data communications facilities between the University Computer Center and the Minneapolis and St. Paul campuses would be necessary if full advantage was to be taken of the Cray's capabilities. Such speed and capacity were not readily available from the telephone utility at affordable rates. Since the prospects for a cable television franchise to provide this service were still nil, we set up a task force to study the feasibility of constructing our own broad-band communications system. The primary problem in doing this was seen to be obtaining access to the right of way needed to bury or hang the cables. Since right of way might involve the telephone company, the interests of the city and of cable television franchise applicants, the bureaucratic inertia of railroads, and/or a multitude of property owners, this was not a task that we could undertake lightly.

The task force prepared a request for proposals for consulting services to assist in testing the feasibility of such a system and obtaining right of way. A well-qualified consultant was retained (locally-based, but with a national reputation in this area: Michaud, Cooley, Hallberg, and Erickson). The work plan for the study included provisions for the eventual extension of a trunk cable system to connect all of the university's disjointed locations in a four-mile-diameter area spanning the borders of the cities of Minneapolis, St. Paul, Lauderdale, and Falcon Heights; the upgrading and extension of the existing closed-circuit television system on the Minneapolis and St. Paul campuses to serve as a general distribution system to most buildings; and the carriage of data, television, and eventually interbuilding voice telephone trunk traffic.

As of this writing, the first phase of this feasibility study has been completed. The results have been somewhat different than anticipated. There is a good chance that an overhead right of way can be obtained exclusively from the electric power utility under quite reasonable rates established for cable television operators. The study required both the University Computer Center and the Administrative Data Processing Division, for the first time, to sit down and determine exactly how much of their data communications costs were associated with leased lines and how much with modem and other interface equipment; this was necessary to establish the amount of money that could be diverted from telephone expenses to pay for a broad-band system. The results of this assessment have indicated that the bulk of these expenses are devoted to modem and related line interface equipment. As a consequence, the payout period for a broad-band system, equipped with necessary rf modems and serving only the computer centers, is about five years. The cost savings, in other words, are not spectacular and compelling. What one gains from a broad-band system are insulation from telephone rate increases (projected recently to be as high as a factor of three for lines under a revised private line tariff proposal to the Minnesota Public Utlities Commission); much higher capacity and speed than any other form of intercampus communications that can be considered; potential cost savings in the future as use of rf modems expands and costs are reduced; and a vast expansion of closed-circuit television capability (for which, however, there is no current operating budget).

Given this mixed bag of marginal current economic feasibility and major (but uncertain) opportunities for future benefits and unit cost reductions, the task force is proposing to proceed with a single cable link between the University Computer Center and the science/engineering portion of the Minneapolis campus to gain experience with such technology and provide the badly needed, high-speed link to the Cray-1. Because of the potential benefits of integrating a broad-band "local network" system with a new digital telephone system, this possiblity is being incorporated into the alternatives under investigation in the Western Electric/Northwestern Bell university telephone system study. The outcome of this study and the university's subsequent analysis of it will be most important in determining the University of Minnesota's intermediate and long-range decisions on its telecommunications systems.

Library Automation

As mentioned above, the University of Minnesota Libraries, Twin Cities has a long record of development work in library automation, focused around a minicomputer system developed in our Biomedical Library with project support from the National Library of Medicine. The expectation was that this system would eventually be developed into a linked or distributed system which would serve all of the major and minor departmental libraries on the Twin Cities campus, and which could be exported for use at other campuses. Use of a national bibliographic data base as a necessary resource for cataloging was always anticipated, but neither of the major bibliographic utilities that operate on a national level showed interest in cooperating with us on this. By mid-1980, after the second outside consultant review in four years, it was decided to discontinue this local development effort; to affiliate with the Research Libraries Group and use their Research Libraries Information Network as the basis for the cataloging, acquisitions, and serials control portion of an automated library system; and to draw upon the resources and expertise of the university's major computer centers for assistance with the local aspects of automation rather than providing this expertise from within the university libraries. These decisions had as much to do with the difficulties encountered by research libraries in managing complex systems development projects as with the particular merits or demerits of the minicomputer system in which the university had invested so much effort.

Given this history, there is an impression within the university community that the university libraries are badly behind peer institutions in automating their operations and services. Although a great deal of progress has, in fact, been made, most of it is in "back-room" operations that are invisible to the university community. The tactical plan which is currently being implemented is to establish a Library Automation Technical Task Force, comprised of a few technical experts from the computer centers and a few experts in library operations from the university libraries. This group will identify immediate needs and targets of opportunity for developing local system components (a circulation control system is a likely objective because of its visibility and provision of on-line location information; we must caution, however, that an on-line circulation system is not an on-line catalog even though it may appear to be this to a library user). At the same time, the library administration is in the process of identifying strategic goals and plans for the next several years; these goals and plans will be reviewed for their implementation implications by the task force and by the university's central administration.

Long-Range Strategic Planning

In long-range strategic planning, an institution needs to set basic parameters that guide its activities in the area of interest. For computer, communications, and information (CCI) services at the University of Minnesota, the necessary parameters include:

1. A long-term sense of direction or general goal.
2. A sense of the fiscal constraints related to CCI services and their priority in claiming institutional resources.

3. An organizational structure to carry out CCI activities, consistent with the goal adopted and with resource constraints.

4. Major operating policies for CCI activities that can guide these activities throughout the institution.

These parameters provide the necessary umbrella under which immediate and intermediate levels of planning can effectively take place.

In the spring of 1981, the university's senior officers authorized a long-range strategic planning study for computation, communications, and information (CCI) services. Their action seems to have been motivated by a general appreciation of the changes taking place in CCI technology and an immediate concern for putting the impending replacement of the telephone system in the proper strategic context. The authors have helped to shape this planning effort. Thus, their views on long-range strategic planning for CCI services are reflected in the following descriptions of:

- Factors inhibiting and supporting the carrying out of long-range strategic CCI planning.
- The initial planning mechanism.
- The results of this planning at the University of Minnesota.

Factors Inhibiting and Favoring Long-Range Strategic CCI Planning

When several staff members suggested a more formal strategic planning activity for CCI services, a number of forces inhibiting and other forces favoring such an activity became apparent. Some of the inhibiting factors were:

1. Lack of full recognition and appreciation of the potential profound, long-range effects of evolving CCI technology on the institution. These effects are related to the conversion of our economy and society to one based on information, and the emergence of office automation as a major tool for increasing productivity. Not everyone recognizes or accepts the reality of this revolutionary change; it is, to some extent, a prediction of an uncertain future. If it comes, it will have profound effects on educational programs and operations; if it does not, we will be wasting some of our time and resources. Thus, some of the senior officers questioned the need for and timeliness of strategic CCI planning.

2. Preoccupation with more immediate crises, such as state income shortfalls. In many large organizations, coping with immediate problems consumes so much energy that time spent on long-range planning—particularly where the future is in doubt or controversial—can easily appear to be a low-priority activity. This has been a particular problem in the last year, with the University of Minnesota facing almost catastrophic budget reductions.

3. The natural tension between planning and action. A plan can sometimes be treated as a constraint that prevents an organization from recognizing and taking advantage of changes in the environment and opportunities that arise independently of the plan. This is why strategic planning must focus on goals and avoid detail, and why tactical planning (which includes some of the detail) must be relatively short-range.

4. Reaction against the potentially detrimental personal and institutional effects of information technology. This problem was characterized most aptly by a university official who urged everyone " . . . to resist the effects of megatechnology on the character of the institution and the values it represents . . . " The threatening aspects of information technology and office automation have been extensively discussed.[6] We can attest that the threats are, indeed, perceived. Successful implementation of this technology, in universities or elsewhere, must recognize and deal with these understandable human reactions in a humane way.

Counter to these real inhibiting factors is a general attitude that there will be a future for the university and that the university can make that future a better environment for its students and society as a whole by charting its own way into the future. In fact, this attitude is a cornerstone of higher education's purpose. In addition to this supportive general philosophy, there are some very pragmatic reasons for the university to embrace long-range strategic planning for CCI services. These include:

1. The centrality of CCI activities to the university's mode of operation. Whatever the role of information technology in society, it is very likely to have a signficant impact on our educational programs; it will require new skills to use it effectively, new ways of teaching and using old skills (writing, for instance), and increased knowledge and wisdom to understand its social and economic ramifications.

2. Potential for increased productivity. Information technology provides significant opportunities to control and even reduce the costs of some necessary operations of universities. The university cannot maintain its credibility in society if it ignores these opportunities.

3. Appearance of good management. Government and society expect their agencies and businesses to plan for the future; failure to do so in conspicuous and effective ways significantly damages our credibility with those who support us.

4. Need for a strategic context in replacing the telephone system. The necessity of making an investment decision involving some $25 million for a telephone system that will affect the entire instituition for many years does not permit the University of Minnesota the luxury of avoiding some effort at long-range planning for information technology; it is simply impossible to make an intelligent decision about an investment this large without thinking about the future of computer and communications technology in the university.

The Initial Planning Mechanism

Considering the above factors and some staff agitation, the Central Officers Group (president, vice presidents, associate and assistant vice presidents, and some key directors) authorized the Vice President for Administration and Planning to establish a committee to address strategic long-range planning in the area of computer, communications, and information (CCI) services. Initially, the committee's work was viewed as planning for planning rather than the development of a detailed plan for CCI resources. Thus, the charge given to the committee was to study the situation faced by the university and to recommend a framework for a long-range plan and the mechanism to conduct the planning. Since there are a large number of stakeholders in the planning for CCI services, the committee consisted of two representatives designated by each of the six vice presidents. Included on the committee were a mixture of administrators with very limited technical backgrounds; administrators with considerable technical backgrounds and responsibilities for CCI service units; and the directors of the three major computer centers (academic, administrative, and hospital). The chairperson of the committee is a special assistant to the Vice President for Administration and Planning and a professor in the School of Management; he is not a stakeholder in existing CCI operations.

One of the first actions of the CCI Committee was to educate itself through reading of reports and articles on information technology, the business plans of the information industry, the social and economic factors driving applications of the technology, and responses of other universities and businesses to all of these factors. In addition to reading, a number of people who could speak to these issues visited with the committee to share their insights and perceptions and to react to the committee's thinking as it evolved. It was also possible for the committee, or some of its members, to take advantage of visits and presentations to the Telephone Resources committee and to other groups studying and procuring word processing equipment on a departmental basis. Some of the people who provided input to the CCI Committee in these ways include:

- Robert Massaro (President, XEROX Office Systems)
- Richard Van Horn (Executive Vice President, Carnegie-Mellon University)
- William Massy (Vice President for Finance, Stanford University)
- Ronald Brady (Executive Vice President, University of Illinois)
- Jack Kinsinger (Associate Provost, Michigan State University)
- Bernard Sheehan (University of Calgary and Manitoba Telephone Company)
- Robert Gillespie (Vice Provost for Computing, University of Washington)

- Albert MacLean (Director of Corporate Computer Operations, Honeywell)

During the course of its work, the committee also used a panel of reactors to its reports. These reactors were administrators from local business and government organizations; they included:

- Nancy Abraham (Assistant Commissioner of Administration, State of Minnesota);
- Walter Bruning (Vice President, Control Data Corporation);
- Herman Cain (Vice President, Corporate Systems and Services, Pillsbury);
- Gene Gross (Director of Data Processing, Cargill);
- Clyde Ingle (Executive Director, Minnesota Higher Education Coordinating Board);
- Carl Kuhrmeyer (Vice President for Administration, 3M);
- George Perry (Vice President for Information Systems, IDS);
- Roland Sullivan (Vice President, Management Services Division, First Bank System).

Since the committee was an administrative entity, it did not include representatives of the University Senate. Informal consultation did occur, however, with individual faculty members and with appropriate Senate committees. Formal presentations of the committee's reports were made to the Council of Academic Officers (deans), the University Senate Committee on Educational Policy, and the Regents Committee on Educational Policy and Long-Range Planning, as well as to the Central Officers Group.

The committee structured its output in the form of three reports. First the committee addressed the changing environment related to CCI services and the issues raised for the university by that change. In the second report, the committee discussed alternatives in the areas of:

1. Institutional goals for CCI services
2. Resource strategies for support of CCI services
3. Organization of CCI activities within the university
4. Major operating policies for CCI activities.

The third and final report contains the committee's recommendations in these four areas. Each of these reports is described in some detail in subsequent sections of this chapter. The development and discussion of the three reports constitutes the process to date of strategic long-range planning for CCI services at the University of Minnesota.

Progress Report 1: Environment and Issues

The committee decided to conduct and report its work to the vice presidents and others in the form of a series of progress reports which could serve as discussion papers. The first of these progress reports was completed and presented in July of 1981. It covered the following information:

1. A summary of existing computer and communications services provided at the University of Minnesota; their scope, staffing, budget, and some information on equipment inventory. This portion of the report established, for instance, that current university expenditures on central CCI services were about $14.6 million per year, or about 2 percent of the operating budget; that about 600 staff members were employed to deliver these services; and the total original value of the computing equipment inventory was about $35 million.

2. An analysis of the technical, economic, and social factors driving the U.S. economy toward intensive use of information technology to improve productivity, and some of the likely implications of these trends for higher education programs and operations. The conclusion of this analysis was that there are some questions about when and how the University of Minnesota will have to adapt to these changes, but that there is little doubt about whether it will happen.

3. Identification of four major areas in which the university must stake out a position to cope in a planned, coordinated, and effective manner with these changes:

a. The adoption of strategic goals for the university's applications of information technology to support its operations and programs. Should the University of Minnnesota, for instance, adopt a long-range goal of providing a computer-intensive environment for its students, as a few institutions have done recently? Or should we opt for a more modest environment or even for resistance to the use of information technology in some cases?

b. The consideration and selection of a resource strategy for providing the capital and operating funds necessary to support whatever level of goal is selected. We recognized quickly that financing the introduction of CCI technology will be one of the major challenges facing the university in the next several years; if nothing else, the problem of replacing our telephone system made this clear. Traditional financing mechanisms (state appropriations) may not be available to do some of the things that need to be done. Many new opportunities are available to take advantage of productivity improvements at all levels (including students). For example, exploiting discount opportunities via bulk purchasing; shifting certain costs to individual users, both departmentally and personally (how many faculty members and students will own microcomputers ten years from now?); and taking advantage of tax laws in imaginative ways (investment tax credit financing, for instance). We are not likely to just "luck out and fall into" some of these opportunities—we will have to plan and work at it if we hope to take advantage of them.

One technique used to explain the importance of resource strategy is shown in Figure 1, which projects schematically the growth in usage and in total costs of computer, telephone, and data communications services, using current technology. These drawings illustrate the consequences of remaining with analog telephone systems for data communications, rather than planning for the integration of digital-computer and telecommunications technology to meet the needs for both data and voice communications.

c. The organizational structure of the institution which will be best suited to manage achievement of the goals selected. The existing organization of CCI resources has operating responsibilities for the major central services assigned to the Vice President for Finance and Operations (telephone services,

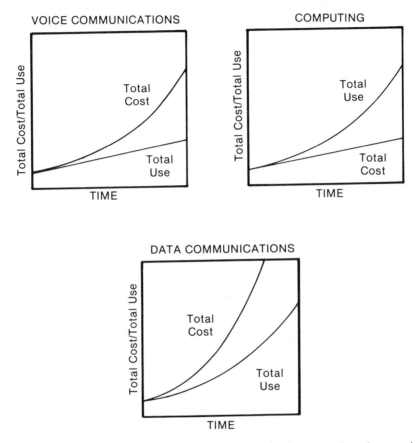

Figure 1. *A schematic representation of the growth of usage and total costs of voice communications, computing and data communications.*

administrative data processing, many other support services including printing and graphics, mailing, central duplicating, and purchasing), and to the Vice President for Academic Affairs (the academic computer centers, the university libraries, and audio-visual, radio, and television services).

There is some loose coordination of these services through the offices of the two vice presidents when the need is sufficiently apparent, and there are many ad hoc consultative arrangements as well. But there are also conspicuous gaps in the needs to which responses can be made, particularly in the area of assistance and support for departments needing access to information and to word processing and microcomputer facilities. The CCI Committee believes that, at least, the current organizational arrangements need to be reviewed and alternatives considered. Models of arrangements at many universities that have positions of associate provost or assistant vice president for computing services were used to indicate part of the range of alternatives.

d. Finally, interim policies and procedures to control the tactical decisions on acquisition and implementation of new projects, facilities, and services while long-range strategic planning is under way. In the face of complex decisions, a natural reaction is to place a moratorium or other controls on such decisions until there is an adequate basis and understanding to make them in an informed and planned manner; the Minnesota legislature did this in 1969. The prolific acquisition of word processing, minicomputer, and microcomputer equipment by departments is an obvious current example of development which could be controlled in this manner. In its first progress report, the CCI Committee recognized this problem and agreed to deal with the advantages and disadvantages of various kinds of control in its second report.

Following the presentation of the first progress report to the president and vice presidents in July 1981, the committee was directed to make similar presentations to three university groups: the University Senate Consultative Committee, the Council of Academic Officers, and the Regents. The purpose was to make them aware of the planning issues and to solicit their reactions and input prior to arriving at any conclusions or recommendations.

The committee was also instructed to consult with state officials for the same purpose and for the purpose of identifying any areas in which the committee could be working together with the state. One particular concern here was the common perception in the state that the university tries to be a pioneer in untested areas at the expense of the state taxpayer; pioneering and excellence are not always highly regarded by those who pay for it. To this end, the committee was asked to determine exactly what the universities of Michigan, Illinois, and Wisconsin were doing and whether we were ahead of them or behind. (At this point, the only public institution from which we had direct input was Wisconsin.)

Briefly, the outcome of these consultations was as follows:

1. The Senate Consultative Committee was skeptical of the value of such planning in the face of other university problems. However, several major committee chairmen expressed strong support.

2. The deans were interested and at least mildly supportive, but somewhat preoccupied with more immediate problems.

3. The Regents were most interested and generally supportive and even enthusiastic for the planning, even though they did not have much time to spend studying the written report; they requested that they be briefed on progress regularly, and this has been done.

4. State agency officials have been interested and supportive because they face most of the same problems. The only clear area of common interest with possiblities for joint action seems to be telecommunications beyond the Twin Cities metropolitan area.

5. Upon consulting formally and informally with other peer public universities (Michigan, Illinois, Wisconsin, Iowa, Washington), the committee has arrived at the following oversimplified generalization: Minnesota may be ahead of most of these institutions as far as strategic planning is concerned, but all of the others are beginning it either formally or in a fragmented, ad hoc fashion; it is almost impossible to deal with telecommunications issues without thinking in terms of a plan and a strategy. Iowa seems to have established a clearer and more systematic planning structure than Minnesota has, but several months later.

6. Minnesota is not pioneering in higher education applications of information technology, and the CCI Committee has not considered proposing this as a realistic alternative. Institutions such as MIT, Stanford, and Carnegie-Mellon, in which development work is being conducted on the use of M68000 and equivalent-scale micr-oprocessors for student and faculty use, are the pioneering institutions. In most cases, much of the pioneering is closely related to activities of computer science groups at these institutions.

Progress Report 2: Alternative Actions

The purpose of the second progress report, completed and presented to the vice presidents in November 1981, was to lay out the alternatives in the four major issue areas identified in the first progress report: strategic goals, resource strategies, organizational structures, and interim policies and procedures. In each of these areas, the report specified three or four alternatives which covered and characterized the range of possible alternatives, recognizing that the university might well select a combination rather than any one of the alternatives proposed.

Strategic Goals

The committee identified three levels of goals:

1. An *INTENSIVE* computer and communications environment for students, research and service programs, and institutional operations. The institution would strive to provide such an environment throughout most programs and operations of the university, and to be in the top quartile of the 20 or 30 leading public universities in this regard, reflecting the important role of high-technology industry in Minnesota's economy and the important role of this industry in the nation's economy.

2. A *COMPETITIVE* computer and communications environment, in which Minnesota would endeavor to maintain equivalence with peer institutions in many selected academic areas, and with peer institutions, state agencies, and local business in the cost-effectve uses of CCI technology in its operations.

3. A *REACTIVE* environment, in which the university would react to pressures to implement new applications of information technology only when necessary to do so for educational purposes or when justified by realizable cost savings.

Table 1 illustrates some of the possible impacts of each of these three alternative goals in eight areas of activity at the University of Minnesota.

Table 1. *Resource strategies*

Resource Strategies	Sources of Funds
Intensive Goal ($10 million per year)	
Major institutional support	Reallocation ($4 million/yr) User fees ($4 million/yr) Public subsidy ($1 million/yr) Private support ($1 million/yr)
Institutional plus significant state support	Reallocation ($4 million/yr) User fees ($2 million/yr) Public subsidy ($2 million/yr) Private support ($2 million/yr)
Major state and private support	Reallocation ($1 million/yr) User fees ($1 million/yr) Public subsidy ($4 million/yr) Private support ($4 million/yr)
Competitive Goal ($6 million per year)	
Institutional support	Reallocation ($2 million/yr) User fees ($2 million/yr) Public subsidy ($1 million/yr) Private support ($1 million/yr)
Institutional plus significant state support	Reallocation ($1 million/yr) User fees ($2 million/yr) Public subsidy ($2 million/yr) Private support ($1 million/yr)
Reactive Goal ($2 million per year)	
Institutional support	Reallocation ($1 million/yr) User fees ($1 million/yr) Public subsidy ($0 million/yr) Private support ($0 million/yr)
Institutional plus some state and private support	Reallocation ($1 million/yr) User fees ($0 million/yr) Public subsidy ($1 million/yr) Private support ($0 million/yr)
Some state and private support	Reallocation ($0 million/yr) User fees ($0 million/yr) Public subsidy ($1 million/yr) Private support ($1 million/yr)

Resource Strategies

In this area, the committee concluded that the order-of-magnitude incremental costs associated with each of the three goal alternatives would be $10 million, $6 million, and $2 million, respectively. (These highly speculative cost estimates were developed so that the audience for the report would have some idea of the resource commmitments that might be required.) It was concluded that there were three significant sources for this incremental cost:

1. Institutional sources, requiring budget reallocation or user fees.
2. State funding as part of the operating budget or as a special appropriation.
3. Private funding, including gifts, grants, and contracts, and payments for services.

Whatever the goals and whatever the strategy, the committee assumed that the institution would take maximum advantage of opportunities to save and recover costs resulting from improvements in technology and productivity, bulk purchase discounts, and standardization of equipment. And whatever the goal, it was assumed that all three sources would have to be drawn upon, but to different degrees.

These three sources of incremental funds were sorted into three resource strategies for each goal, as shown in Figure 2.

The purpose of laying out these resource strategies with order-of-magnitude guesses on dollar amounts is to permit those who will eventually be faced with making decisions to assess the relative probability of success for the various scenarios represented—something that could not be done without including some quantitative estimates.

Organizational Alternatives

The second progress report reviewed the existing organizational arrangements for CCI services in some detail. Five functions were identified for inclusion in any central management structure, and four different combinations of these were presented as reasonable alternatives.

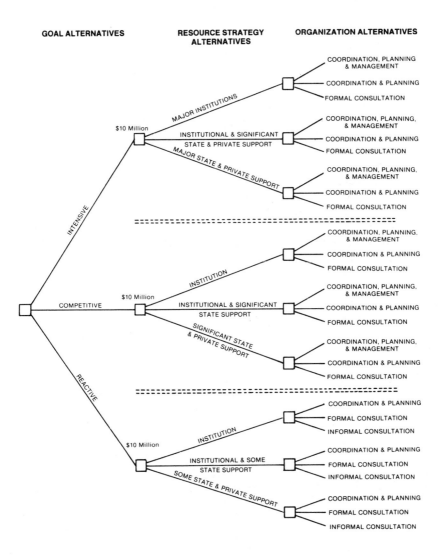

Figure 2. *Goal, resource strategy, and organization alternatives for computation, communications, and information services.*

The five functions are:

1. Coordination
2. Planning
3. Policy administration
4. Support and review
5. Line management

The four alternative combinations are:

1. Coordination, planning, and management
2. Coordination and planning
3. Formal consultation (committee method of coordination and planning)
4. Informal consultation (ad hoc arrangements)

A synthesis of the alternatives for goals, resource strategy, and organization is shown in Figure 2. The tree structure of this figure is intended to indicate the paths, patterns, and relationships between decisions in each of the three areas.

Interim Policies, Guidelines, and Procedures for the Management of CCI Services

The committee identified the following as primary candidates for interim coordination and control:

1. Any CCI proposals that carry with them implications for systems interconnection should be subject to central review. The choices in mode of interconnection could sorely limit future networking of separate systems. A review should be made of all current and proposed data and communications systems with the intent to standardize and integrate them as appropriate.

2. Word processing and departmental administration systems should be reviewed centrally to ensure favorable purchase and support arrangements and to ensure consistency and compatibility with central data processing, text processing, and communications facilities and developments.

3. Any peripheral equipment, data systems, or new systems development acquired or undertaken by university departments, schools, or service units should become solely the responsibility of that group. They should know that future university-wide changes are likely and that they are at risk if such changes make their acquisition incompatible with new systems. Purchases of this kind may have real merit and should be encourged if they may return their investment during an interim period.

4. No departmental or collegiate CCI service that duplicates a central service should be sold outside of that college or department unless rates are negotiated with the central agency also offering the service.

5. If new CCI systems or services are proposed that would derive income from sales to non-university users, a review should be made centrally to guard the university's non-profit status.

As mechanisms to carry out the implementation of these interim policies or guidelines, the committee considered the designation of a single central officer or office; establishment of a small administrative committee to conduct such functions; or distribution of the various functions among a few designated administrative officers who would consult with one another.

Progress Report 3: Recommendations

In March 1982, the committee forwarded its final recommendations to the senior officers. These recommendations were as follows:

1. The university should establish, as one of its highest-priority general goals, the development of an "intensive" CCI environment. It should be recognized that this development may require incremental resources which eventually may exceed $10 million per year in 1982 dollars.

Rationale: Factors supporting this recommendation include the following:

  a. Students are expected to demand an intensive CCI environment.
  b. Society is rapidly increasing its dependence on CCI technology.
  c. Substantial improvements in the operations of the university can be achieved.

d. Other universities, government agencies, and business and industry will use this technology effectively and extensively, creating expectations and demands that it be used comparably at the University of Minnesota if that institution is to remain competitive.

e. Certain social and scientific problems can be attacked more effectively by using CCI technology that permits the integration of data from many locations (regions, nations, etc.) and disciplines.

2. In order to support the development of an intensive CCI environment, the university should plan to obtain incremental resources which will grow eventually to as much as $10 million per year (1982 dollars) in the following way:

Direct reallocation from existing budgets: $4 million per year
Increased user fees: $2 million per year
State support: $2 million per year
Private support: $2 million per year

These funds are in addition to an expected $4 million per year tnat should be provided by direct productivity savings resulting from applications of the technology.

Rationale: Factors supporting this strategy of heavy reliance on internal resources include:

a. The weak fiscal condition of the state of Minnesota.
b. A reluctance of the public and elected officials to support CCI development as a capital expenditure.
c. A prevalent social philosophy that those who benefit should carry most of the financial burden.
d. The need for stable, long-term support.

3. The university should use its bonding authority or some similar mechanism to establish a fund of at least $5 million that can be used to finance the development of administrative system improvements that can pay for themselves through cost savings. In addition to developing the fund, the university should develop the necessary decision and control systems to ensure the integrity of the development fund. Within these control systems, care must be exercised to ensure that operating units have real incentives to undertake cost-saving projects.

Rationale: This recommendation provides a necessary mechanism to overcome the lack of investment capital in units that have the potential for substantial cost savings through the use of CCI technology.

4. The university should immediately establish as a general policy that the commitment to and direction of growth in CCI services will be subject to policies, plans, and priorities established centrally by the senior officers. A single central administrative office should be made responsible for proposing, interpreting, and enforcing CCI policies. This same office should also be responsible for the planning and coordination of CCI activities at the institutional level. Initially, the university should establish the specific policies noted below:

a. *Interconection.* The system design interface criteria, development goals, and priorities related to telecommunications interconnect system(s) will be defined by plans prepared by the office responsible for coordinating CCI activities. Any purchases of equipment or system development that have the possibility of using the central university interconnect system or a limited interconnect system (local network) must receive prior approval from this office.

b. *Microcomputers.* The university will try to standardize its purchases of microcomuters to a relatively limited number of types, for the purpose of facilitating acquisition, maintenance, and software, hardware, and communications support. Favorable purchase terms will be arranged through the purchasing department. Maintenance and support of software, hardware, and communications will be provided through the coordinated activities of the university's major computing and telecommunications centers.

c. *Word and Text Processing.* It is necessary to distinguish three kinds of word and text processing: (1) administrative office word processing; (2) student text processing; and (3) faculty text processing. Each kind will play a major role in the university's future programs, and it will be difficult to afford separate systems for each; hence, all three kinds will need to be integrated and supported to some appropriate degree. It will also be important to integrate administrative office word processing with the major central administrative systems. Departments and colleges that propose to install or significantly improve administrative office word processing systems must ensure that their proposals are consistent with university plans for administrative systems development. Departments and colleges that propose new or improved text processing systems for faculty and student use must ensure that their proposals are not inconsistent with plans for administrative office word processing and with institutional CCI support plans for programs of instruction and research.

d. *Data Bases.* Institutional data bases containing administrative data (student, course, personnel, payroll, financial, space, equipment, library) must have appropriate logical interfaces to permit the extraction and combination of data to support central administration as well as collegiate and departmental information needs. Each data base is, appropriately, the responsibility of an operating department; these departments must make trade-off decisions between structuring data bases to support operations which collect and use the data, and structuring them for easy retrieval of information. While provision of information from individual data bases should remain a responsibility of operating departments, the responsibility for providing information across individual data bases should be assumed by a central CCI service operation, advised by operating units on questions of release and integrity of data to be extracted. Specific design features and development priorities within and among the major administrative data systems will be defined in plans prepared by the institutional CCI planning and coordinating office.

e. *Printing, Graphics, and Duplication.* All major equipment and systems proposals dealing with printing, graphics, and duplication services should be addressed as part of an integrated institutional printing and graphics program. This integrated program should, in turn, be part of the overall institutional plans for CCI activities.

f. *Departmental System Support.* The central administration and central service units have no responsibility to assist with the

maintenance or support of a collegiate or departmental CCI
system unless that system has been specifically accepted as
part of the overall institutional CCI plans and programs.

g. *Internal Competition.* Any college or department providing CCI
services to another unit or member of the university community must have approval for such activities under the Regents'
Policy on Business Enterprises (1980). The Vice President for
Finance and Operations is responsible for administering this
policy and for approving rates under it. Units seeking such
approval should refer their requests through the CCI planning
and coordinating office for review and submission to this vice
president.

h. *External Sales.* Any college or department providing CCI services to parties outside of the university must have approval
for such activities and associated rates under the Regents'
Policy on Business Enterprises (1980), administered by the
Vice President for Finance and Operations. Units seeking such
approval should refer their requests through the CCI planning
and coordinating office for review and submission to this vice
president.

Rationale: These policies provide an initial basis for bringing some
institutional control to the proliferation of CCI services and equipment in the university. The purpose of this control is to better integrate CCI components and services to provide the maximum level of
service to the university community at the lowest total cost. Without
this optimization, it is unlikely that the goal of an intensive CCI
environment can be achieved.

5. The university should establish an office at the associate vice
president level to carry out the following responsibilities:

a. Development of institutional CCI plans, policies, and programs (including appropriate organizational change).

b. Integration of major unit and institutional planning in the CCI
area.

c. Coordination with the Office of Development and Alumni
Relations and the Office of Institutional Relations in presenting the funding needs for CCI services to potential supporters.

   d. Monitoring and evaluation of both centralized and decentral-
      ized CCI services to ensure efficiency and conformance to uni-
      versity policies.
   e. Assistance in developing resource allocation methods for CCI
      developments and operations.
   f. Review of the capital and operating budget plans of the major
      central CCI service units and presentation of them to the Bud-
      get Executive.

Rationale: This recommendation is the result of a careful analysis
of the scope of activities to be covered by a central administration
office and the appropriate level of control to be exercised by this
office.

6. The university should immediately establish a single office
responsible for the operation and maintenance of all CCI interconnection systems, including telephone systems, broad-band and
closed-circuit cable television systems, microwave systems, building
management and security systems, and similar facilities.

Rationale: The major issue here is simply the consolidation of the
line management responsibility for systems that will be increasingly
integrated and potentially competitive. Substantial cost savings may
result from careful design and sharing of these facilities. The total
capital investment and annual operating cost of all of these systems
together can provide a pool of funds which should support each one
of them better than would be possible separately.

7. The university should establish immediately an interim group,
under the general supervision of the senior officers and the day-to-
day direction of the Vice President for Administration and Planning,
to begin the planning and coordination of activities expected of the
proposed permanent organization. This group should consist of
appropriate individuals on full-time or part-time temporary assignments. One person should be clearly designated with responsibility
and authority to direct the efforts of the group.

Rationale: This recommendation recognizes the urgency of some CCI issues at the University of Minnesota, especially those related to severe budget restrictions imposed by the state of Minnesota. It also recognizes the benefits of taking specific action to demonstrate a real commitment to the goal of an intense educational CCI environment.

Expected Response to the CCI Committee's Recommendations

The CCI Committee made its final report to the president and vice presidents in early April 1982. The committee also plans to report to the deans, the Senate Consultative Committee, and the Regents to explain and discuss its recommendations. At this point, the committee expects the vice presidents to manage further consultation with these groups and to receive advice from them and from the line managers of departments and service units on the recommendations made and their implementation. Although individual members of the committee will surely be called upon to participate and advise in these consultations, the committee itself will cease to function following its final report. It will be up to the president and vice presidents to take action on the recommendations and the advice received through this consultative process. Should many of the recommendations be accepted, the committee expects that the final details of their implementation will be worked out by the person or persons to whom major responsibility is assigned for implementation.

In any case, the decisions will be made at the highest policy level of the university, and any implementation will have to be carried out with the active support and understanding of the president and vice presidents. The support and active cooperation of the vice presidents, who are responsible for the line operating units of the university, are essential to the credibility and effectiveness of whatever policies and planning and coordinating mechanisms are established.

Opportunities

As mentioned during the course of the above exposition, there are several major opportunities for the University of Minnesota to exploit in adopting the kind of long-range strategic plan that has been under development. These include:

1. A major enhancement of the university's educational programs—its ability to attract students, to prepare them better to cope both personally and vocationally with a rapidly changing, technology-intensive society.

2. Major enhancements of the university's research and service programs, enabling it to contribute more and more effectively to state and national needs, to the advancement of technology and its applications, and to the advancement of our understanding of and sensitivity to its effects on people and society.

3. A framework to evaluate, explain, and justify future developments at the university. Many of these CCI improvements will be necessary whether or not there is a strategic plan. Planning will permit such developments to be viewed as part of an overall design rather than as a surprise, thereby enhancing rather than compromising the university's credibility.

4. An effective theme for attracting substantial external resources from the private sector.

5. Increased prospects for recapturing and saving money by coordinating development and other activities to take best advantage of economies of scale and bulk purchasing, reducing unneeded duplication of facilities and services, increasing standardization and compatibility of equipment, and designing incentives to reward actions and decisions which are consistent with all of these interests.

The end product of the CCI Committee is a plan for planning. The structure it proposes will be responsible for the actual detailed planning and for implementation. The acceptability of the proposed recommendations depends on the response of the university community and on the actions of the university administration.

References

1. Governor's Advisory Committee for State Information Systems. "Computers and Information Systems in Higher Education"; a part of the report, *Information Systems in the State of Minnesota, 1970-1980.* State of Minnesota: Office of the Governor, 1970. *
2. President's Science Advisory Committee. *Computers in Higher Education* (the Pierce Report). Washington, D.C.: U.S. Government Printing Office: 1967.
3. Governor's Joint Committee on Computers in Education. *A Proposed Educational Computing Services Organization: Its Facilities and Services.* State of Minnesota: Office of the Governor, revised edition, 1973. *
4. Task Force on the Future of Computing at Stanford. *Future Directions: Information Technology in Support of Scholarly and Administrative Activities.* Stanford University: Center for Information Technology, 1981.
5. "Universal Access to Personal Computers is Urged for College Students, Professors." *Chronicle of Higher Education,* January 19, 1981.
6. Marcus, Jane. "Report of the Study Group on Text Processing, Appendix G." An annotated bibliography found in *Future Directions: Information Technology in Support of Scholarly and Administrative Activities.* (See reference 4).

* Copies of these reports are accessible through the Minnesota Educational Computing Consortium, 2520 Broadway St. NE, St. Paul, MN 55113.

11

HUMBOLDT STATE UNIVERSITY
CALIFORNIA STATE UNIVERSITY, CHICO
SONOMA STATE UNIVERSITY
CALIFORNIA STATE UNIVERSITY, SACRAMENTO
SAN FRANCISCO STATE UNIVERSITY
CALIFORNIA STATE UNIVERSITY, HAYWARD
SAN JOSE STATE UNIVERSITY
CALIFORNIA STATE COLLEGE, STANISLAUS
CALIFORNIA STATE UNIVERSITY, FRESNO
CALIFORNIA POLYTECHNIC STATE UNIVERSITY
SAN LUIS OBISPO

CALIFORNIA STATE COLLEGE, BAKERSFIELD
CALIFORNIA STATE POLYTECHNIC UNIVERSITY,
POMONA
CALIFORNIA STATE UNIVERSITY, NORTHRIDGE
CALIFORNIA STATE UNIVERSITY, LOS ANGELES
CALIFORNIA STATE UNIVERSITY, DOMINGUEZ HILLS
CALIFORNIA STATE UNIVERSITY, LONG BEACH
OFFICE OF THE CHANCELLOR, LONG BEACH
CALIFORNIA STATE UNIVERSITY, FULLERTON
CALIFORNIA STATE COLLEGE, SAN BERNARDINO
SAN DIEGO STATE UNIVERSITY
IMPERIAL VALLEY CAMPUS, CALEXICO

The California State University

THOMAS W. WEST
Director, Division of Information Systems

Introduction

The mission of The California State University (CSU) is to provide a quality learning environment for its teaching, research, and public service functions. Primarily, this involves transmitting knowledge from faculty to students using various modes of communication.

During the history of civilized mankind, there have been three major revolutions in the modes of human communication—the advent of the spoken word, the discovery of writing, and the invention of printing. As the 21st century approaches, our society finds itself in the midst of the fourth major communications revolution—the explosion of electronic communication, utilizing solid-state electronics advanced by the development of computing. This revolution is making it possible to electronically transmit voices, images, data, and words in an integrated fashion from one remote point to another. This phenomenon currently affects every person in many ways and promises to expand its impact, especially in higher education where the primary function is the transmission of knowledge.

To stay at the forefront in the delivery of knowledge, The California State University needs to capitalize on the opportunities this fourth revolution offers. Presently, faculty, staff, and students communicate with each other using individual media items such as voice, pen and paper, telephones, computer terminals, mail service, conferences, classrooms, etc. The converging technologies which are allowing the integration of communication through the electronic technology will provide greatly enhanced delivery of the services of computing, telephone, electronic mail, library activities, word/text processing, printing/duplicating, and micrographics. This will substantially improve the ability of faculty to transmit knowledge to students.

Currently, the planning and the management of these services are divided among various units on most campuses and within the chancellor's office. This fragmentation is the natural result of the distinct historical and evolutionary paths each of these services has followed. However, as the CSU confronts the opportunities afforded by the electronic communications revolution, each campus and the system need to pursue a coordinated approach to planning. The result must be an appropriately integrated technological environment on and across campuses to enable students, faculty, and staff who use these services to fulfill their respective roles.

The period from 1982 to 1987 will be crucial to each campus's success in attaining a comprehensive integrated technological approach by the beginning of the 21st century. During the next five years, significant gains can be made if the management at the campuses and in the chancellor's office focus on planning and implementing strategies that appropriately integrate the information technologies and, where appropriate, consolidate the campus management structures associated with these various services.

This chapter identifies the major opportunities and issues facing the information-technology management function of the campuses and the system* at the CSU over the next five years and, where pos-

*The scope of the information-technology management function as conceived in this strategic plan includes: computing services communications (data, telephone and television); office systems technologies (word processing systems, electronic mail, dictation, copying/printing); administrative information systems development and maintenance; instructional computing support; and technological resources which impact the library and learning resource services of the campuses.

sible, focuses on an action designed to make significant progress toward the long-range goal of technological integration. A framework is provided for the campuses and the system to use in the on-going planning of information-technology resources, but the framework must be viewed as just a snapshot in time.

Within this overall statement of future direction and foci, each campus will develop its own operational plan of projects and priorities to be accomplished over a three- to five-year period, and annual system-wide priorities and plans will be developed. These operational plans will be updated annually, and will be closely tied to the budget planning cycle. This overall framework will be re-examined and updated annually.

The Planning Environment: Present and Projected

Demography

The California State University (CSU) is a system of 19 campuses enrolling over 300,000 students . It employs over 30,000 faculty and staff members and has an operating budget of nearly $1 billion. It is one of three major public systems of higher education in the state of California and has as its primary mission the education of students.

The CSU offers a wide range of academic programs at its 19 institutions. Each institution has its distinctive characteristics, yet in this heterogeneous system there are many large, common needs which apply to all campuses.

Instruction

The uses of information technology in support of the instructional programs have been developing in recent years. Each year an increasing percentage of faculty uses computing and other information resources as aids in the instruction of students. Yet, there is a large untapped potential for the use of information technology in instruction.

As information-technology literacy becomes increasingly important to being an educated person, it is anticipated that nearly every academic discipline and a very high percentage of the faculty will use some facet of information technology as an aid in the instruction process by the year 2000.

Management

The uses of information technology in support of the operational and management activities of each campus and the system have been evolutionary. Most computerized information-systems activity currently augments manual office procedures and there has been very little exploitation of the emerging office-systems technology. Major interest and activity is brewing on all fronts to develop on-line computer-information systems and office-automation technology to support the operational and management needs of each campus and the system. By the beginning of the next century it is projected that each campus will have a fully integrated, comprehensive, information-management system and will be utilizing the full range of office-automation technology.

Vision

As we forecast into the future and envision the interaction of people and technology in the year 2000, the following scenarios may well depict a typical day on the campuses of the CSU:

- Vice presidents and deans start the day by signing onto desktop terminals to check their calendars and act on documents in their electronic "in baskets." They send memos, correct and print drafts of reports, set up and conduct meetings, and pore over management reports—all without touching a pencil or paper, or leaving their desks.
- Middle managers and supervisors start by checking appointments, checking and sending memos, correcting and printing reports, listing all the day's tasks for secretaries, and asking for records.

- Secretaries and clericals sign onto their workstations and review the day's work. One requests mailing labels for a promotional letter. Another prepares the form letter of request, which will "merge" with the mailing list to several memos and letters—again, without touching a pencil or paper or leaving the station.

- Faculty check and answer mail, and send memos and reports to each other for review. They analyze data and incorporate the resulting tables and graphs directly into reports. On a typical morning a faculty member might set up an experiment to run and feed data directly into the computer. While it runs, he drafts a few pages of class notes or an article and makes minor corrections on another—moving one paragraph, deleting another, adding items to the list of references, running the document through the spelling checker, and reviewing the final product before printing. He later calls up the record of a student with whom he is counseling academically.

- Students do assignments, take tests, evaluate classes, write and print papers, leave notes for teachers, and check library indexes for articles and books on topics they are studying using a portable workstation that can be used from a residence hall room, an on-campus laboratory, or from home.[1]

Mission and Goals

Mission

The mission of the information-technology management function within The California State University, at both the campus and system levels, is to plan, develop, implement, maintain, and manage in a cost-effective manner those technologies and resources necessary to assist:

- The faculty and students in the teaching/learning process and the faculty in their acquisition of knowledge through instructionally related research, scholarly publications, and creative works.

- The administration in the effective and efficient management of the programs and resources entrusted to it by the state and the Board of Trustees as it serves the students.
- The faculty and administration in rendering appropriate public services to citizens, agencies, and organizations throughout the state of California.

Instructional Goals

The campuses of the CSU have in common several basic information-technology management goals for the accomplishment of their instructional and instruction-related research missions in this changing e ment. These goals are to:

- Develop a higher degree of information-technology literacy among students.
- Improve the problem-solving capabilities of students in a technological society.
- Facilitate the teaching/learning process by using information technology as an aid.
- Enhance the instructional research and scholarly efforts of the faculty.

Within these general goals, each campus and its various academic departments will have specific goals for the uses of information technology as a tool, as an academic discipline (computer science), as an aid in learning, or as a skill requirement for the completion of a degree.

Management Goals

The administrators of the campuses and the system have several common information-technology-related goals for managing the 19 institutions and the chancellor's office. These are to develop for each campus and the chancellor's office an information management system and the technological capability which will:

- Satisfy the need for information, and thereby aid all academic and administrative departments in their day-to-day operations and decisions.
- Make readily available to the campus, the system administrators, and the Board of Trustees, information needed for their short-term and long-range strategy decisions.
- Enable the CSU to provide reports to the external agencies relative to the "state of the CSU."
- Provide effective services to the students and faculty who are engaged in the activities of learning and to the staff who provide support for the learning process.
- Increase the productivity of the management and staffs of the campuses and chancellor's office through the effective use of information technology in their office functions.

Public Service Goals

The CSU is in the initial stages of developing information-technology goals in support of its public servic. These goals will be designed to provide special resources and services which will enable each campus to more effectively serve constituent organizations and agencies throughout its service area.

Support of Instruction and Research

Goals

In contrast to the current industrial-based society, The California State University will be operating in a knowledge-based environment by the year 2000. The lives of educated people in such a society will be inextricably linked with information technology. An increasing level of information-technology literacy will be needed to enable them to take advantage of the challenges and opportunities of the new environment. This literacy should include a level of knowledge that enables a student to:

- Appreciate the broad implications of this technology.

- Use computing and communications technology in his or her professional, vocational, social, family, and personal environments.
- Maintain a high degree of confidence in the effectiveness, efficiency, and security of the systems.

Already the information-technology revolution has penetrated business, government, and industry. Each campus in the CSU must integrate the technologies of word, data, image, and voice processing in the academic environment to better serve and motivate students entering this society. The long-range objective is to enable an individual student or faculty member to access a wide range of internal campus and external resources via a personal technology workstation.

Current Status

Faculty and students on all 19 campuses have access to a solid core of computing resources in both applications software and hardware. The recent installation of a new Cyber computer on each campus has enabled increased usage among current users and has ignited interest among potential users. Unfortunately, there is a shortage of professional staff to meet the burgeoning needs. Only in the last two years have there been funds for an Instructional Computing Coordinator for each campus. As the number of users grows, additional professional consultants will be needed to assist the users in effectively using computing and other technology resources.

Thrusts

For the next five years, efforts will involve building on the current program capabilities and developing new ones. Specifically, the major tasks involve planning and managing:

- The development and skills training of faculty and staff.
- A variety of programming languages and applications software used by students preparing for careers in education, business, government, and industry.

- The large statistical analysis needs of an ever-increasing number of users.
- The growing academic text-management activities of faculty.
- The emerging need for graphics.
- The phenomena of personal microcomputers.
- The role of computer-based education as a pedagogical tool.

Basic Services

Two primary foci of the CSU program activities will be to continue to take advantage of the economies of scale through system-wide acquisition and maintenance of major proprietary software and data bases, while increasing the quantity and quality of professional staff on each campus to provide user consulting and user-education services.

Each campus computing center, through its Instructional Computing Coordinator and staff, will be responsible for:

- Developing and expanding the consulting services to faculty and students.
- Designing and conducting user education and training programs for faculty and students.
- Working with academic departments to ascertain and plan for their future needs.
- Managing, where appropriate, staff and technological resources to meet the needs of the users.

To enhance the system-wide acquisition, maintenance, and delivery of programming languages, software, and data bases to meet new and changing requirements of the instructional programs, the Instructional Support Group within the Division of Information Systems will continue to be responsible for:

- Coordinating the acquisition and installation of new applications software.
- Providing system-wide, high-level technical support for the existing applications software library.

- Providing consulting and coordination services to the campus Instructional Computing Coordinators and their respective staff members.
- Working with appropriate CSU-wide academic-discipline user groups to ascertain and plan for their special academic needs which can be satisfied on a system-wide basis.
- Developing and presenting seminars and consultant workshops on the use of instructional software and hardware resources.
- Maintaining a liaison with state, national, and international professional associations and other organizations.

New Foci

In addition to building on the existing activities during the next five years, particular attention must also be given to developing and implementing capabilities which provide students and faculty training and access to the emerging technological resources.

Faculty/Staff Training

An increasing number of faculty and staff members are aware of the importance of, and recognize the need for, the ability to use information technology in the performance of their work. A vast majority of these individuals have not had an opportunity to acquire the knowledge and skills necessary to make effective use of these tools. Consequently, a major focus of the CSU must be on faculty and staff development programs which provide education in the use of these productivity tools.

Word/Text Processing

Of major importance is the emergence of word/text processing which portends significant demands on existing and projected hardware resources of the CSU. Historically, the manipulation of words has been the lifeblood of the academician. As more faculty members become aware of the power of technology to improve scholarly production, the campuses must have in place the resources to meet this demand. This will involve acquiring the necessary software and hardware to assure the individual user technical concurrence in his uses of both word and data processing.

Graphics

The growing availability of sophisticated graphics hardware and software is an opportunity to provide an important capability for the instructional program. The foci here will involve:

- Acquiring hardware and software resources to implement basic graphics capability on each campus.
- Acquiring hardware and software resources to implement a computer-aided design (to be located where appropriate) and computer-aided manufacturing (CAD/CAM) capability.
- Investigating the requirements for image processing of large data bases such as satellite-generated LANDSAT and SEASAT (to be located where appropriate).

Computer-Assisted Instruction

The use of computer-assisted instruction (CAI) in teaching the basic skills and in the acquisition of advanced special skills has been evolving over a number of years. Planning on campuses will call for providing the effective and efficient use of such tools. Specifically, it involves:

- Developing plans for the appropriate uses of microcomputers in the delivery of CAI.
- Developing plans for the appropriate use of system-wide and campus mainframe computers.
- Stimulating development of quality courseware by faculty members.
- Planning appropriate mechanisms to ensure and maintain the quality of courseware offered to students.

External Data Bases

Increasingly, faculty members and students have the need and desire to access bibliographic data, library catalogs, census data, and other forms of specialized data bases that are maintained on separate computing networks scattered across the United States. To be responsive, the CSU must determine cost-effective methods of acquiring access to specialized information resources such as national network facilities in software and data bases residing at governmental and industrial sites and at other universities.

Specialty Centers

As new service opportunities emerge, an integral part of future planning will involve developing specialty resource centers on various campuses to serve the needs of the entire CSU system. For example, Sacramento has been designated as the location of a computer-based education (PLATO) distribution center to serve the CSU, other educational institutions, and non-profit organizations. One of the campuses may very well be designated the center for high-level graphics services. One or more of the campuses with strong engineering programs may be asked to provide the leadership and support for CAD/CAM for the CSU. Such a strategy is designed to capitalize on the special talents of professional personnel located throughout the university system.

Support of Institutional Management

Goals

The CSU faces the challenge of managing its resources more effectively and efficiently while maintaining and enhancing its academic quality. This calls for more informed decision making at all levels of the campus and the system, and for improved productivity on the part of the members of the administration. Improving decision making and productivity will involve:

- Developing a comprehensive integrated management system for each campus, as depicted in Figure 1.
- Putting into place the technological resources and organizational changes that will enable an individual staff member to handle information in its many forms, using a single technology workstation as a tool, as depicted in Figure 2.

As in the academic environment, the CSU must integrate the technologies of word, data, image, and voice in order to serve the staff needs and to increase the output of the administration.

Current Status

The campuses of the CSU have been developing and implementing operationally oriented systems for the past decade. Much of this effort has been through centralized system-wide applications. However, most campuses out of necessity have developed special modules of various systems to meet unique campus needs. As a consequence, the quantity and quality of integration of a campus's

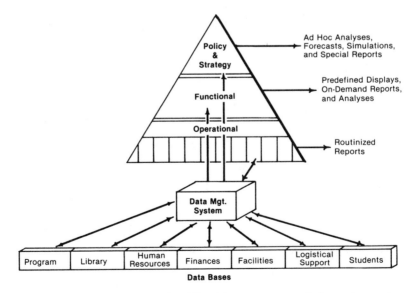

Figure 1. *The desired state of California's management information system.*

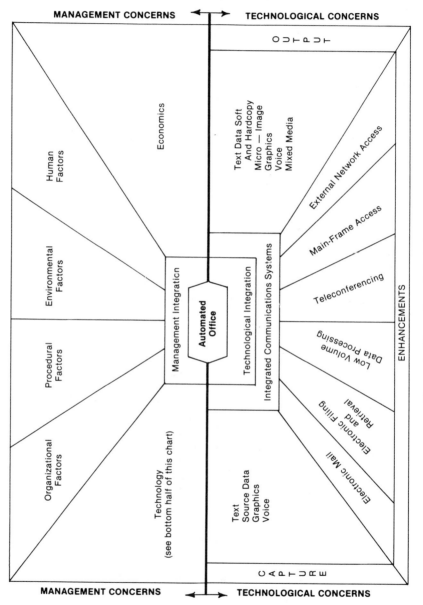

Figure 2. *The socio-technical system.*

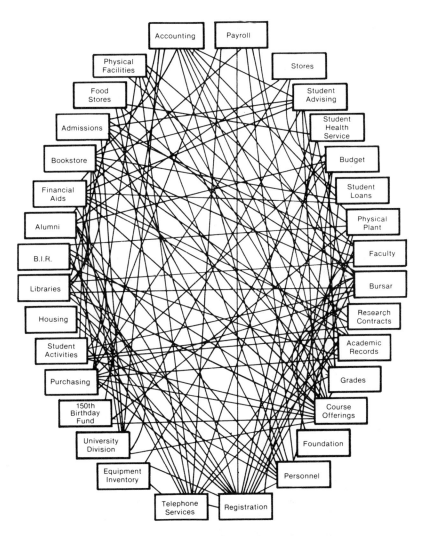

Figure 3. *Before a management information system.*

information management system varies from campus to campus. Figure 3 depicts the worst case of the fragmentation. In addition, most of the existing systems are technologically dated, using batch computing methods for entering and accessing data/information files.

In automating the office to gain greater productivity, the CSU campuses have followed the typical path of most organizations. While there exists a wide mixture of tools and devices to process words, handle dictation, copy materials, and facilitate voice communications, very little has been done to coordinate their implementation and integrate their uses. In essence, the campuses of the CSU run the risk of developing a technological jungle in the office unless there is some coordinated planning.

Information Systems Thrust

Very few corporations or institutions have been successful in making a quantum leap from fragmented operationally oriented systems (see Figure 3) to a comprehensive fully integrated information management system (see Figure 1). Most institutions of higher education that achieved a modest degree of success over the past decade did so by evolving toward a total integration. The first step is to put into place systems that integrate data as a corporate resource to meet needs of multiple operations on each campus.

As the CSU and its campuses focus on the institutional management needs of the next five years, the emphasis will be given to developing on-line integrated information systems in the following system categories: student, program/curriculum, human resources, business/financial, facilities, library, and logistical support. To be effective in developing and implementing these systems there must be cooperative efforts—sharing of human and financial resources—between the chancellor's office and the campuses. For instance, certain modules of these systems will be acquired and developed on a system-wide basis for implementation at all 19 campuses. The chancellor's office resources will be heavily dedicated to these modules.

Other modules will have utility and importance for several but not all 19 campuses. In these instances, the resources of the campuses involved should be pooled with one campus serving as the leader and pilot for implementation. The chancellor's office will assist in coordination and software acquisition.

There will always be information system modules that have utility and importance for a specific campus. In these instances, the campus affected will dedicate its own resources and the chancellor's office will assist where possible and serve as a clearinghouse to ensure that such a module does not already exist elsewhere.

Table 1 shows the breakdown of systems modules and how the CSU plans to approach their development and implementation.

To ensure that development and implementation of the information system module will move each campus toward an integrated information management system in a timely fashion, the CSU strategy involves:

- Treating data as a campus-wide and as a system-wide resource. This means utilizing standardized data-element definitions and establishing campus-to-campus system controls and management procedures.
- Developing and implementing on-line systems which give the users immediate access to update and inquire into the various data bases.
- Managing systems development projects, utilizing a standard project management system.
- Acquiring packaged applications whenever cost-effective.
- Providing the tools so users can make ad hoc data inquiry and retrieval.
- Operating the systems and managing the data for all campus modules on the campus computing facilities.
- Maintaining and updating the systems as the user needs change and technology advances.

Office Automation Thrust

Automating the office offers an opportunity for each CSU campus and the chancellor's office to significantly improve their management productivity and create a quality working environment for the staff. Office automation offers a major opportunity for each campus and the system, but will necessitate solid planning and implementation of word processing, electronic mail, records management,

Table 1. *CSU Information Management System*

Assignment category	All-campus modules	Multi-campus modules	Single-campus modules	Chancellor's office modules
Student	Admissions Records Transcript Alumni Financial aids Student billing and collection	Articulation Housing Prospective students Student employment Scholarship	Student program reporting Student certification Graduate admissions Athletic scheduling International studies	Census auditing Enrollment reporting EOP CPEC reporting Disabled students
Program	Curriculum (class schedules) Registration			Academic planning
Human resources	Employee history Payroll Position control/salary savings Leave accrual Applicant tracking Skills inventory		Telephone directory	Statistical analysis

Table 1. CSU Information Management System (cont.)

Assignment category	All-campus modules	Multi-campus modules	Single-campus modules	Chancellor's office modules
Financial management	Financial Accounts payable Accounts receivable Purchasing Budgeting Student accounts Financial aid billing ATSS			Budget data CFIS Financial reporting/auditing
Facilities	Space and facilities			Space and facilities utilization
Library	Circulation Public access Acquisitions Union shelf list			
Logistical support	Work order control Planned maint. Plant op. chargeback Equip. inventory	Health services	Vehicle registration Parking Key control	

executive scheduling, teleconferencing, and other capabilities, as depicted in Figure 2. Specifically, the system and each campus's planning and implementation must focus on:

- Acquiring office automation software and hardware that is technologically compatible with the campus communications network.

- Standardizing and acquiring word processing software and hardware that will enable the staff member to use one workstation for both word and data processing, and will provide for easy transfer from one campus department to another.

- Establishing procedures and allocating professional human resources to conduct office systems studies in various campus units to determine need and plan for the organizational changes and technological hardware installations.

- Studying and recommending the appropriate approaches and implementation plans for the use of electronic mail, executive calendar scheduling, electronic filing, and teleconferencing.

Support of Public Service

As the CSU examines its missions, program activities, and resources in service to its supporting constituencies, the information-technology function should play a significant role. In essence, our sophisticated information-technology network should serve as the backbone of a 21st-century delivery system of knowledge services, similar to what the Agricultural Extension System of the land grant universities has done since the late 19th century.

Given that the CSU would take a more proactive posture toward public service, information technologies might be used to:

- Establish computer-based education distribution centers for northern and southern California to serve elementary and secondary schools, community colleges, and other post-secondary institutions.

- Establish the CSU network as a center for the newly developed computer-aided design/computer-aided manufacturing (CAD/CAM) technology capability.
- Provide applied-research and service centers for corporations and organizations that cannot afford to acquire their own CAD/CAM system.

Through public-service activities, campuses can strengthen relationships, secure financial support, and enhance institutional images with their constituencies.

Governance and Management

Goals

The CSU is a complex, dynamic, and organic system of heterogeneous campuses. The development and implementation of the electronic communications revolution demands more coordinated strategic planning and operational management of the services encompassed in the information-technology function, both at the system-wide and campus levels.

It is important for the chancellor's office to have in place policy and management mechanisms that optimize the commonality of information-technology needs across campuses while recognizing the distinctive characteristics and special needs of individual campuses. Likewise, each campus must have policies and mechanisms in place to optimize the mission of the campus while recognizing the uniqueness of the various academic schools and departments.

To manage the information-technology services toward our long-range goals, these campus and system-wide mechanisms must strive to achieve:

- Viable system-wide and campus adaptive-planning and policy-formulation processes that are responsive to opportunities and constraints.

- Effective management of system-wide and campus planning and monitoring systems that can translate strategic plans into operating plans, allocate scarce resources, measure performance, and monitor progress.
- Prudent, cost-effective, and efficient system-wide and campus management of all resources necessary to our mission, including human, budgetary, technological, and facility resources.
- The management of information as a campus and system resource.
- An architecturally sound, stable, and effective electronic information service system for the campus and throughout the CSU.
- An adequate system of applications that can satisfy the needs of each campus in its instructional, administrative, and public-service programs, and the chancellor's office for its corporate management.
- An adequate support system composed of staff, equipment, and managers which will assure viable operation of the service and application systems at each campus.
- A view of the campus and CSU information-technology environment as a positive indicator of academic quality.
- A sufficient measure of satisfaction with the quality and cost-effectiveness of the campus and the CSU networks from concerned constituencies, including: students, consumers, faculty, and staff users.
- A high level of public accountability to those who provide direction and support; in particular, the State Legislature, state agencies, and the Board of Trustees.

Current Status

The governance and management mechanisms that foster and control the development of information technology throughout the CSU are multiple and fragmented. These various entities exist at the state government level, in the chancellor's office of the CSU, and on all campuses. There are many managers and staff in place to deal with various pieces of the information-technology arena.

At the state level, the State Office of Information Technology, the Division of Communications, the Department of General Services, and the Legislative Analyst's Office all impact the planning, budgeting, procurement, and implementation of information-technology projects of the campuses in the CSU. Because the CSU is treated like a state agency, it currently falls under the rules and regulations of Section 4 of the State Budget Act. Therefore, the CSU is subject to the policies and procedures of the State Administrative Manual as they pertain to data processing, word processing, and communications.

Already, the uses of information technology are being fostered on several fronts on each campus. While few campuses have integrated their policies, strategic planning, and management mechanisms, most have approached new developments in data processing and office automation as separate tracks. The same could be said of the chancellor's office for system-wide efforts, with the Division of Information Systems being responsible for computing and the development of voice communications, while video communications are in two other units.

Historically, the operation of computing services within the CSU has been fostered and administered from a central perspective with the Division of Information Systems (DIS) providing both policy and management guidance. The Division of Information Systems also represents the CSU with state agencies to ensure compliance with the controls and policies of the state of California.

Over the past two years, the environment for the development of technology has been changing in California. The State Office of Information Technology (SOIT) has been charged with being an advocate for the development of technology, and at the same time for continuing its control functions. SOIT is now advised by the California Information Advisory Board, consisting of executives from the various agencies, including the CSU.

For the CSU, there are two system-wide policy and management-advisory groups—the Information Systems Policy Board and the Management Advisory Committee—which have functioned over the past few years. Most campuses have had a policy or users, advisory committee. These boards have focused their attention on the computing-related aspects of the information-technology function. The specific management responsibilities have been divided among the chancellor's office Division of Information Systems, the campus computing centers, and the campus user departments.

Over this same period, The California State University has moved toward decentralization of its hardware and software resources, as well as its human resources base. With the installation of a major new computer, each campus now has a nucleus of resources to serve most of its own campus needs.

Thus, the time is right for the development of a coordinated, cohesive, information-technology management function for the CSU, one which utilizes the growing strengths of the campuses while refocusing the efforts of the Division of Information Systems to most effectively service the needs of the students and faculty throughout the system.

Governance

As the view of information technology broadens and its uses become increasingly a part of the on-going programs of each campus, the governing mechanisms, state statutes, the CSU policies, campus policies, and procedures must be adapted to the new level of user need and campus maturity. Specifically, this necessitates:

- Redefining the relationship of the CSU to Section 4 of the Budget Act and the related state agencies.
- Reconstituting the Information Systems Policy Board to formulate—and advise the chancellor on—plans, policies, and priorities for system-wide efforts.
- Reorganizing the Management Advisory Committee to more adequately represent the wide range of users throughout the CSU. This committee would advise the information-technology managers of the CSU on needs and problems.

Management

To achieve coordinated planning, management of the information-technology function at the system and campus levels must focus on:

- Differentiating the Division of Information Systems' responsibilities for system-wide planning, monitoring, and external liaison from its systems development and service roles to the campuses and chancellor's office.
- Examining potential consolidations of management responsibilities for the information-technology services on each campus.

Specifically, to provide system-wide leadership and coordination, the director of Information Systems should focus on:

- Coordinating the development of strategic plans, system-wide priorities and guidelines, and policies and procedures for information-technology management for the CSU.
- Reviewing the annual information-technology operating plans and budgets of all campuses and the chancellor's office, ensuring compatibility with the strategic plan of the CSU.
- Approving and certifying those information-technology projects and services of the campuses and chancellor's office divisions, that cost over $75,000, to ensure compliance with Section 4 of the Budget Act.
- Acting as the official CSU liaison with state and federal agencies, national associations, and other professional organizations for the information-technology function.

To assist and advise the director, a management council consisting of associate directors of the Division of Information Systems, campus computing center directors, and directors of other campus information-technology services could be established. The management council would focus on the on-going management, planning, and operating issues facing the CSU in information-technology management.

Roles and Responsibilities

The Division of Information Systems' responsibilities for providing on-going services and resources include:

- Acquiring and providing high-level technical support and training for common instructional-support software to each campus computing center.

- Developing and maintaining the administrative information system modules designated as system-wide for all campuses.

- Developing and maintaining a common comunication system for all intercampus voice, data, word, and image processing.

- Installing and maintaining common operating systems for all campus-wide and system-wide macro- and minicomputers in the CSU network.

- Providing large-scale specialized computing power for instructional users on all campuses.

- Acting as the data processing center for all of the divisions within the chancellor's office.

- Providing coordination and staff support for new technological developments to all campuses and the chancellor's office.

- Arranging for necessary resources from networks external to the CSU.

The involvement of the campuses in information-technology management responsibilities would include:

- Formulating campus operational plans, policies, and procedures for information-technology management within the CSU system-wide strategic plan, policies, and procedures.

- Managing the information technologies and services of the campus including computing, communications, office automation, etc.

- Planning, developing, and maintaining administration information systems designated as campus-specific.

- Providing the liaison, training, and information-retrieval services to the administrative users on the campus.

- Providing the consulting services to the faculty and students involved in the teaching, learning, and research activities of the campus.

- Instituting and assessing software application needs for instructional computing use on the campus.

- Providing the technical support for campus automation.

- Developing feasibility studies and monitoring all software/hardware procurements for the campus.

- Participating in, and assisting the chancellor's office with, the strategic planning and development of services and resources.

- Assisting the chancellor's office with the technical support of operating systems on the host and minicomputers located on campus.

- Acting as the campus liaison to the chancellor's office, with other campus computer centers, and professional associations and organizations.

- Approving and certifying all information-technology projects and activities on campus in accordance with campus and CSU policies and in compliance with Section 4 of the State Budget Act.

Finally, the campus user departments also have responsibilities for information technology including:

- Effectively and efficiently using the information resources and services provided by the campus and the CSU network.
- Providing quality services to the students and other public sectors of the institution.
- Identifying and justifying the need for additional resources and services to meet the needs of the department.

- Participating in the campus planning committees and task forces and those of the chancellor's office when so requested.

Human Resources

Having sufficient hardware and software in place, and having effective policy and management mechanisms, will meet only a portion of the needs. As the number of students, faculty, and staff who use information technology continues to grow, the key to success will be the availability and the quantity and quality of professional staff in the information-technology function to serve these users.

The university must focus on human resource development which will:

- Properly forecast the appropriate number of staff members needed on each campus to meet the growing demand.
- Properly describe the qualitative characteristics (training and skill), and the organizational locations into which these professionals will be placed on campus.
- Ensure the securing, retention, and development of these professional people by utilizing effective staff development and training programs at the campus and system-wide levels.

Campus and Network Technological Configuration

Trends

We are truly living in an Information Age, as evidenced by the growing uses of computing, satellite communications, and a variety of telecommunications networks that enable an individual to communicate with remote points. Today, there are personal computers sitting on desks that have power equivalent to the major computers of a decade ago, which occupied 2,000 to 4,000 square feet. This trend of increasing computer power while using less space will continue, suggesting that a student in the year 2000 may have a personal computer with power equivalent to what is currently installed for one entire campus.

The processing of information, whether it be words, data, or images, has moved from the cumbersome state of producing reams of paper to the streamlined method of on-line access, via television-like terminals, which provides an individual with the ability to manipulate data and make inquiries from remote locations. The utilization of such technology has enhanced the decision-making process and knowledge base of individuals and organizations.

Current Status

The CSU has just completed the largest single multi-campus installation of mainframe computers in higher education. New Cyber Computer Systems (Cyber 720s and 760s) were installed on 17 of the 19 campuses during 1981. An additional two were installed at the State University Data Center. The last system will be installed at San Diego and San Jose in 1982-83.

These new mainframe computers, coupled with the existing DEC PDP-11/45s or DEC PDP-11/70 local timesharing computers located on each of the 19 campuses, provide a nucleus of computing power equal to any university system in the country. Figure 4 depicts the current configuration of the CSU Network.

This configuration, connected by a statewide data communications system, provides a very solid foundation on which to develop an information-technology utility for the CSU system. However, technological developments are moving in many directions, especially within the personal computing area. Consequently, in configuring its technological environment, each campus must focus on combining the strengths of the large centralized campus computing resources with the capabilities of distributed mini- and micro-computers, as well as linking the campus resources to special centralized facilities at the CSU State University Data Center and elsewhere.

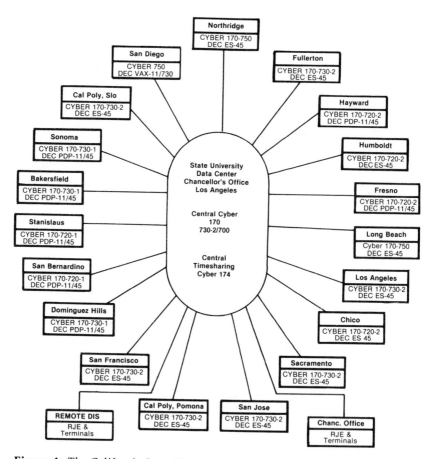

Figure 4. *The California State University System computing network.*

Projected Configuration

In the foreseeable future, each campus will have a campus information-technology network consisting of communications utilities serving as a hub. This network will include campus mainframes ringed by minicomputers. In many cases, these minicomputers will be designed to serve special functions—work processing, real-time laboratory data collection, a specialized application or a specific instructional program area. In addition, microcomputers will be used in classroom laboratories as individual tutorial computers providing

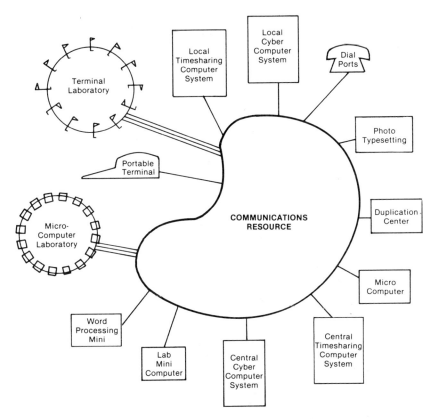

Figure 5. *The potential campus communications network.*

greater access to large numbers of students, especially in the lower division level courses. This will be done where it is determined to be cost effective. Microcomputers will also be used in administrative offices where the operation needs are quite independent of the major campus information systems and where it is cost effective.

At the nexus of each campus's information-technology network will be a communications system which provides for data, voice, word, and image transmission capabilities. Figure 5 depicts a typical configuration projected for a campus.

The local campus network will be linked to other CSU campuses, the State University Data Center, and external facilities via an inter-campus communications system. Using standard and common protocol for all CSU communications will enable an individual to use one workstation to interface with the appropriate information resources, whether they be on campus, on another campus, at the State University Data Center, or elsewhere.

Foci

To move in the direction of a totally integrated network, campus and system-wide foci in planning will involve:

- Planning, developing, and installing a comprehensive local campus communications utility which is capable of handling data, words, images, and voice. This implies the need to look at the computing services, telephone services, television, and other communication services on campus to determine and install a cost-effective utility.

- Planning, developing, and installing an appropriate inter-campus communications network which also handles data, words, images, and voice. Such an intercampus network must also provide access to external networks and application systems through the state network, EDUNET, ARPANET, and others.

- Reassessing and deciding on appropriate uses to be made of each campus's major host computer (Cyber) and minicomputers (DEC) to meet the projected users' needs.

- Establishing standards for the use of microcomputers in support of instruction and administration, and determining which vendors are technologically compatible with our network architecture.

- Defining and allocating Cyber resources (storage disk space, CPU, etc.), to the administrative uses versus the instructional uses on each campus.

- Forecasting the quantity and quality of peripheral equipment (terminals, communication speeds, etc.) to meet the projected usage of each campus.

Facilities

Based on the needs of the users, the organizational design of the information-technology function, and the technological configuration of each campus, the campus space needs for the next five-to-twenty years must be identified, designated, designed, and developed. These space needs will fall into two major categories—user space and information-technology management space.

While we envision individual users having individual portable workstations by the year 2,000, over the next five years our foci must be to assess the long-range space needs of each campus and the chancellor's office. This assessment will be in terms of computing center space, instruction laboratories, and administrative work space, leading to a space plan for each campus for submission to and endorsement by the CSU Physical Facilities Planning Division, the State Office of Information Technology, and the Legislative Analyst's Office.

Financing Strategy

Issues

It has become obvious that state and federal funding of higher education will not keep pace with the rising costs of educating students. As an industry, higher education has reached a static state, at least temporarily, in financial growth from public funds.

If the CSU is to maintain and extend its academic quality, new sources of revenue must be cultivated. The most expedient course of action to increase funding would be to assess student's tuition. A second source of funding would increase philanthropic gifts and grants. A third source of funding would involve the CSU campuses, and other institutions of higher education, entering the marketplace with their services, resources, and talents on a cost-reimbursement basis. Clearly, the line between non-profit and profit organizations has become blurred over the past decade. Though higher education has attempted to avoid openly competing with private industry in the knowledge business, this has happened.

Foci

Since the uses of information technology are becoming absolutely essential to the academic quality of the 19 campuses, their growth must be nurtured. However, the current strategy of using only general funds to support these technological services will be insufficient. As research has pointed out, it is in times of shrinking organizational resources that funding for information technology may need to be increased. Therefore, the strategy for financing information technology on each campus should consider a mixed approach involving:

- Continuing and, where appropriate, increasing the direct appropriations of general funds to support instructional and administrative information-technology activities on campus.
- Fostering the reallocation of departmental funds to the information-technology function utilizing direct chargebacks for new and additional services.
- Cultivating gift and grant income in support of this function.
- Developing policies and procedures for charging for services to external agencies utilizing information-technology support.

The successful implementation of this strategy will necessitate:

- Developing an extensive system to account for the uses of information technology.
- Exploring and developing plans of action for the use of information technology in bona fide public service programs on a full cost-plus-overhead recovery mode.
- Establishing mechanisms to recover the full cost of such services to external agencies.
- Establishing mechanisms to reallocate and transfer campus funds to support new and add-on services beyond the normal general fund allocation to the information technology unit.

Action

To address the issues and opportunities for cultivating alternative sources of funding, a special system-wide task force needs to be established to articulate a basic framework and guidelines for use by the campuses in pursuing new funding.

Reference

1. Mullins, Carolyn J. and West, Thomas W. *The Office Automation Primer.* New York: Prentice-Hall, forthcoming.

Note:

This chapter is a proposal and working draft. It has not been endorsed as an official statement of The California State University.

Trademarks

Apple Computer, Inc.
Apple, Apple II, Apple II Plus

Bell Systems
Centrex, ESS1A6, ESS#1, Horizon, UNIX

Bendix Corporation
Bendix G-21

Burroughs Corporation
Burroughs 1700

Commodore International, Ltd.
Commodore Pet

Control Data Corp.
CDC 1604, CDC 6400, CDC 6600, Cyber 70/71, Cyber 74, Cyber 170/720, Cyber 170/730, Cyber 170/750, Cyber 170/760, Cyber 171, Cyber 172, Cyber 174, Cyber 203, Cyber 720, Cyber 760, CYBERNET

Cray Research, Inc.
Cray-1, Cray 1-B

Data General
Eclipse

Dartmouth College
Avatar

Digital Equipment Corporation
DEC, DECsystem-10, DECSYSTEM-20, DECnet, DECtape, DIGITAL, LSI-11, LSI-11/23, PDP-11, PDP-11/23, PDP-11/34, PDP-11/44, PDP-11/45, PDP-11/60, PDP-11/70, RSTS, RSX, TOPS-10, TOPS-20, VAX, VAX-11/750, VAX-11/780, VMS, VT-100, digital

EDUCOM
EDUCOM, EDUNET, EFPM,

Hewlett-Packard Company
HP1000, HP2000

Honeywell, Inc.
Honeywell DPS-3, Honeywell DPS 8/44, Honeywell 66/DPS-3, H200

International Business Machines Corporation
IBM 360/50, IBM 360/67, IBM 370/155, IBM 370/158, IBM 370/168, IBM 407, IBM 650, IBM 1130, IBM 1401, IBM 1460, IBM 3031, IBM 3033, IBM 3033N, IBM 3270, IBM 4341, IBM 7044, FPS 190L, FPS 164, IBM Displaywriter, SCRIPT

Prime Computer, Inc.
PRIME 550, PRIME 750, PRIME 850

Software AG
ADABAS, NATURAL

Sperry Corporation
UNIVAC 90/60, UNIVAC 90/80, UNIVAC 1103, UNIVAC 1108, UNIVAC 1160

Stanford University
ARAMIS, CONTACT/EMS, Context, ORVYL, SPIRES, SUMEX-AIM, SUNet, SPIRES

Tandy Corporation
TRS-80

Teletype Corporation
Teletype

University of Iowa
CONDUIT

Westinghouse
Data Score

XEROX Corporation
Ethernet, STAR, XEROX 860, XEROX 9700

Index